'S

1981 GUIDE TO
HAWAII

by Faye Hammel

Published by Prentice Hall Press
A Division of Simon & Schuster, Inc.
Gulf + Western Building
One Gulf + Western Plaza
New York, NY 10023

ISBN 0–671–62337-0

Manufactured in the United States of America

*Although every effort was made to ensure the accuracy
of price information appearing in this book,
it should be kept in mind that prices
can and do fluctuate in the course of time.*

CONTENTS

MAPS

INFLATION ALERT: We don't have to tell you that inflation has hit Hawaii as it has everywhere else. For this reason it is quite possible that prices may be slightly higher at a given establishment when you read this book than they were at the time this informaton was collected in 1986. This may be especially true of hotel and restaurant prices. Be that as it may, we feel sure these selections will still represent the best travel values in the islands.

Chapter I

WHYS AND WHEREFORES

TO GET THE MOST for one's travel dollar in thriving, prosperous (and inflationary) Hawaii, the tourist today must be more *akamai* (smart) than ever before.

For Hawaii is no longer the remote, end-of-the-rainbow place it once was. Waikiki once knew only the sound of the surf. Today it bustles with over a million tourists a year, scores of hotels, literally hundreds of eating spots, and a wealth of sightseeing, entertainment, and sports activities. It is the most popular vacation spot in these United States.

Hawaii has something for everybody. It has luxurious $1,000-a-day suites with broad lanais (balconies) and views of the Pacific, and plain $40-a-day rooms with views of somebody else's kitchen. It has $35 luaus and $2 bowls of Japanese noodle soup. It has some of the most breathtaking vistas in the world, some of the most exciting cultural activity, and some of the most splendid stretches of sand and surf anywhere. And it has, like any other center of such attraction, its tourist traps.

That's where this book comes in. It takes know-how to get the best accommodations for the price, no matter what the price; to find the most delectable and adventurous food for the money, the most authentic Polynesian entertainment, the most thrilling Hawaiian sights. It takes know-how, too, to make every day count in Paradise. And what we intend to do in these pages is to give you that know-how, to let you in on the inside tips that separate the *kamaainas* (oldtimers) from the *malihinis* (newcomers). We'll show you the best way to enjoy the major sights and take you, too, off the beaten path to surprising places that most tourists never hear of. We'll show you the best way to escape to this best of all escape places. In short, we'll tell you how to get such good value for your dollar in Hawaii that you'll have enough money left over to come back again next year. And the year after that. For Hawaii is one of those places that, once experienced, has a way of getting in the blood.

Some Elementary Hawaiian Georgraphy

The Hawaiian Islands were spewed forth from the bottom of the Pacific in great volcanic explosions that occurred many thousands of years ago. The entire archipelago includes some 122 islands, most of them merely tiny mountain peaks of a submarine mountain range that stretches for 1,600 miles. The eight largest islands make up the Hawaii we know: the four major ones—Oahu, Maui, Hawaii, Kauai—which belong to the world of the visitor; Lanai, a plantation island totally owned by the Dole Pineapple Company; Molokai, the place where Father Damien made history at Kalapaupa by caring for the lepers (there is still a sanatarium there, but the island is also gaining fame as a retreat for those who really want to get away from it all); Kahoolawe, which is a target range for American planes and ships; and Niihau, where the old Hawaiian way of life is still maintained and which is kept *kapu* (tabu) to all but those invited by its owners, the Robinson family.

Contrary to popular belief, the Hawaiian islands are not in the South Pacific; they are much closer to the U.S. mainland, 2,500 miles away, and lie in the northern Pacific Ocean at a latitude about even with the southern part of the United States. With increasing technological advances, a journey from the West Coast to Hawaii takes only about five hours by plane and four days by ship.

What Hawaii is Like

Hawaii is at once like everything you dreamed it would be and totally unlike anything you imagined. It is both a tropical paradise and a cosmopolitan boom town, a place where the old island gods still hold sway and where speculators and builders and real-estate men have been riding high. It is one of the most fascinating paradoxes of old and new, of beauty and razzle-dazzle, of serenity and show business anywhere. It is an island world that went from the Stone Age to monarchy to statehood in less than 200 years. It is a place where Japanese and Chinese and Polynesians and Americans and Filipinos and Koreans, merchants and missionaries, whalers and working men from all over came together to form a new world. And where, despite everything, the old Hawaiian gentleness, the warmth and hospitality that have come to be known worldwide as *aloha,* still pervades all. This is what makes Hawaii someplace special: no matter how many new hotels and condominium apartment buildings rise above the Waikiki skyline, it will never be as cold and commercial as Miami Beach. The spirit of the Hawaiians still holds forth.

The Hawaiians—A Brief History

To know the Hawaiians of today, it helps immeasurably to know a little bit about the Hawaiians of the past. The very earliest settlers to these volcanic islands arrived from various parts of Polynesia, probably Tahiti and Bora Bora, about A.D. 750. Guiding themselves by a primitive and probably intuitive navigational science, they crossed thousands of miles of ocean in pairs of large outrigger canoes, connected by long bamboo poles that supported a tiny hut between the canoes. They brought with them their animals and plants, introducing such foods as the sweet potato into a climate that had never yet supported it.

They settled primarily on the largest islands of the Hawaiian archipelago—Hawaii, Kauai, Maui, Molokai, and Oahu. The islands were fragmented into little kingdoms, each ruled by its own chief, with its own *kapus* and particular customs. Power belonged to the strongest, and the bloody overthrow of leaders was quite common. But life was stable, and very probably even comfortable. None of the settlers ever made any attempt to return to the tribes from which they had come. In the warmth of the sun, these Stone Age people, living primitive lives, worshipping their own gods, and keeping the old ways of life, remained undisturbed and untouched by outsiders until the 18th century.

In 1777 Capt. James Cook, who was really looking for the Northwest Passage, stumbled on the island of Kauai. The natives, who had long believed that their great god Lono would one day return to them, mistook Cook and his crew for the god and a full entourage of lesser deities. At first he received a god's reception, but soon fighting broke out between the natives and the sailors, and eight months later, on another voyage, Cook was clubbed to death by natives and drowned off the Kona shore of the island of Hawaii. But from that time on, the Sandwich Islands, as he had named them in honor of the Earl of Sandwich when he claimed them for Great Britain, became part of the modern world. By 1790 King Kamehameha the Great, operating from his home island of Hawaii, conquered the other islands in the chain in a series of bloody forays (except for Kauai, which surrendered) and united them under his rule. Hawaii was already one nation when the first emissaries from the Western world—

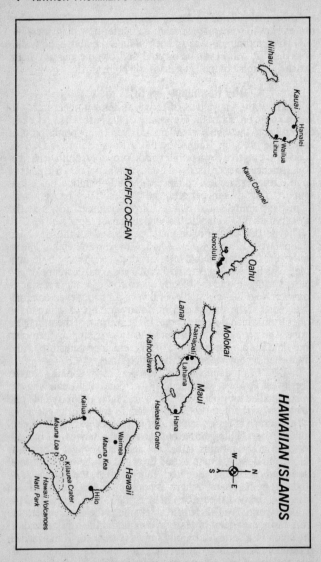

merchants, fur traders, whaling men—started their invasion of the islands.

In 1820 a band of New England missionaries arrived in Hawaii, determined to save the heathen islanders from the devil. They brought piety, industry, and the Congregational religion to the natives; their coming speeded the end of the old Hawaiian life. (Their story is told eloquently in James Michener's *Hawaii,* in both the novel and the film.) They smashed the idols and continued the destruction of the rigid *kapus* (already weakened by the king prior to their arrival), taught the people to read and write, and "civilized" the natives. And although they undoubtedly did an enormous amount of good, many of the natives here have never forgiven them, as the island saying goes, for doing so well. Some of the missionaries' children turned into businessmen, bought up the land, started industries, and it is their descendants who are still among the ruling forces of Hawaii's great corporate empires.

The native Hawaiians never really adjusted to the white man's world, refused to work his plantations, died from his diseases in horrendous epidemics. Today, just a few thousand pure-blooded Hawaiians remain. The rest have disappeared or become intermingled with the other races—mostly Japanese and Chinese—that came to do the white man's work.

The Orientals began to arrive around the 1850s, when the whaling trade was dropping off and the sugar plantations were becoming big business. The Chinese came first to work the plantations, then the Japanese, last the Filipinos. The Hawaiian melting pot began to simmer.

Meanwhile, the reign of the second Kamehameha, Kamehameha II, had been short. He and his queen died of measles in London in 1824. Kamehameha III reigned for 30 years, during which time the independence of the islands was declared from Britain. An English-language newspaper was started and a public school opened at that time, both in the islands' capital, Lahaina, on the island of Maui. But the capital remained there only until 1845, when the king and his court moved to Honolulu. Commerce was picking up in the Honolulu harbors, and in 1850 that city was declared the capital of the 19th-century kingdom.

The line of the Kamehameha descent ended after Kamehameha IV and V had passed out of the picture, by 1872. William Lunalilo was elected successor by the legislature, but he died within a year; David Kalakaua succeeded him. Queen Emma, the widow of Kamehameha IV, appeared to have a rightful claim to the throne, and it was to this end that many riots where staged. American and British marines were called in.

In the latter part of the 19th century, industry continued to boom, with sugar the leading crop and coffee a close second. (Rice, now of small importance in the state, was once the number-two crop.) Finally, in 1875, the Hawaiian sugar planters worked out a reciprocal agreement with the U.S. government, by which Hawaiian sugar companies were assured an American market and the Americans were given the freedom to use Pearl Harbor as a coaling station. The American Age was arising in Hawaii; the annexation of the Republic of Hawaii took place in 1898, but statehood would not be achieved until more than half a century later, in 1959.

King Kalakaua, "The Merry Monarch," was followed by Queen Liliuokalani, the last reigning monarch of the islands. When her plans for a new constitution were violently opposed, she was removed from office in the bloodless uprising of 1893 and replaced by Sanford B. Dole, a *haole* (white man) representing American commercial interests. It was while she was under house arrest that she wrote the poignant "Aloha Oe," now a song of good-bye to those leaving the islands. But it was also a lament, a farewell to the days of the past when kings and queens, and even an occasional god, walked the earth.

The 20th-century history of Hawaii began with the booming of the pineapple industry, a boom that has never stopped. The U.S. Armed Forces moved into the area and made Hawaii an independent army department in 1913. Although Hawaii was not directly involved in World War I, many islanders had volunteered for the French and German armies before the U.S. entered the conflict. The depression of the '30s blew through the islands with the relative calm of a trade wind, compared to the hurricane-like devastation on the mainland. Big business was not yet too big, industry not yet well developed.

But Hawaii felt the impact of World War II more than any other American state. Because the U.S. had developed the harbors and military installations on the islands so greatly, they were a prime target area for the enemy. After the dreadful bombing attack of December 7, 1941, Hawaii entered a period of martial law. Liquor consumption was regulated, curfews were imposed, and blackouts were common. Fortunately, the islands' Japanese population was not herded off into concentration camps as it was in California. In fact, a group of Nisei volunteers became one of the great heroic regiments of the U.S. Army fighting in southern Europe. The 442nd Regimental Combat Team has been called "probably the most decorated unit in United States military history," and one of its members, Daniel K. Inouye, is the senator of Watergate fame. This participation in the war did a great deal to break down race lines in Hawaii. Today, the Japanese are the largest single ethnic group, and one of the most powerful, in the state.

After the war, increasing lines of transportation developed between the American mainland and Hawaii. Tourism became a major industry and the already existing industries grew at phenomenal rates. Years of labor disputes in the 1940s, spearheaded by the militant ILWU, raised the standard of living for the Hawaiian working man to an all-time high. Finally, in 1959, after a 30-year struggle for statehood that began with Hawaii's first representative to Congress, Prince Jonah Kuhio Kalanianaole, delegate John A. Burns (later Hawaii's governor) effected passage of the bill that made Hawaii the 50th American state. Dancing in the streets celebrated a goal long promised and arduously won.

Since statehood, Hawaii has blossomed and boomed and burst forth into a new era. Now largely Democratic in politics, with a mostly Japanese legislature, it is liberal in its outlook, proud of its ability to blend the races, to let the newcomer "do his own thing." Garment industries, steel mills, and cement factories are growing. Agriculture uses the most advanced techniques, and pineapple and sugar are still big business. So are tourism and the military. Technology has moved in and made Hawaii the mid-Pacific outpost in America's space efforts and oceanography research. The University of Hawaii and the East-West Center for Cultural and Technical Interchange have raised the level of education in the state remarkably, bringing in scholars from all over the world. Population swings near the three-quarters-of-a-million mark; over a million tourists are expected annually. Despite economic uncertainty here as everywhere, it looks as if Hawaii is still on the way up.

Chapter II

HONOLULU LOGISTICS

YOU'RE OFF THE PLANE and standing in the Hawaiian sunshine. If you're lucky, some doting friend—maybe even the representative of your hotel—has greeted you with an aloha kiss and draped a fragrant lei around your neck. If not, don't worry; there are lei stands all over the islands and you'll have worn dozens by the time you're ready to go home.

Your biggest problem, right now, is getting from the airport to Waikiki, where you'll most likely be staying, a distance of about ten miles. If you've reserved a car in advance, it's easy; just pick it up and you're on your way. Or you could grab a taxi (they're always waiting at the airport). The tab to Waikiki will run you about $14. It makes more sense for the individual traveler to catch one of the limousine services right into Waikiki. These cost about $3.50 to $4 and will take you right to your Waikiki hotel.

Although we are great believers in the City Bus System, "TheBUS" (as it is called) is not ideal for baggage-laden tourists. Buses do operate from the terminal into Waikiki, but they have no provisions for your luggage. If, however, you can contain all your belongings in your lap, the price is certainly right—60¢ a ride. And you'll get a head start at meeting the local population.

Transportation Within the City

BUSES: Once settled at your hotel, however, you should definitely learn how to use TheBUS. They run all over town and maintain frequent schedules between Waikiki and downtown Honolulu. The best way to figure out how to go where is to pick up a copy of "Hawaii Visitors' Guide to TheBUS," a free handout available all over town. If you need further information, call TheBus information department at 531-1611. The fare, again, is 60¢; have exact change ready. If you want a free transfer to a connecting bus, ask for it as you board. Senior citizens can get free

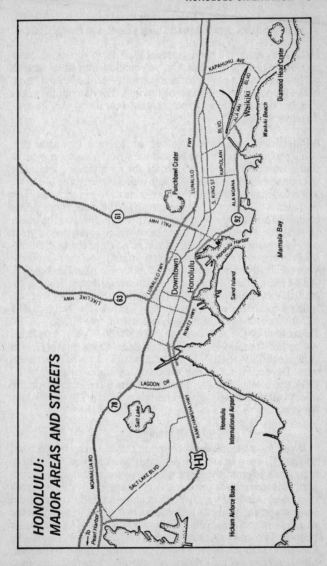

HONOLULU:
MAJOR AREAS AND STREETS

passes after a four weeks' processing period (phone 524-4626 for details). Students, age 6 through high school, are charged 25¢.

TAXIS: They cruise the main streets of Waikiki, so you should have no trouble picking up a cab. Or, you can ask your hotel desk to get one for you, or phone for one yourself (see the Yellow Pages of the Honolulu phone-book for listings). They are quite expensive, but could be cheaper than renting a car if you only have to do minor traveling.

U-DRIVES: At some time or other during your Hawaiian stay you'll probably want to get behind the wheel of a car, maybe to tour around the island of Oahu, or for a sightseeing excursion over on the windward side. The car-rental business (or U-Drive, as it is called here) is one of the most competitive in the state. The best idea is to check the companies out on the scene, since prices change so quickly; the tourist newspapers will give you the leads. If, however, you know in advance that you're going to do a great deal of driving (and especially if you're going to the neighbor islands where your own set of wheels is a must), you should reserve your car in advance from one of the reputable island companies. All of them offer "flat rates," which means that mileage is included: they usually turn out to be less than the regular rates plus mileage for extensive driving. **Budget Rent-A-Car** (toll free 800/527-0700), **Holiday Hawaii Rent-A-Car** (toll free 800/367-2631), **Dollar Rent-A-Car of Hawaii** (toll free 800/367-7006), **Avis Rent-A-Car** (toll free 800/331-1212) and **National Car Rental of Hawaii** (toll free 800/CAR-RENT), are all reputable firms to do business with. Depending on the car, the company, and whatever special deals are available at the time you're there (be sure to inquire about "all-island" specials), expect to pay from $20 to $40 daily for your car.

Camping

If you must be on wheels, but don't want to pay for both car and hotel, here's an idea that just might work for you. If you have a camper's adventurous spirit, a group of two or three, and a minimum of three nights, you can save considerably by carrying your own hotel—and fully equipped kitchen—around. You can rent some surprisingly comfortable campers in Honolulu and on the neighbor islands, from about $45 to $90 per day, for two to six people. Two companies rent recreational vehicles: **Beach Boy Campers,** 1720 Ala Moana Blvd., Honolulu, HI 96815 (tel. 955-6381), renting on four major islands; and **Travel/Camp, Inc.,**

P.O. Box 11, Hilo, HI 96720 (tel. 935-7406 or 961-2001), serving
the Big Island only. Camping is very popular among island residents, and the public campgrounds, usually on the shores of secluded beaches, are quite beautiful. There have been recent
reports of vandalism, but these are usually from tent campers,
not from RV users.

Island Geography

Now that you're navigating around the city, either on foot or
by bus or car, you should know something about where you are.
Honolulu is, of course, the state capital, and the only major city
on the island of Oahu. But before we get you oriented, we have
to tell you that people here have no use for such terms as "north"
or "south" or "east" or "west"—not even "uptown" or "downtown" are much help. For the Hawaiian Islands sit in a kind of
slantwise position on the map, and the only reference points that
are used are either place names or directional signals meaning
"toward the mountains" or "toward the sea."

Here's how it works. Let's suppose that you are standing on
Waikiki Beach, looking at Diamond Head crater; this means you
are facing in a Diamond Head direction. You are, of course, at
the beach area, but just a few miles away from this Pacific Riviera
the water is deep enough for ocean-going vessels to dock in Honolulu harbor, which fronts on the downtown business district. (It
was, in fact, that harbor's depth that made Honolulu a logical
center for international commerce.) The downtown area is in an
Ewa (eh-vah) direction, toward the village of Ewa, from Waikiki,
and farther out in this section of the island low plains of rich, red
volcanic earth give birth to tons upon tons of sugar and pineapple. Anything toward the ocean is *makai*. Over to your left
from the beach area, in a *mauka* direction, are the striking Koolau Mountains, which form the dramatic backdrop for the city.
On the other side of the Koolaus is Windward Oahu, miles of
verdant countryside bordering on the water's edge. This is fast
being transformed into suburbs, the bedrooms of Honolulu from
which commuters speed into the city's offices every day via tunnels bored through the mountains.

The Weather and When to Visit

Hawaii is one of those rare, blessed places on earth where the
weather is always—well, almost always—wonderful. Any time of
the year that you can get here is the right time to come. Most people come during the summer months of June, July, and August
(mostly mainland families and young people); or during the dead

of the winter (the Christmas to Easter "high season" when prices go up), when the crowd is older and as much Canadian as it is American. But the weather is always good. An average temperature throughout the state would probably settle at about the 74°F. mark; in the summer it's usually in the 80s. Leave your warm coats at home; bring a sweater or light topper for some mountain areas at night; pack a light raincoat too, just in case.

During the summer, a Hawaiian "rain" will probably be a ten-minute light shower during which nobody bothers going inside. During the winter months, there may be an occasional thunder-and-lightning storm, and sometimes it rains for several days in a row. Some winters it hardly rains at all. The varying amounts of rainfall can be explained in terms of northeasterly winds bringing rain clouds that are subsequently blocked by the main mountain range on the northern side of each island. Each island, therefore, has its windward side (where the rain falls) and leeward side (to which the storm clouds seldom get). Most tourist centers are, naturally, leeward. The gentle trade winds keep the weather on a pretty even keel.

Average Monthly Temperatures in Hawaii

Month	Temp	Month	Temp
January	72.2	July	77.7
February	71.9	August	78.4
March	72.2	September	78.3
April	73.2	October	77.4
May	74.9	November	75.4
June	76.8	December	73.3

A Matter of Language

You don't have to go to Berlitz before you go to Hawaii. English is the one language spoken everywhere in the state, although many first- and second-generation immigrants still use their native languages at home, and the Chinese and Japanese communities even have their own daily newspapers. But some of the old Hawaiian words have become charmingly intertwined into the language, and it's fun to know and use them. So that you'll know your *kanes* (men) from *wahines* (women) and your *kamaainas* (oldtimers) from *malihinis* (newcomers), here are some tips.

Remember, first, that Hawaiian is a very simple language, much simpler than English. It contains only the five vowels plus these seven consonants: *h, k, l, m, n, p, w.* Vowels are sounded as they are in Spanish; consonants, as they are in English. The written language was the work of the missionaries who wrote down the native oral language. Mary became *Malia*, John became *Keone*, Britain turned into *Beretania*. Remember that every syllable ends in a vowel, and that you pronounce every syllable, and it all becomes quite simple. You always put the accent on the next-to-the-last syllable. For example, *kamaaina* is pronounced kah-mah-*eye*-nah, *wahine* is wah-*hee*-nay. Don't worry too much about the details, though.

Everyone will think you're pretty *akamai* (smart) if you know that a *haole* is a white person (Caucasian), a *hapa-haole* is half-white, *kau kau* is food, a *keiki* a child, a *luau* a feast, a *hukilau* a fishing festival. *Pupus* means hors d'oeuvres (they're usually served free with cocktails during Happy Hours), a *punee* is a couch, and *lomi-lomi* means massage (lomi-lomi salmon is literally "massaged"). If you want something done fast, it's *wiki-wiki,* and when something is finished, it's *pau.* The *alii* were royalty, the nobility of old Hawaii, and breaking their *kapus* (taboos) could get a person into plenty of *pilikia* (trouble). You'll most likely have a hotel room with a *lanai* (a porch). A pregnant woman is *hapai.* Everyone, of course, knows that a *lei* is a garland of flowers, a *muumuu* a long, loose-flowing Mother Hubbard–type dress (actually, the nightgowns of the missionary ladies— the only clothes that would fit the ample frames of the old Hawaiians). *Kokua* means cooperation or "take care" (you'll often see road signs saying *kokua)* and *mahalo* is the island way of saying thank you. And once you've been in Hawaii for a couple of days you'll have no need of definitions of *aloha.* The warmest greeting you can give in the islands: *aloha nui loa.*

Chapter III

MOST-FOR-THE-MONEY HOTELS

SOMEWHERE IN HONOLULU there is a hotel that is exactly right for you—whether *you* are a budget-conscious family counting pennies or a retired millionaire clipping coupons or, like most of us, the average tourist who wants a good time and a good deal for his money. For the Honolulu hotel scene covers an incredible variety of accommodations, everything from bohemian haunts as rundown as you'd expect, to hotels where the bedrooms are as big as ballrooms and where presidents, movie stars, Arabian princes, and Greek shipowners feel right at home. And the price range is just enormous. You can rent an oceanfront suite for $2,000 a night at one of the seaside palaces, or a cute little kitchenette apartment a few blocks from the beach for about $30.

What we have attempted to do in this chapter is to pick out what we consider the best accommodations in whatever price category you choose. If you want to pay anywhere from $80 to $150 and up for a double for the night, make your selections from the first category, "The Great Ladies." If a nightly tab of $50 to $80 suits your fancy better, stick to the second category, "The Moderately Priced Hotels." And if you're watching your pennies, turn to the third category, "Budget Discoveries." Here we've described clean, comfortable, and sometimes surprisingly lovely accommodations where the nightly tab begins at $50 and under, double.

You'll notice that most of our hotel recommendations are in Waikiki, rather than in downtown Honolulu or other parts of the island of Oahu. To our mind, Waikiki and the areas near it are the best places for the typical visitor, who wants to stay close to the turquoise waters and sparkling sands that have lured him perhaps thousands of miles from home. And Waikiki is ideal because it's so small. Bounded on one side by the Pacific, on the other by the Koolau Mountains, it's small enough so that everything important is within walking distance, or just a short drive or bus ride away.

To help you get your bearings geographically, you should know that there are three major arteries in Waikiki, all of which run parallel to each other. Fronting on the beach is **Kalakaua Avenue,** Waikiki's main street and its choicest location, full of big hotels, shops, restaurants, thousands of tourists. About three short blocks *mauka* (toward the mountains) is **Kuhio Avenue,** a bit quieter and less crowded. And a few more blocks *mauka* of that is the **Ala Wai Boulevard,** next to a peaceful waterway close to the mountains, created back in 1920 when a brilliant entrepreneur got the idea of draining the swampland that was Waikiki. It is adjacent to the public and inexpensive Ala Wai Golf Course, and joggers love it.

As you read the hotel descriptions below (and remember there are many other good hotels in Waikiki; these are simply our choices), you'll become aware that, regardless of price structure, there are two general categories of hotels in Hawaii: the big, lively, resort-type hotels that are ideal for active singles and unencumbered couples; and the usually smaller, apartment-type hotels that are better suited for families with children or for anyone who wants to stay in the islands more than the usual week or two. These smaller apartment hotels (many of which are condos) all have a money-saving (and child-pleasing) advantage—a kitchenette, perfect for making breakfast coffee, storing Junior's chocolate milk, and fixing a quick snack when you don't want to eat out. (Most of the large hotels do not have kitchenettes, but some will furnish you with small refrigerators if you request them.) By and large, the apartment hotels are on the side streets that run between the three major thoroughfares, and on the Ala Wai Boulevard. Remember, all the hotels are within easy walking or busing distance of each other, and all are near the important attractions of Waikiki. In general, prices are higher the closer you get to the beach; rooms get bigger and tariffs lower as you head toward the Ala Wai.

Note: The telephone area code for all phones in the state of Hawaii is 808.

Hotel Know-How

Now, a few words about some miscellaneous matters.

RATES: You should know that most hotels have different rates for high season (usually mid-December to April 1) and low season (the rest of the year). High-season rates add an average of $8 to $20 to your bill per day. During slack periods, rates may come down considerably, especially in the smaller establishments. And many hotels offer special considerations for weekly and monthly stays.

Also note that we cannot be responsible for any change in the rates quoted here. The prices listed are those supplied by the hotels as we go to press in the middle of 1986. Even though prices may rise in these inflationary times, we feel these hotels will offer the best value for the money.

PRIVATE BATHS AND MAID SERVICE: Every hotel described below offers private baths; maid service can vary from daily to every other day to weekly. Always check with condominiums to see how often maid service is provided.

AIR CONDITIONING: Most of the newer hotels offer air-conditioned units; where this is not so, trade winds and cross ventilation will usually offer enough comfort. If you suffer a lot from the heat, though, you may find an air conditioner important, especially in the warm summer months, July through September. Also remember that it's easy and inexpensive to rent a fan if you need one.

RESERVATIONS: It is always advisable to reserve a hotel room in advance. This way, you can be sure of getting the type of accommodation you prefer at the rate you want to pay. Even without reservations, you will probably find a room in Waikiki; there are usually more hotel rooms than there are guests, unless a big convention is in town. A few weeks' notice is usually adequate, but remember that the more popular the hotel, the more essential is a reservation a good deal in advance—perhaps even several months. And reservations are particularly important in the high season, from December through Easter and, again, from June until Labor Day. Some very popular hotels request that one reserve at least *a year in advance* for the Christmas–New Year's holidays. The general rule is this: as soon as you know you're going to Hawaii, start making reservations.

BABYSITTERS: The desk clerks at any hotel can put you in touch with qualified people who will look after Junior while you're out seeing the town.

The Great Ladies: Expensive

If anyone were to ask us to name our favorite hotel in Honolulu, we would have to go right out on a limb and say the **Kahala Hilton,** 5000 Kahala Ave., Honolulu, HI 96816 (tel. 734-2211). About a 15-minute ride from the razzle-dazzle of Waikiki, in the beautiful Kahala residential area, it is a rare combination of island tranquility and jet-set sophistication, a place where the warmth and graciousness of the staff perfectly match the charm and serenity of the surroundings. So conducive, in fact, is the Kahala to relaxation that about one-third of the guests are repeat visitors who never leave the grounds. We don't blame them.

One could, in fact, spend days here just celebrity-watching. Was that really Sammy Davis, Jr., or Carol Burnett or Shirley MacLaine? Or you can concentrate on more mundane things, like lazing on the gentle beach; tooling around in a pedal-boat or kayak; taking a plunge in the pool; working out at the new Manualua Bay Club, a seaside super-spa that includes six night-lighted tennis courts, sauna, weight room, and aerobics classes. If you have an eye for beauty, take a stroll inside and outside the hotel, and bring your camera. Inside, note the immense, multi-colored, glass chandeliers that suggest the drift glass of Hawaii's beaches, the teakwood parquet flooring from Thailand, the Polynesian-inspired circular rug masterpieces. Outside, wander through the acres of beautiful gardens, with their bamboo groves, waterfalls, rare plantings. There's even a lagoon stocked with fish, giant turtles, penguins, and dancing dolphins who will entertain with the hula.

Where to stay? You have your choice of 370 spacious guest rooms, all with elegantly tasteful appointments, including a large seating area, a lanai in many of the rooms, quiet air conditioning, color television, and knockout his-and-her bathrooms with two separate bath vanities and a small refrigerator. The price range depends on whether you face the mountains ($145 to $185 for a double) or the lagoon or ocean ($205 to $295). Magnificent suites run from $340 to $1,100 a day. There is no charge for children of any age sharing their parents' room, and there are daily activity pro-grams for them during the high seasons and at holiday times. extra person is charged $25. If you're alone, deduct $2 on the price of doubles. Rates are subject to change.

This, however, is not the place to be alone. You should be here with someone you love—the better for enjoying the romantic nights on the seaside Hala Terrace where Danny Kalekini presents one of the last authentic Hawaiian shows on the island; for enjoying the lavish Sunday-night buffet; for candlelight dining à deux in the *Travel-Holiday*-Award-winning Maile Restaurant; or just for the sheer beauty of being in a place that combines the charm of the old and the excitement of the new Hawaii.

Reservations can be made through Hilton Reservation Service or any Hilton Hotel.

The most spectacular hotel in Waikiki itself? That accolade might go, perhaps, to the **Hyatt Regency Waikiki at Hemmeter Center,** 2424 Kalakaua Ave., Honolulu, HI 96815 (tel. 922-9292; reservations, toll free 800/228-9000), a $100-million caravanserai by the sea that ranks as one of the great showplace hotels of the country. Occupying an entire city block, the 1,234-room hotel accomplishes the seemingly impossible: creating an oasis of calm and tranquility and lush tropical beauty in the midst of the most bustling, heavily trafficked area in town. Christopher Hemmeter and his team of architects and designers created the effect by placing all the public areas around a lushly landscaped, huge atrium or Great Hall, above which the guest rooms rise in twin, 40-story towers that afford maximum views of ocean and mountains, and maximum amounts of privacy and peace. The Great Hall, one of the most beautiful spots in Honolulu, replete with tumbling waterfalls, fountains, cascades of greenery, South Seas-scented flowers and plantings everywhere, magnificent sculptures, and dotted with art, antiques, and intimate conversation areas, is, quite naturally, one of the most popular shopping (see Chapter VII), restaurant, and promenade areas in town.

The guest rooms have also been designed with an eye to the utmost in both comfort and glamour. Among the largest in town (425 square feet), each has a lanai with outdoor furniture, a sofa, huge closets, wall-to-wall carpeting, TV, air conditioning, and either twin beds, doubles, or double doubles. Cheerful color schemes and quality artworks everywhere create a harmonious feeling. These units rent from $80 to $150, depending on the view and floor. The ocean-view Parlour Suites have all this plus a spacious living room and rent for $300. And the incredible two-bedroom Presidential Suites, veritable mansions in the sky, complete with living room, library, and no fewer than six lanais, are $1,200 per night. The Regency Club offers penthouse rooms at $350 to $800.

The beach is directly across the street, but guests can also swim and sun at home at the third-floor pool and enjoy drinks at the

Elegant Dive poolside. Regency Club guests enjoy rooftop sundecks with a cool-water Jacuzzi. All told, the hotel has six restaurants and six cocktail lounges including the Terrace Grille, an indoor-outdoor restaurant overlooking the ocean; Musashi, a stunning Japanese restaurant; and Harry's Bar, tucked into a corner of the open-air atrium, with the mood of a European sidewalk café. Bagwells 2424, the ultimate in continental dining; Spats, a Roaring '20s speakeasy; The Colony, a steakhouse; and Trappers, a fashionable club with stylish entertainment, deserve detailed reviews in themselves (see Chapter IV).

The elegance of old Hawaii has been born again in the brilliant new interpretation of the classic Hawaiian seaside hotel, the **Halekulani**, 2199 Kalia Rd., Honolulu, HI 96815 (tel. 923-2311; reservations, toll free 800/367-2343). The new, 456-room resort, right on the beach at Waikiki, is a reincarnation of the famed hotel that dates from the 1930s; one of the original buildings has been incorporated into the new design—five interconnecting buildings of stepped heights surrounding courtyards and gardens overlooking the ocean. Understated elegance might be the words to describe the style of this new "House Befitting Heaven." Arriving guests are escorted directly to their rooms where registration is completed in privacy, and a porter offers to unpack the luggage! Guest rooms, most of which face the ocean, are very large, and have separate sitting areas, no fewer than three telephones (one at bedside, another in the bath, a third at a full-size business desk), cable color TV (operated by remote control and housed discreetly in an armoire), plus a small refrigerator stocked with bottled water and ice. Rooms are done in tones of beige, white, and gray, with blue flecks in the wool carpets; only silks, cottons, and wool are used. The tile lanais, with their chaises longues, tables, and chairs, are large and comfortable, many with views of the ocean beach and the magnificent pool, its huge cattleya orchid design made of a million imported South African tiles sparkling at its base. The orchid and pool have become the symbol of the new Halekulani.

Dining facilities are as superb as one would expect, from the greenhouse-like Orchids, to the elegant French restaurant La Mer (dinnertime here is a three-hour haute cuisine experience, one seating per evening only, about $50 per person), to the famous House Without a Key, rebuilt oceanside under a century-old kiawe tree, surely one of the most romantic spots in the world for sunset cocktails and entertainment (breakfast and light lunch are also available here).

The Halekulani recalls the graciousness of living in the Hawaii of old, in a new and distinctive setting. Its rates are a little higher than they used to be back in the '30s: single or double, garden view is $155; courtyard view, $185; ocean view, $245; ocean-front, $245; Diamond Head oceanfront, $275. An extra person is charged $35. Knockout suites run from $325 to $2,000 per night. There is no charge for children under 14 sharing their parents' room.

As much a landmark on the Waikiki skyline as Diamond Head is the pink stucco Moorish-style hotel called the **Royal Hawaiian,** 2259 Kalakaua Ave., Honolulu, HI 96815 (tel. 923-7311; reservations, toll free 800/325-3535 in the continental U.S.). Standing on the site of King Kalanikapule's home by the sea of a century and half ago, it was Hawaii's original luxury hotel and has been the subject of newspaper and magazine stories, and the scene and site of scores of television shows and movies, since it opened back in 1927. Now under the Sheraton banner and with all its rooms, suites, and public areas recently redecorated and refurbished, the Royal Hawaiian wears its regal heritage like a proud mantle. You can't help saying, "They don't build hotels like this anymore."

Surrounded by acres of lush tropical gardens (note the splendid monkeypod tree) and fronting on a handsome stretch of beachfront, the hotel exudes that unmistakable aura of regality—in the black terrazzo marble of its lobby floors; the coral-toned, hand-loomed rugs; the high-ceilinged splendor everywhere. Its famed Monarch Room is one of the best places in the islands for top-name entertainment.

Despite its regal bearing, the Royal Hawaiian has become quite democratic now that it's part of the swinging Sheraton hotel chain. Single or double rooms go from $105 (garden view) on up to $150 for an ocean view. And all are beautiful, immense, and in the old style. Views are superb, and service is immediate and gracious. As you would expect, suites are splendid, priced from $180 up. You can stay either in the older, original six-story hotel building or in the new, 17-story Tower wing, where all rooms overlook the pool and the Pacific. Guests at the Royal can use the food, beverage, and shopping facilities of the four other Sheraton resorts in Waikiki—the Moana, Surfrider, Sheraton-Waikiki, and the Princess Kaiulani—as well as the Sheraton Resort and Country Club in Makaha—and charge them to their bill.

One of the newer skyscrapers directly on the beach, the **Sheraton-Waikiki,** 2255 Kalakaua Ave., Honolulu, HI 96815 (tel. 922-4422; reservations, toll free 800/325-3535 in the continental U.S.), is a light, gay, vibrant place where everybody seems to be having a good time. The lobby has a wonderfully open feeling about it, and the breezy summerhouse mood extends into all the public rooms and the 1,900 newly redecorated, air-conditioned bedrooms as well. The "standard mountain view" rooms here—$99 double—are quite large as hotel rooms go, and the appointments bespeak charm. Flower murals in soft pastel shades dominate the color scheme, bathrooms and closets are roomy (so are the private lanais), and, of course, there's color TV. The ocean-view rooms are dazzlers. Most nearby hotels have a view of the Sheraton, but at the Sheraton your views are of a vast expanse of blue Pacific, the sun dancing on the waves in daytime, the lights from Diamond Head to downtown Honolulu glistening under the night sky. These rooms go for $160 double. Suites start at $195, and some, fit for diplomats and royalty, boast a vast 20-foot living room with an outdoor lanai, and can easily accommodate four people. The best values here are the $75 doubles in the adjoining Manor Wing, all recently redecorated. There is a $10 surcharge in winter.

You'll probably find you're spending a lot of time right at the hotel, what with all those great little shops in the lobby, that vast expanse of beach at your doorstep, and one of the biggest and sunniest pools in Waikiki on the beachfront. When you're hungry, there's the pretty Ocean Terrace for casual meals, the glamorous Hanohano Room for gourmet dining in a spectacular setting 30 stories up (take the glass elevator just for the view), as well as the Kon Tiki Restaurant, Safari Steak House, and Oahu Bar for drinks, steaks, and entertainment. If you decide to leave "home," you can, of course, "play and charge" at the other Sheraton hotels in Waikiki, as well as at the Sheraton Makaha Resort with its golf and tennis facilities.

To use the word "hotel" to describe the **Hilton Hawaiian Village,** 2005 Kalia Rd., Honolulu, HI 96815 (tel. 949-4321), is really an understatement. With over 2,600 rooms, 20 acres of grounds, 3 swimming pools, a man-made lagoon, its own U.S. post office, supper-club theater, acres of shops, and more than a dozen places for wining, dining, and catching the celebrities, it's a swinging little world of its own. Henry J. Kaiser built it, Hilton bought it, and the visitors love it. Now, with a vast, multimillion-dollar renovation being completed, it's greater and grander than ever.

If you're a guest here, you may not find it necessary to leave the Village during your entire stay. You can surf, take outrigger-canoe rides, or just plain swim off one of the finest stretches of beach in Waikiki, with acres of white sand even at high tide. During the day there are free hula and ukulele lessons. Come night-

fall, you can have your drinks under the stars in the beachside
Garden bar, dine on Cantonese cuisine in the Golden Dragon
Dining Room, feast on prime ribs of beef in the Rib Room, or
enjoy superb continental cuisine in the elegant Bali Room, or for
a change of pace, dine on fresh pasta at the Pasta Korner. Then
on to the Don Ho show in the Hilton Dome or a nightcap in the
Pot O' Gold Lounge—among other possibilities. You could
spend your entire vacation shopping; there are some 100 regular
stores here plus a slew of exotic Oriental ones in the Rainbow
Bazaar.

There is also a wide choice of accommodations. You can live in
either the Rainbow Tower (which has possibly the finest rooms in
Waikiki), the Ocean Tower, or the Diamond Head Tower. View
is the main factor in determining price. You can have a good-size
double room in the Ocean or Diamond Head Towers from $80
and up, with only court or garden views. Broader mountain and
garden views start at $100. All regular rooms in the Tapa Tower,
the 35-story addition to the Hilton are $120 and $130; there are
also more expensive corner and penthouse suites here. Yacht
harbor and ocean views begin at $140, and the world of luxury is
yours—private lanais, refrigerators, color TVs, etc.; complete
apartments and penthouse suites run from $160 to $1,000.

An extra person in a room is $20; quoted rates are for single or
double occupancy. There is no charge for children regardless of
age staying in the same room with their parents. If you want to eat
your meals "in"—and there are so many restaurants that you
won't get bored—you can choose a Modified American Plan ar-
rangement (two meals) for $39, or a three-meal American Plan at
$52.

Another self-contained resort community that provides
enough glamorous diversion for weeks of Hawaiian living is the
Westin Ilikai, 1777 Ala Moana Blvd., Honolulu, HI 96815 (tel.
949-3811, or toll free 800/228-3000 from mainland U.S. and Canada). Inside this unique island-within-an-island you can choose
from more than 800 of Waikiki's largest luxury accommodations
housed in two buildings overlooking both the Ala Wai Yacht
Harbor and Ala Moana Beach Park, with its acres of green lawns
shaded by huge monkeypods, banyans, and coconut palms. Your
vacation here can be as lazy or as lively as you wish: there's sunning and swimming in two pools or the nearby blue lagoon; for
the more adventurous, there's sailing, surfing, or scuba-diving in
the waters beyond. One of the rare hotels in Waikiki with tennis
facilities, the Westin Ilikai has six courts. You can shop until you
run out of travelers checks, eat your way through a variety of fun

restaurants, watch top island entertainment under the stars, and stay in some of the nicest hotel rooms in town.

We are great believers in hotel apartments, and here the Westin Ilikai really shines. The typical room in the main building is the largest in Waikiki, offering all the conveniences of a full apartment. A large sliding glass door opens onto magnificent ocean and mountain views. Closet and bathroom are liberal, and the kitchen and dinette are both fully equipped. Now for the prices. Based on view, rather than height (the hotel is right on the beach, so ocean views are unobstructed), rooms in the Tower Building run $126 to $141 double. There is no charge for children under 18 occupying the same room; over 18, the extra charge per person is $15. Yacht Harbor Building rooms start at $96, but are sans kitchenettes and smaller, although elegantly furnished.

Much of the Westin Ilikai's excitement is in its restaurants and nightclubs. Its coffeeshop, Pier 7, looks out over the Ala Wai Yacht Harbor. You can lunch outdoors under the shade of palm trees and umbrella tables at the Centre Court. When night falls, everything goes into high gear, for sunset signals the start of the hotel's traditional torchlighting ceremony. Then you must choose between Opus One cabaret for the sounds of music, or at the Top of the I for dinner, dancing, and gazing at the lights of Honolulu blinking 30 stories below.

If what you crave is elegant living, glorious views of the ocean, and plenty of room to stretch out, then the **Colony Surf,** 2895 Kalakaua Ave., Honolulu, HI 96815 (tel. 923-5751), is an excellent choice. It's located in the quieter Diamond Head section of town, across from Kapiolani Park, and the size of the rooms is matched by the splendor of the vistas—would you believe a 25-foot windowed panorama of ocean in many of the rooms? There are two buildings: the **Colony Surf,** whose elegant one-bedroom suites have fully equipped kitchens, two double beds, color TV, every nicety, and cost from $105 (single or double occupancy) on the limited-view lower floors, all the way up to $250 for direct ocean frontage; and the **Colony East Hotel,** whose studio rooms go from $85 to $105, single or double, to $115 to $125, depending on the view. Although they are smaller than the immense suites in the hotel building, they are luxuriously appointed, have kitchenettes, air conditioning, two double-size beds, plenty of closet space, and large bath vanities. You can't go wrong in either building.

The Colony Surf is also the home of the famed Michel's, which we'll describe later in the chapter on restaurants. Elegant and expensive haute cuisine is served here at dinnertime, but breakfast and lunch are both reasonably priced, and the mood and views

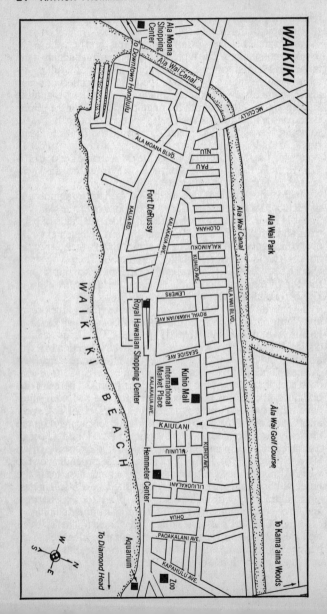

are superlative. The Colony Surf is a *kamaaina* hangout, a spot where the knowledgeable locals go just to get away from it all. It's that kind of place.

Although it's in the midst of the Waikiki madness, at 2552 Kalakaua Ave., Honolulu, HI 96815 (tel. 922-6611, or toll free 800/367-5370 in the continental U.S.), there's an air of retreat about the **Hawaiian Regent Hotel.** It's wrapped around a cool, lush inner courtyard and the architectural details are striking. The third-floor swimming pool and sitting area, with glorious views of recently widened Waikiki Beach just across the street, is a stunner. The good looks continue in the rooms, which are large and exquisitely furnished in teak and rattan, with divided baths and vanitorium and tub-shower combinations. Breathtaking views of sea, mountains, or Diamond Head are enjoyed from spacious and private lanais. There are TV, radio, air conditioning, direct-dial phones—the works. Prices begin at $86 double for mountain-view rooms, and go to $145 for oceanfront corner deluxe rooms. It's $12 for an extra person in the room. One-bedroom suites are $275; two-bedroom suites, $395; there is no charge for children under 18 sharing a room with their parents. You can eat at the attractive Summery Restaurant or dine on fine continental cuisine in the multiple-award-winning Third Floor. Have a drink at the Library, a contemporary wine bar and lounge overlooking Waikiki Beach, or a cup of espresso at the Café Regent, a Parisian-style café set in the gardens of the hotel courtyard. For beef and seafoods, it's the Tiffany Steak House, on the third floor; for Japanese dining, the Regent Marushin. The Lobby Bar hosts Hawaiian entertainment nightly in the center of all the hotel activity in the main lobby. The Ocean Terrace Bar and Snack Shop offer casual lunches and poolside cocktails. And for tennis buffs, there's a court, plus pro instruction available daily from dawn to dusk.

A striking 37-story, 495-room Tower has recently been added to the popular **Pacific Beach Hotel,** right across from the beach at 2490 Kalakaua Ave., Honolulu, HI 96815 (tel. 922-1233), making it more exciting than ever—especially since the Tower boasts a fantastic, three-story, 250,000-gallon saltwater Oceanarium, from which lobby and restaurant viewers can observe the marine life of the Hawaiian coral reefs without ever having to take snorkel in hand!

Both glamour and practicality are available at the Pacific Beach: glamour in the good views in all of the 850 rooms, whether they face ocean, mountain, or Diamond Head; and practicality in such conveniences as the kitchenette-bars, color TV, air conditioning, shower-tub combinations, double-double or king-size beds throughout in the large and luxurious rooms. The decor is elegant green and brown, the furniture ultramodern. Rates begin at $80 for a standard single or double and go up to $120 for those rooms in the front of the building that have the ocean just outside and a sunset spectacular such as few hotels can boast of. From May 1 to December 26, rooms are $10 less.

The hotel also boasts two professionally designed tennis courts, a pool, and several restaurants and lounges that include, within view of the Oceanarium, the Oceanarium Restaurant (see Chapter IV for details) for light dining, Neptune for continental fare, and Shogun, a Japanese steak and seafood restaurant.

It could take an entire book to detail the charms of the **John Guild Inn,** 2001 Vancouver Dr., Honolulu, HI 96822 (tel. 947-6019), a three-story gingerbread mansion in Manoa Valley near the university of Hawaii, which has been authentically restored to the resplendence of the 1920s. Furnished with antiques of the period, each of the seven guest rooms and the intimate cottage has its own unique personality; each is named in honor of a well-known person who lived in Hawaii. From the Dole Room on the third floor, furnished with a double bed, at $65, on up to the John Guild Suite, with a private sitting room and bath, at $125, they all resemble some wonderful movie set. All rates are double occupancy, and include a generous continental breakfast complete with island fruits, juices, Kona coffee, and freshly baked goodies; fruit, wine, and cheese are served in the afternoon; and soft drinks, juice, tea, and coffee are available at all times. Sherry and port wine are left out for a nightcap. The game room offers an antique piano and nickelodeon for fun; the living room, a collection of art nouveaux boxes and hula dolls. There's also a billiard room, and a lanai with a hypnotic view of Waikiki's city lights. Board games, books, and magazines are everywhere—and a croquet set is available, too. The Inn does not cater to children under age 14, but it does cater to the curious traveler and the romantic.

If you're not going to the neighbor islands this time but you do want a resort vacation in a glamorous, country setting, then you can't do better than to choose the **Turtle Bay Hilton and Country Club,** P.O. Box 187, Kahuku, HI 96731 (tel. 293-8811), a self-contained resort and country club on the island's North Shore, not far from Sunset Beach, and about an hour's drive from Waikiki. Set amidst five miles of white sand beach, this gorgeously landscaped hotel is an ideal place for active sports, with its ocean-view championship golf course, 10 plexipave-court tennis complex, horseback riding, motorized dune cycles, idyllic beach, swimming pools, and facilities for snorkeling, scuba-diving, and windsurfing. Guest rooms, located in either the low-rise main building or one of the cottages, are beautifully furnished in Polynesian decor. Each room has a private lanai, tub and shower, color TV, and all the amenities. Single or double rooms with a view of Kahuku Bay are $80; ocean-view, ocean-lanai and ocean-front rooms are $90, $100, and $110; cottages are $140 a day. Add $15 for a third person. There is no charge for children, regardless of age, when they stay in the same room with their parents. You could just about have a vacation here without ever leaving the 880 acres that comprise Turtle Bay—shops abound adjacent to the spacious lobby, and there's even a branch of Liberty House. The Palm Terrace is a big, handsome restaurant with a view of the ocean on three sides. It's open all day and serves an excellent buffet lunch for under $10.

For reservations, write to the resort at Kahuku, or contact your local Hilton Reservation Office.

The Moderately Priced Hotels

Most of the hotels described below offer accommodations ranging in price from approximately $50 to $80 for double occupancy. So that you'll know where you're at, we've divided them into three major categories: those fronting on or very near Kalakaua Avenue, Waikiki's main drag and the street closest to the beach; those along or near Kuhio Avenue, which runs parallel to Kalakaua; and finally, those on or near the Ala Wai Canal, a five-or six-block walk *mauka* from Kalakaua Avenue.

ALONG KALAKAUA AVENUE: The veteran classic South Seas hostelry on the beach at Waikiki is the **Moana Hotel,** 2365 Kalakaua Ave., Honolulu, HI 96815 (tel. 922-3111; reservations, toll free 800/325-3535 in the continental U.S.), a handsome white colonial building in the Sheraton family. Old Hawaii hands always like to say, "I remember Waikiki when just the Moana was here," and indeed some seven generations of visitors have danced and dreamed under the stars and twinkling lights of the huge banyan tree on the beach that, along with the hotel, has become a Honolulu landmark. The hotel's decor is colonial, for the Moana Hotel bridges the monarchy to territory to statehood periods of Hawaiian history. Rooms are larger than the standards of contemporary hotel construction. Rates at the Moana go from $60 to $85 single or double in the main building (ceiling fans but no air conditioning), and from $100 to $140 single or double in the completely renovated, air-conditioned Ocean Lanai wing. And $15 for a third person. There is no charge for a child under 17 occupying the same room with an adult.

You will, of course, want to dine in the oceanside Captain's Galley Restaurant and take in the Polynesian Revue at the Banyan Court, a festive nightly ritual.

The Moana is one of the few oldtime spots where the graciousness of the plantation days of Old Hawaii still survives.

The **Waikiki Beachcomber** at 2300 Kalakaua Ave. (tel. 922-4646), located as it is between Seaside Avenue and the International Market Place, sits astride the heartland of Waikiki. It's an attractive hotel, across the road from the beach, with smartly Polynesian lobby and dining rooms, plus a pool and terrace looking over the avenue. This is the site of the Bora Bora Showroom, where you can catch one of the best Polynesian shows in Waikiki. Considering their luxurious appointments and generous size, the rooms are a very good buy. You can count on TV, air conditioning, dial-out phones, refrigerator, divided bathroom, and a furnished lanai for your $68, single or double. At this price you'll look toward the mountains or toward the ocean, the latter view partially blocked by the Royal Hawaiian Hotel across the street. Higher up, it's higher up—$82 and $90, single or double; with a third person it's an extra $10. Rooms are $5 less April 1 to December 20. We like these rooms, especially the grass-textured wallpaper with its floral designs and the welcome spaciousness. Reservations: phone Dunfey Hotels toll free at 800/228-2121.

Walking into the lobby of the regal **Queen Kapiolani Hotel,** 150 Kapahulu Ave., Honolulu, HI 96815 (tel. 922-1941), is like walking back in time to the Hawaii of a century ago, when royalty was in full bloom. This towering hotel overlooking Kapiolani Park, less than a block from the beach, is the representation of all the elegance that Queen Kapiolani, the consort of Kalakaua, Hawaii's last reigning king, meant to her people. A bubbling fountain surrounded by tropical plants on the outside of the building leads the way to the lobby, which is worth a visit in itself, lavishly done in green wallpapers and accented by magnificent chandeliers of kerosene lamps, reminiscent of the days of the whalers in Hawaii. The bentwood wicker chairs are stunning replicas of Old Hawaii furniture. The Kalakaua Dynasty decor carries over to the rooms too; they are almost royal chambers in themselves, decked out in gold and royal blues. The door to each room, in fact, has a full-color reproduction of the seal of the state of Hawaii over it. The views, too, are splendid, since the hotel is across the street from Kapiolani Park, and there is no new construction to block the view from here to Diamond Head or the ocean. Besides the elegance, there are such modern creature comforts as air conditioning, an open-air restaurant and pool on the third floor, and a full dining room. Single rooms start at $47, twin-bedded ones at $50. Prices go up to $67 and $70 for more luxurious accommodations, and there is a charge of $8 for each extra guest. Kitchenette rooms are available at $74 single, $77 twin; suites run $155 double. There is a $6 seasonal surcharge per room from December 21 through March 31. For reservations, write Hawaiian Pacific Resorts, 1150 South King St., Honolulu, HI 96814, or phone 800/367-5004 toll free.

For luxury-plus accommodations at not unreasonable prices, the **Outrigger Prince Kuhio,** 2500 Kuhio Ave., Honolulu, HI 96815 (tel. 922-0811; reservations, toll free 800/367-5170 in continental U.S., 800/826-6786 in Canada), is the place. Everything about this hotel is a delight, from the handsome, white-haired Hawaiian gentleman who greets guests with a lei and a welcoming "Aloha," to the spacious and beautiful lobby, to the luxuriously appointed guest rooms. The temptation to sink into one of the huge basket chairs or chaises in the lobby and never move is great. Each of the 620 guest units offers a choice of king-size bed or two doubles; all have private lanais, and there is a small refrigerator and wet bar in every room. The bathrooms are Italian marble and feature lighted makeup mirrors—just like a star's dressing room. Colors throughout are cool blues and greens. The tenth floor is the recreation area, with sundeck, big swimming pool, and Jacuzzi, as well as a snack and cocktail bar. The morning newspaper is delivered to your room every day; coffee and tea are served in the lobby every morning. At night, when your bed is turned down, you'll find an orchid and a chocolate on your pillow! Doubles are priced from $65 to $100 (the price goes up as you move from the lowest floors up into the 20s and 30s). An extra person in the room is charged $10. On the top floors, with access by key only, is the Kuhio Club, whose guests receive special niceties, like complimentary continental breakfast in the morning and hors d'oeuvres in the evening. Guest rooms are $115 to $125, single or double; one-bedroom suites go for $195 to $375.

Since its takeover by the New Otani Hotel Corporation of Japan, the **Kai'mana Beach Hotel,** Diamond Head Way at 2863 Kalakaua Ave., Honolulu, HI 96815 (tel. 923-1555), has been totally refurbished and looks very good indeed. The open-air lobby, with its wicker bucket chairs and sofas, looks out on the Hau Tree Lanai cocktail lounge and a beautiful view of the Pacific. The little shopping arcade outside boasts an antique shop, Suzie France, and an ice-cream parlor, Scoop du Jour. Rooms are spacious and well appointed; the corner rooms have lanais on two sides for a stunning view. Furniture in the guest rooms is dark rattan, and the color scheme is soft green. There is a tremendous variety of types of accommodation here. We'll cover a few to give you an idea of what's available. Standard rooms go for $56 single, $72 double. Then you get into the type of view: Diamond Head is $62 single, $65 double, Ocean and Waikiki is $76 single, $80 double. Junior suites, with one bedroom, are $160 and $165, single or double. Garden apartments are $74 single and $77 double for the studio kitchenette and $100 single or double for the one-bedroom with kitchenette. From December 20 to March 31, rates are $10 higher in all categories. An additional person is $10. Naturally, all accommodations are air-conditioned and have color TV. Rates are subject to change.

Now that we've gone in a Diamond Head direction about as far as we can go, let's head back along Kalakaua Avenue, into the center of Waikiki. Here, about a block away from the beach, at the corner of Kalakaua and Lewers Street, you'll find the **Pleasant Holiday Isle Hotel,** 270 Lewers St. (tel. 923-0777; reservations, toll free 800/242-9244), a nicely appointed hotel with a superb location smack in the middle of everything. Many of your fellow guests here will be spending up to $56 a day for a double, but they're paying for the glorious views; if you're willing to forgo that view, you can have the same rooms they have—on the third and fourth floors—for just $47 a day double, $42 single. Each extra person is charged $7 a day, but there's no fee for children under 2, unless they need a crib. A cool, blue-green color scheme runs through the hotel; all rooms are air-conditioned and nicely laid out, and all have refrigerators. There are radios and color TV in every room, and the staff is hospitable. For those too lazy to get themselves to the turquoise Pacific less than a block away, there's a nice-size pool on a deck outside the hotel lobby that offers a beautiful view as well as privacy. Downstairs, you can get good food and modestly priced drinks.

One of the first high-rise hotels to be built in Waikiki, and still one of the largest (885 rooms), is the **Reef Hotel,** right on the beach and in the center of things at 2169 Kalia Rd., Honolulu, HI 96815 (tel. 923-3111); reservations, toll free 800/367-5170 in U.S., 800/826-6786 in Canada). With a top beachfront location, plenty of activities, warm hospitality, and nicely furnished rooms, the Reef offers excellent value for the money. During the regular season, April 1 through December 18, small "tourist" rooms are $45, standard rooms are $50, moderate rooms are $70, deluxe partial ocean-view are $85, and oceanfront are $100; during the winter months, these rooms are $50, $55, $75, $90 and $125, respectively. Suites for up to four people run from $90 to $150. Add $15 for an additional person. The Reef boasts one of the largest freshwater swimming pools in Waikiki, and many water activities on the beach. Lots of interesting shops line the extensive lobby and the lower-level lobby. At poolside is the famous Sadie Thompson's Bar & Grill, and the cozy Harry's Underwater Bar is different and fun. The Shorebird Lounge and Broiler, right on the beach, is great fun for giant burgers, inexpensive broil-your-own dinners, sunset cocktails, and disco later. If you're planning to rent a car, inquire about the excellent Reefmobile rates, from $32 per person, including a hotel room and an automatic compact car with unlimited free mileage.

In this era of high-rise Hawaii, it comes as a shock to find a low-slung, two-story hotel cozily nestled into a tropical garden, complete with pools, plantings, and that oldtime Hawaiian feeling you weren't sure still existed. And that's the kind of pleasant shock you'll get when you walk into the courtyard of the **Hawaiiana Hotel,** 260 Beach Walk, Honolulu, HI 96815 (tel. 923-3811; reservations, toll free 800/367-5122). Located on a side street, half a block from the beach on one side and Kalakaua Avenue on the other, the Hawaiiana is not well known among tourists since it doesn't go about blowing its own horn; but those who know it treasure it and wouldn't dream of going anywhere else. All of the units are attractively furnished as studio rooms or suites, with complete electric kitchens; all catch the trade winds, most have lanais, and all have views of either the garden or one of the two pools (there's a shallow one perfect for kids). The studio rooms run from $47 to $62 single, $50 to $64 double (the lower-priced ones are closest to the street and office); a third person in a room is $11 per day; the one-bedroom suites run $86 for up to four persons. From December 17 to April 20, add $3 per category.

But the comfort and charm of the rooms is just the beginning of the story here. The hotel believes in doing extra little things for its guests, like serving them free coffee and pineapple juice out by the main pool in the morning; placing a pineapple in their rooms when they arrive; giving them leis on departure; presenting two Hawaiian shows a week (free); and leaving a newspaper at the door every morning. Use of the washing machines and dryers is free, and so is parking on nearby Saratoga Road. The Hawaiiana is the kind of place where you get to know your neighbors, and many couples who have met here now plan their vacations together and reunite at the Hawaiiana every year! Mapuana Schneider, the hospitable manager, suggests advance reservations, especially during the busy midsummer and midwinter seasons.

After you've seen the Hawaiiana, it's almost a case of déjà vu when you see **The Breakers,** 250 Beach Walk, Honolulu, HI 96815 (tel. 923-3181). The mystery is cleared up when you learn that the same architect designed both. Like its neighbor, it has that low-slung, relaxed, Hawaiian-garden feeling. There are about 66 rooms in the five ranch-style buildings, all of them nicely appointed, with complete electric kitchenettes, modern Oriental decor, air conditioning; many have lanais. The studio rooms go at $47 and $59 single, $51 and $61 twin. There are also 15 garden suites that rent at $96 single or twin, $103 triple, $109 quad. You'll enjoy the large pool, the leis on departure, the beach facilities down the road, and the lovely garden setting.

A real find, one you'll not see advertised anywhere, is the **Waikiki Shore Apartments,** 2161 Kalia Rd., Honolulu, HI (tel. 926-4733; reservations, toll free 800/367-2353). This is a condominium apartment building, with each unit privately owned; in fact, it is the only apartment building we know of right on the beach at Waikiki. Many of the owners have purchased their apartments here as investments, and make them available year round for short-term rentals.

Studio apartments start at $60 regular, $50 off-season (April 16 to December 15). One- and two-bedroom apartments start at $84 and $120, respectively, $74 and $110 off-season. Two-bedroom oceanfront apartments begin at $150 ($146 off-season). Prices advance a few dollars depending on the floor. Rates for the one-bedrooms are for up to three people; rates for the two-bedrooms are for up to four people; add $7 per day for each extra person.

The rooms are spacious. Each apartment has its own private lanai that runs across its entire width, so you have views of both sea and mountains, and of the green, spacious lawns of Fort DeRussy, next door. Each apartment is furnished and decorated differently, of course, but all are attractive, and all have complete kitchens with garbage disposal and laundry facilities, as well as private telephones. Request air conditioning if you desire it; many of the apartments have it, and even in those that do not, cross-ventilation is excellent and there are ceiling and desk fans as well. The beach is one of the loveliest around, and dozens of restaurants and shops are just a few steps from the front door of the cool, inviting lobby, decorated in rich shades of turquoise. You get the feeling of apartment living here, not a tourist hotel. Ample parking is available in the basement.

The cool and peaceful **Best Western Waikiki Plaza Hotel,** 2045 Kalakaua Ave., Honolulu, HI 96815 (tel. 955-6363; reservations, toll free 800/367-8047, ext. 101, in the U.S. or 800/423-8733, ext. 101, in Canada), is outstanding among the newer hotels. We like the location, near Fort DeRussy and the good beaches in that area. The two-level lobby gives a feeling of coolness, with its terrazzo floors and tasteful furnishings. And you certainly won't go hungry or unentertained here. The Makai Sugar Company Restaurant on the mezzanine floor offers excellent food impeccably served. There's cocktail and sandwich service at the pool. And at night, the Sugar Mill Lounge features entertainment of high quality.

The rooms are quite lovely, all air-conditioned, with color television, telephones, and private lanais. And every room has a fine view of either ocean or mountains, not too common in many Waikiki hotels. Most rooms have two double beds or a king-size one. From April to December 23, one-room accommodations go from $45 to $62 for singles, from $49 to $66 for doubles. Add $4 to $5 more for the winter months. There is a charge of $12 per extra person when using the existing equipment, $10 extra if a rollaway bed is required.

Located at the entrance of Waikiki, adjacent to the Ala Moana Shopping Center and overlooking the Ala Wai Yacht Harbor, is the **Ala Moana Americana Hotel,** 410 Atkinson Dr., Honolulu, HI 96815 (tel. 955-4811; reservations, toll free 800/228-3278). This 1,193-room luxury building is a beauty, certainly the closest to the "mostest"—for shopping as well as to downtown Honolulu. Ala Moana Beach Park is within walking distance, but the main action of Waikiki Beach is about a ten-minute bus ride away.

The handsome lobby is the ideal place for talk and a drink. The second-floor level is worth a look for the outstanding examples of art of the islands, including a mural of the King Kalakaua era executed by Juliette May Fraser, and some charming paintings from modern Hawaii. And despite the wealth of shops and restaurants in the adjoining Ala Moana Shopping Center (you need only cross a footbridge to be smack in front of Liberty House), there are more shops lined up in the lobby, plus a snack café, a poolside bar, a lounge, and a show room in the hotel. The Mango & Miso restaurant is open around the clock and adjoins Rumours, one of the largest nightclubs in Honolulu.

Every room in this tallest of Hawaii's resort hotels has air conditioning, color TV, radio, tub-shower combinations, direct-dial telephones, and automatic wake-up system. The color schemes are attractive, most of the rooms have twin beds and lanais. Singles and doubles go from approximately $65 to $95, depending on the floor and the view. There is no charge for children under 14 sharing the same room with their parents, but there is a maximum of three people in a room.

ALONG KUHIO AVENUE: It's hard to ask for a more central location in Waikiki than the one enjoyed by the handsome **Coral Reef,** 2299 Kuhio Ave., Honolulu, HI 96815 (tel. 922-1262). It's next door to the bustling International Market Place, and the mood here too is one of excitement and fun, with shops, restaurants, and a supper-club all holding forth on the main floor. Upstairs are some 243 rooms, each good-size and nicely furnished in island style, with private lanais, shag carpeting, air conditioning, a desk, and a cable color TV set in every room. Rooms have either two double beds or one double and one single. Rates are $43, single or double, from April 1 to December 20; $63 from December 21 to March 31. Add $10 for a third person. The hotel also specializes in moderately priced suites, eminently suitable for large families, at around $95. For $5 more, you can request cooking facilities in any category.

For reservations, phone Aston Corp. toll free at 800/367-5124.

The attractive **Outrigger Malia,** 2211 Kuhio Ave., Honolulu, HI 96815 (tel. 923-7621; reservations, 808/926-0679, or toll free 800/367-5170, 800/826-6786 in Canada), has a lot going for it—including a rooftop tennis court, a therapeutic spa, and a wonderfully central location. And right off the colorful, breezy lobby is the Wailana Malia, one of the best coffeeshops in town, open 24 hours a day. And we haven't even told you about the rooms yet! Each of them, cheerfully decorated with cane furniture, crimson carpeting, and printed bedspreads, has a lanai, air conditioning, and color TV. One entire floor features rooms designed especially for physically handicapped guests, with wide doors to accommodate wheelchairs and grab-bars in the bathrooms. The junior suites consist of a sitting room with two daybeds (or *punees,* as they are called in Hawaii), plus a bedroom. They can accommodate up to four people; rates are $60 to $65 for up to four. Regular rooms contain two double beds and have a small refrigerator. Rates for these rooms are $45 to $60 single or twin. From December 19 to March 31, add $5 per category.

The walkway to the airy lobby of the **Sherry Waikiki,** 334 Lewers St., Honolulu, HI 96815 (tel. 922-2771), is surrounded by plant beds filled with lau'e ferns, croton, and palm trees, making for a charming entry into this cozy and friendly little hotel. Off to the left is the sparkling pool, surrounded by a carpeted sundeck and serenaded by soft Hawaiian music that comes out of nowhere. All 100 of the units have kitchenettes, lanais, and full baths with tub and shower. The small studios, which accommodate two, go for $54 a day; the larger studios, maximum four persons, go for $64, and the deluxe one-bedroom suites, maximum five persons, are $84.

The **Waikiki Resort Hotel,** 2460 Koa Ave., Honolulu, HI 96815 (tel. 922-4911), has a breezy, open lobby that looks out at the pretty fountains just outside. Rooms here are decorated in golds and browns with dark-green carpeting; all have lanais. The hotel is air-conditioned throughout, and all rooms have the comforts of refrigerator and radio as well as the usual TV. Double rooms run from $52 to $69, depending on the height of the floor and which way the rooms face. The higher-priced rooms are on a high floor and face the ocean; the lower-priced ones are below the eighth floor and face the mountains. Rooms with kitchenettes (as opposed to just a refrigerator) all face the ocean and are $69 per day double. For a touch of luxury, you might try the one- and two-bedroom suites at $170 and $270. Children under 12 are free, provided that additional beds are not required; add $10 per day for an additional adult. The Falls Coffeeshop is just off the lobby for good and moderately priced food, and there's a lovely swimming pool too, even though a nice stretch of Kuhio Beach is just down the street.

The **Marine Surf** at 364 Seaside Ave. (corner Kuhio), Honolulu, HI 96815 (tel. 923-0277; reservations, toll free 800/367-5176), boasts a central location just a block from bustling Kalakaua Avenue. And that's not all it boasts. For $44, single or double, from April 1 to December 20 ($54 the rest of the year) you get a studio apartment, not just a hotel room. This means a fully equipped electric kitchen and a dining area. Give them points too for color television, sliding glass doors to a furnished lanai, and two extra-length double beds. The views get better as you go up, and the rates go up accordingly: $51 or $61 for superior rooms (single or double); $57 or $67 for deluxe rooms (again, a single or double); some penthouse suites available at $85 to $95. No charge for children under 12 unless they require a rollaway bed; extra adults, or rollaway or crib, $8. And the swimming pool in this 23-story building is on the fourth floor. You'll find a quiet, conservative lobby, but bright, colorful apartments. Inside the building is Matteo's, for superb Italian food, and Jameson's Restaurant, a cheerful pub. Parking is available.

At the new 625-room **Island Colony Hotel** at 445 Seaside Ave., Honolulu, HI 96815 (tel. 923-2345), elegance begins in the spacious, airy lobby, with its stylish rattan furniture and big, beautiful tapa banners that hang from the ceiling and sway in the breeze. It continues in the pool and sundeck on the sixth floor, the restaurant off the lobby, and on into the rooms, all of which have very large lanais; some of the views are breathtaking. The rooms are lavishly appointed in subdued Polynesian prints with rust-colored rugs, and all have phones and color TV sets. You have your choice here of several accommodations. If you want to do only some light cooking, take the "deluxe hotel rooms," which have two double beds, a large refrigerator, hotplate, cookware, and tableware; prices range from $43 a day on the lower floors to $48 on the upper floors. Or you can have a studio with full kitchenette (although the refrigerator is smaller than in the above rooms); these are priced at $59 for the lower floors, $85 for the top ones. Then there are one-bedroom apartments with full kitchen—there are four of these per floor—that go for $89 to $109; add $10 for an extra person. Between December 20 and April 10, add $7 per category. There are prints by Allen Akina and Pegge Hopper on the walls of the guest rooms, as well as in the lobby.

The Island Colony is a truly beautiful place, abounding in aloha. For reservations, write Aston, 2299 Kuhio Ave., Honolulu, HI 96815, or phone toll free 800/367-5124.

Pacific Monarch Hotel and Condominium, 142 Uluniu Ave., Honolulu, HI 96815 (tel. 923-6292), is right across the street from one of our old favorites, the Royal Grove (see below, under "Budget Discoveries") and, in fact, the Fong family manages several of the attractive units here. Most of the units, however, are managed by Silver, Ltd., at the address above, and by Colony Resorts (call toll free at 800/367-6046 in the U.S., 800/663-1118 in Canada). The Pacific Monarch is a handsome, modern skyscraper, choicely located just a block from Kuhio Beach. Rooms are pleasant and nicely decorated, with air conditioning, TV, phones, full baths, all the amenities. Studio rooms all have wet bar/refrigerator/hot plate and rent for $60 to $70 superior, $70 to $80 deluxe. One bedroom apartments boast full kitchens, and cost, for up to four persons, $85 to $95 superior, $90 to $100 deluxe. Many of the lanais are quite large and offer views (depending on the floor and angle) of Diamond Head, the ocean, and the lights and sights of Waikiki. Facilities are excellent: a secured building, sky-top pool, sundeck, Jacuzzi, and even a sauna with a picture-window view of Diamond Head! Car and condo packages are often available. Tops for comfort, convenience, and easy living.

If comfort and convenience mean a lot to you, then we think you'll be as happy as we were to discover the **Ilima Hotel,** 445 Nohonani St., Honolulu, HI 96815 (tel. 923-1877). Every room in this attractive hotel has a modern, fully equipped kitchen, color TV, private lanai, radio, telephone, double beds, and full tub-shower combinations. Sun-worshippers will love the two sundecks atop the tenth floor, as well as the ground-level pool area with its ample sunning space on one side and tree-shaded comfort on the other.

As for the rooms, they are impeccably clean and attractively furnished in Polynesian style. The studios, which have two double beds and can easily accommodate four, rent for $36 to $52. They're all the same, but the rates get progressively higher as you go up and the views get better. It's $8 for each additional grown-up and $8 for a crib or rollaway. There are also one-bedroom suites: the small ones with two double beds rent from $54 to $72; the larger ones with three double beds go from $62 to $78. Two-bedroom suites rent for $72 to $88. The penthouse units can be utilized as a one-, two-, or three-bedroom suite, and rent for $58 to $173. Add $8 to these rates from December 15 to April 15. Parking and local phone calls are free.

The Ilima is close to the Ala Wai, so it's slightly removed from the hustle and bustle of Waikiki, but just a few minutes' stroll takes you to where the action is.

The **Hawaiian King Hotel,** 417 Nohonani St., Honolulu, HI 96815 (tel. 922-3894; reservations, toll free 800/367-7042 in the U.S., 800/426-8328 in Canada, 008-033134 in Australia, and 03-348-6535 in Japan), is the kind of hotel one stumbles upon only rarely. The five-story condominium apartment building centers around a lovely garden and pool area, the place to chat with fellow guests. And accommodations are definitely superior to many in Waikiki. Each unit, designed with the family in mind, is a handsome, beautifully decorated suite, with large living room, separate bedroom, a full kitchenette (and we mean full, down to the disposal unit in the sink) separated from the living room by a counter, and carpeting in the living room and on the lanai. As further blessings, all the apartments are air-conditioned, and as quiet as they are attractive. There's a cocktail lounge, minimart, boutique, and laundry at hand. Units are serviced daily, and there is 24-hour front desk and telephone switchboard service. Considering all this aloha, you get good value for your money. During the summer season, April 15 to December 15, a standard unit, single or double, is $44 per night, $250 per week; superior units are $54 and $300; deluxe go for $60 and $350. In winter, rates are $52, $62 and $68, with no weekly rates. Children 12 and under are free; an extra person is charged $6 per day, $35 per week.

The **Waikiki Banyan,** 201 Ohua Ave., Honolulu, HI 96815 (tel. 922-0555; reservations, toll free 800/367-8047, ext. 125, in mainland U.S., 800/423-8733, ext. 125, in Canada), is perfect for those who want the at-home comforts of a condominium apartment combined with the attentions of a full hotel—daily maid service, bell service, a 24-hour front desk, and much more. That "much more" includes an enormous sixth-floor recreation deck, complete with a pool, tennis court, sauna, barbecue areas, snack bar, and a children's play area—a great choice for families—all within sight of glorious mountain views. The Waikiki Banyan is a huge place, 38 stories high, with about 295 rental units. Each of these is a two-room suite, nicely if not elaborately decorated, but very comfortable; each has a large living-dining area, a well-equipped kitchen, a sofa bed in the living room, two twins in the bedroom, air conditioning, color TV, private phones. You're well set up for vacation living here.

Prices are best during the summer season: April 16 to December 16. It's then that singles and doubles with a city view go for $71, $79 mountain view, $87 ocean view; triples are $81, $89, and $97; quads are $91, $99, and $107. Weekly rates are $449, $479, and $499. Winter rates are about $10 more per category (no weekly rates), plus a surcharge of $10 per night per room from December 21 to December 31. There is no charge for children under 12 using existing bedding; a rollaway bed or crib is $10 per day.

Right at the corner of the Ala Wai and Seaside Avenue is the **Seaside Surf,** 400 Seaside Ave., Honolulu, HI 96815 (tel. 922-2383; reservations, 800/367-5170 in the U.S., 800/326-6786 in Canada). Another member of the ubiquitous Outrigger Hotels chain, this 56-room high-rise offers facilities for very comfortable living. Attractively styled in Polynesian decor, these are all one- and two-bedroom apartments, each boasting two bathrooms, kitchenette with microwave oven, two or three color TVs per unit, two telephones, and air conditioning. From April 1 through December 18, standard one-bedroom apartments are $75 and $85 for up to four people; moderate one-bedroom units are $80 and $85; deluxe one-bedroom units are $85 and $90; and two-bedroom suites are $105 to $125; add $5 more the rest of the year. There's plenty of covered parking; no pool or restaurant.

Budget Discoveries
Rooms in this category will average $50 or under per night.

NEAR KALAKAUA AVENUE: There's a friendly feeling about the modest little **Royal Grove Hotel,** 151 Uluniu Ave., Honolulu, HI 96815 (tel. 923-7691), where the Fong family is in charge. Just a block away from Kuhio Beach, the six-story pink hotel has a small pool right on the premises, a grocery shop, healthfood store, and restaurant off the lobby, an attentive staff, and some 100 nicely put-together rooms whose prices begin as low as $28 for a single or a double. Comfortable kitchenette units begin at $34.50, and for $38 and up you can have your choice of kitchenette units with their own lanais. The one-bedroom apartments are good buys too, from $36 to $75 and it's $10 for an extra person. It's not at all fancy, but good value for the money.

Note: You'll probably find TV reception at low-rise hotels like this to be poor: if you're going to do a lot of TV watching (we can't imagine why), you're better off staying at a high-rise hotel. Because of the mountains, in high-density areas like Waikiki, only the tall buildings with very high rooftop antennas can get really good reception. Just one of the facts of Hawaiian life.

One of the newer hotels in the Waikiki area is the big, beautiful, bustling **Waikiki Village** at 226 Lewers St., Honolulu, HI 96815 (tel. 923-3881). The enormous lobby boasts several shops and a swimming pool located just behind the reservations desk! The staff members are very attractive young people who clearly like their work and enjoy being helpful and dispensing aloha.

The hotel is air-conditioned throughout, and there is a television set in each of the attractively furnished rooms. The decor is modern with a Polynesian flair. Double-room rates are $50 to $60 per day for rooms without a kitchenette. Two-room suites with kitchenette are $68 and up for up to four persons. Add $10 per day for each additional person. The kitchenette units here consist of a unit with a sink, half-size refrigerator with cupboard and counter space, and hotplates—perfectly adequate for light meals. Waikiki Village also boasts an attractive coffeeshop and a cocktail lounge, and one of the prettiest stretches of Waikiki Beach awaits you just across Kalia Road.

If there is a "heart" of Waikiki, the **Reef Towers** must be it. Located at 227 Lewers St., Honolulu, HI 96815 (tel. 923-3111;

reservations, toll free 800/367-5170, 800/826-6786 in Canada), half a block from the beach in one direction and half a block from busy Kalakaua Avenue in the other, it is right in the midst of everything, as well as being the home of the Al Harrington show at the Polynesian Palace. Accommodations here lean toward the living-room-by-day, bedroom-by-night feeling; most rooms are equipped with a refrigerator, and some—at higher price levels—also have a kitchenette. Standard rooms are a good buy at $30, single or double. Don't expect much in the way of views here, or in the moderate rooms ($40 double), since the Reef Towers is really socked in by big hotels. Be satisfied with a glimpse of the ocean or mountains or the pool of a nearby hotel. Moderate rooms with kitchen are $45, deluxe units with kitchen are $50. Add $5 to these rates during winter (December 19 through March 31), $10 more for an extra person. Lanais are small but private, bathrooms have just a stall shower, and closets are adequate. Inquire about their "Wheels Deal," which offers good rates for a hotel room and automatic compact car with unlimited free mileage.

Another very popular part of this chain is the **Waikiki Tower of the Reef Hotel,** 200 Lewers St., Honolulu, HI 96815 (tel. 922-6424; reservations, toll free 800/367-5170 in U.S., 800/826-6786 in Canada), and very pleasant it is. The back of the attractive open lobby looks onto the pool area of its sister hotel, the Edgewater, whose pool it shares, and the beach is a very short walk away. Just off the lobby is the attractive and moderately priced Waikiki Broiler Restaurant, which is not just the usual hotel coffeeshop. The rooms are smartly decorated in brightly colored floral schemes, bathrooms have full tub and shower, and all rooms have a direct-dial phone, color TV, and air conditioning. Most rooms have a lanai; corner rooms have two lanais; and to create a suite, two corner rooms can be opened up so that you have three lanais and two TV sets! All corner rooms have a kitchenette (they are the only ones that do). The one thing that determines whether rooms here are standard, superior, or deluxe is the height of the story (not the fact that it has a kitchenette, special view, etc.). Rates are $45, single and double, for standard accommodations; $50 for moderate; and $55 for deluxe. Add $5 to these rates during winter (December 18 to March 31), $10 more for a third person. Junior suites for three persons are $65 to $75.

Like its sister Reef hotels, the Waikiki Tower has attractive car and hotel packages. Inquire for details.

The **Malihini Hotel,** 217 Saratoga Rd., Honolulu, HI 96815 (tel. 923-9644), occupies an ideal location between beach and town; the beach in front of the Reef Hotel is just a hop across the street, and Kalakaua is a few minutes' walk away. The Malihini is a fine family choice. The large rooms are pleasantly furnished, have either king-size or double beds, fans, full electric kitchens, and some have lanais big enough for dining room tables and a border of plants. Outside, in the brick courtyard, you'll often find fellow guests barbecuing their steaks or throwing a cocktail party for the rest of the crowd. Children are warmly welcomed. Laundry facilities are right at hand. Prices are reasonable: $22 to $24 for a compact studio; $28 to $32 for larger studios with lanais; $38 to $44 for the one-bedroom apartments with lanais for four. Family rates can also be worked out. Prices go up a few dollars during the December 15 to April 15 high season.

Look out any streetside window in the **Waikiki Surfside,** 2452 Kalakaua Ave., Honolulu, HI 96815 (tel. 923-0266; reservations, toll free 800/367-5124 from continental U.S.), and you're practically within "spitting distance" of Waikiki Beach, which is just across Kalakaua Avenue. Its location is its greatest asset, for this is an older hotel, with an unprepossessing façade and mini-lobby. Within are well-worn but still okay rooms. They are clean and cheerily decorated, with pile carpets and brown marble tabletops. They are all air-conditioned and have color TV. The best time to come here is between April 1 and December 20, when standard rooms are $29, single or double; rooms with a slightly better location are $35; and oceanfront rooms with lanais are $40. In winter, there is a $20 surcharge in all categories.

With only 196 rooms, the **Waikiki Gateway Hotel,** 2070 Kalakaua Ave., Honolulu, HI 96815 (tel. 935-3741, or toll free 800/367-5124), isn't one of the "big" Waikiki hotels, but this small charmer is pure Hawaiiana (pre-missionary). Prominent artist Joseph Feher's pictures depicting the Hawaii of long ago were reproduced as murals and now decorate the barkcloth walls of each room. They are beautifully complemented by the rich-toned cane furniture and the deep red-and-gold color scheme. Even the bathrooms are beautiful!

Each room has a large lanai (some have two), a direct-dial phone, and a television set (color in the suites). One of the island's finest restaurants, Nick's Fishmarket, is in the lobby. And there are laundry facilities on the fourth floor adjacent to the sundeck and the delicious blue pool backed by a wall of lava rock.

The Waikiki Gateway is not at the beach, but TheBUS, which stops right out front, will get you there promptly. Rates start at $36 for a double room and advance up to $56 on the higher floors. Add $8 for each additional person. Winter rates—December 20 to April 1—are $8 to $9 more. Reservations should be made about two months in advance.

ALONG KUHIO AVENUE: There's a very comfortable feeling about the **Ambassador Hotel of Waikiki,** 2040 Kuhio Ave., Honolulu, HI 96815 (tel. 941-7777). It's neither too large nor too small, has an excellent location in the middle of Waikiki convenient to the beach and shopping, and the rooms are comfortable and attractive. All are done up in studio style, and they have air conditioning, telephones, and sliding glass doors opening onto private lanais. The views are bigger and better in certain locations, but prices are reasonable throughout—from $40 to $52 single, from $44 to $56 double. We especially like the one-bedroom suites, which include full electric kitchens, and the corner suites with their great views of the ocean and Diamond Head. Here the price is $70 to $90, single or double; add $8 for an extra person. You can have breakfast, lunch, or dinner at the Café Ambassador Coffeeshop, or drinks at the Embassy Bar, right on the premises. And if you're too lazy to walk to the Pacific, there's a large pool and sundeck lanai one floor above the bustle of Waikiki; drinks and snacks are at the ready too.

At the Ala Wai end of Lewers, the **Waikiki Holiday,** 450 Lewers St., Honolulu, HI 96815 (tel. 923-0245), is about a ten-minute walk to the beach and a block from the bus line. From the sweeping entrance and free-form pool outside to the 90 handsomely appointed rooms, lobby, and charming Indian restaurant, Shalimar, the place exudes a quality of charm and comfort that is hard to come by in this price range. All the rooms are air-conditioned and completely refurbished, and parking is available on the premises. Here's the easy-to-take price tab: doubles with kitchen are $31 to $46; without kitchen $24 to $50. An extra person is $5. One-bedroom apartments are $48 to $58 for four. The rooms have private balconies with views that get better the higher up you go.

ALONG THE ALA WAI: For those who like the feeling of a big and coolly efficient hotel, the newly renovated **Aloha Surf,** 444 Kanekapolei St., Honolulu, HI 96815 (tel. 923-0222), is an excellent choice. The hotel looks out on the Ala Wai Canal and is about a ten-minute walk to the beach. A beauty shop, gift shop, outdoor coffeeshop, and pool all adjoin the almost wide-open lobby. Rooms are air-conditioned, and have wall-to-wall carpeting and bright but tasteful color schemes. All rooms have television, most have a lanai, and some have a kitchenette. As for the views, which start a few floors above street level, they are of the Koolau Mountains and a tiny bit of ocean. The rates remain stable all year round, so don't worry about higher winter rates. Even so, these rates compete well with others in less favorable locations. Standard rooms rent for $42, single or double; moderate rooms with private lanai go for $46; and rooms with kitchenette cost $56. Suites run from $65 to $80. An extra person is $8.

ALONG THE ALA WAI: The **Waikiki Sand Villa** at 2375 Ala Wai Blvd., Honolulu, HI 96815 (tel. 922-4744; reservations, toll free 800/367-5072 from U.S. except Alaska, 800/421-4545 from Alaska, 800/663-3602 from Canada), looks like a sandcastle. It's made of sand-colored material and is castle shaped. All of the rooms have a lanai, color TV, and tub and shower in the bathrooms. There are no kitchenettes, but the Royal Rooms and junior suites do have refrigerators. The guest rooms are good-size and attractively decorated in rattan furniture and printed bedspreads. And the young staff is cordial and helpful. Rates depend solely on the floor and view, and run $28 single, $38 double for standard accommodations; $36 to $48, superior; $46 to $58, deluxe, $56 to $68 premium. For a triple or quad, add $8 per person. A one-bedroom junior suite is $94, single or double. Children under 8 stay free unless they require a rollaway crib.

A BIT FARTHER AWAY: The **Pagoda Hotel,** 1525 Rycroft St., Honolulu, HI (tel. 941-6611), comes complete with a scenic floating restaurant right on its premises. The studio rooms are very pleasant, well-set-up for housekeeping with a full refrigerator and stove, and air-conditioned. They go from $46 to $54 single or double, depending on the floor. You're not too near the ocean here, but your own car or the free shuttle bus will have you in all the excitement of Waikiki in just a few minutes. There's a pretty pool on the grounds.

Closer to Waikiki, across Ala Moana Boulevard from the Ilikai, and equaling it in prime proximity to both the beach and the Ala Moana Shopping Center, is the **Hawaii Dynasty Hotel,** 1830 Ala Moana Blvd., Honolulu, HI 96815 (tel. 955-1111). Rising 17 stories, this 206-room resort is set well back from traffic noise, and since all rooms are air-conditioned, peace and quiet are doubly assured. Hawaii Dynasty Hotel rooms are standard size, but the bed sizes are deluxe. When you ask for twins, you get two double beds. Closets, too, are big, and a smart vanitorium extends the whole length of the tub-shower-equipped bathroom. The rooms, done in either beige and green or gold with yellow, all have a telephone; most have peeks at the ocean; some feature a lanai.

Rates go from $27 to $42 for singles, $37 to $42 for double doubles. Better views, lanais, and king-size beds account for the higher rates. There are also penthouse suites for $110. Cribs are free, and there is no charge for children under 18 sharing a room with their parents. Extra adults pay $10 a night, and up to three people can share one room. From December 21 to April 15, there is a high-season surcharge of $7 per category. Babysitters are at the ready.

Chapter IV

DINING DISCOVERIES

DO TOURISTS spend more time eating than doing anything else? Statistics could never prove it, of course, but it has always seemed to us that dining out is one of the most popular pastimes under the Hawaiian sun. And with good reason: although Hawaii is not one of the true gourmet capitals of the world, it embraces a wealth of cultural traditions from all over, and dining here can be more fun—and more adventurous—than almost anyplace else. Honolulu itself has perhaps a dozen great restaurants, scores of unusual and interesting ones, and many where the food is hearty, well priced, and just what you would expect from a good restaurant back home. Because there are so many restaurants in Honolulu, however, and in so many price categories, some guidance is in order. You're not going to spend every evening dining out with wine and candlelight and haute cuisine; neither are you going to eat all your meals at beachside burger stands or in the coffeeshop of your hotel. What we've done here, then, is to track down several dozen of what we consider the best restaurants in town, no matter how much or how little you want to pay or what kind of dining experience you're after. And we've divided these restaurants into three categories. To wit:

1. Elegant and Expensive. Here we'll give you the details on a group of restaurants that are at the top of our list, where the cuisine, the service, the ambience, the view—or any combination thereof—all make for a memorable experience. Expect to pay at least $30, maybe a good deal more at those places with an all à la carte menu, for dinner. A few cocktails before, the proper wine during, and a bit of liqueur after will, of course, add up. Not to mention the tax and the tip. When it's feasible, we'll also tell you how you can enjoy the same glorious surroundings and superb food for a much lower tab—at lunch. At these places, reservations are a must. And when you phone, inquire about dress; although most Honolulu restaurants are eminently casual, a few prefer that men wear jackets and ties. (At some island restaurants, "dress" means pants and shoes.)

2. Medium-Priced Restaurants. The bulk of the restaurants we'll describe covers the range from $10 to about $25 for dinner. Many of these offer excellent table d'hôte dinners for reasonable prices. Here you'll continue to sample some of the international cuisines that have found a home in the islands—Japanese, Chinese, Mexican, Indonesian, Thai, French, Hawaiian, Italian, continental. And there'll be no shortage of that old Hawaiian favorite, the steakhouse. (This is the 50th *American* state, remember?)

3. Informal and Inexpensive. Which means exactly what it says. These are casual, come-as-you-are places, a few of them coffeehouses (but in the islands, even the coffeehouses are exotic), where you can expect to get dinner for $10 or under. Some are open around the clock, in case that hungry feeling should strike at an unexpected hour.

You'll note that under each main category we cover restaurants in Waikiki, in the downtown Honolulu area or beyond, or near the Ala Moana area. With one exception, all our choices are a short drive, or bus ride, or taxi ride away. (We'll tell you about a few restaurants in Windward Oahu when we take a later tour around the island.)

Elegant and Expensive

The Third Floor, in the Hawaiian Regent Hotel, 2552 Kalakaua Ave. (tel. 922-6611), has won a name for itself as one of the most fabulous restaurants in town. It received *Honolulu* magazine's "Restaurant of the Year" award in 1985. The decor is extraordinary, the service unbelievable (at least six waiters and waitresses served us at a recent meal, all addressing us by name!), and the continental cuisine of a very high order, filled with unexpected touches. You dine beneath open-beam ceilings, magnificent copper chandeliers, and multicolored Camelot banners against a romantic background of rippling fountains flowing over black river rocks, tropical wall plantings, and koa wall mosaics. You certainly have the right to expect the very best cuisine, and the menu of chefs Jan Rabe and Wolfgang Horndlein lives up to expectations.

We said the touches were unusual, and that they are. Instead of ordinary bread, you are served a slice of Indian *naan* bread, made by a master baker from New Delhi in an imported clay charcoal-heated oven. Instead of butter, you are served a combination of butter and duck liver—a whole crock of it. A tray of tiny relishes (miniature baby corn, pickled tomatoes, onions) is yours to nibble on while you study the wine list (the house has an excellent cellar) and order your entree. These range in price from $21 to $28.50, all à la carte. You could start your meal with the unique iced appetizer buffet, your pick, for $8.50, of such surprises as blue-point oysters, poached salmon medallions, marinated herring, vinaigrette shrimp, and fresh artichoke hearts. For the main course, you may want to try, as we did, the scampi provençale, sautéed in garlic butter and tomato with saffron rice, or the splendid seafood casserole. Both dishes were excellent. And one person, instead of the usual two, may order the rack of spring lamb provençale, served with mint sauce and fresh vegetables. New continental dishes are always being added to the menu, authentically prepared with air-flown imported delicacies. If you have room for dessert, there are European cheeses, French and Viennese pastries, and a very good Polynesian fruit salad flavored with kirsch wine—plus a dozen different European coffees. But do save some room for the surprise of the evening, as your waitress places a Plexiglas tub on your table with white (dry ice) clouds drifting down from it, like a stage setting of a dream. On it are chocolate-covered ice-cream bonbons—courtesy of the house. And, oh yes, while you're feasting, strolling musicians wander from table to table to play your requests.

The Third Floor is open for dinner only, 6:30 to 11 p.m. daily. Reservations are a must; jackets for the men are recommended; validated parking.

Hidden away in the far reaches of Waikiki, down steps, around corridors, and behind doors, is a small restaurant to which the gourmets of the world have beaten a path. This is **Michel's**, in the Colony Surf Hotel at 2895 Kalakaua Ave. (tel. 923-6552). The reason? Michel's chefs, whose culinary artistry is every bit as magical as the view from your table, which can rival anything on the Riviera—you're practically next to the incredibly blue-green Pacific, and you can watch the boats and bathers of the Outrigger Canoe Club as you dine on the fruits of Michel's wizardry. For example, some chefs simply cook snails; at Michel's they're sautéed in burgundy wine and topped with a tantalizing mixture of garlic (ever so slight), parsley, and butter. Some chefs just toss salads; at Michel's, island bibb lettuce is graced with ripe tomatoes, green peppers, hard-cooked eggs, green onions, exotic herbs, and Michel's own French dressing, all gently tossed at your table. Little matter that the snails are $9.50 the half dozen or the salad $5 per person or that the entrees range from $20 to $35. How can you put a price on ecstasy? We might as well tell you right now that Michel's is not the place to go if you are in a hurry. This is no steam-table operation, and one of the ingredients of the culinary art is time. Many discriminating diners who have been coming to Michel's over the years phone a day ahead for their favorite special dishes. You cannot rush such delights as canard rôti à l'orange, or Chateaubriand for two, or poulet rôti à l'estragon. For dessert, how about strawberries Romanoff, at $6? The very best wines and liquors, *mais certainement*. Check, please.

Inside Information Department: If you can't afford to have dinner at Michel's more than once (or not even once), why, live like the rich at lunchtime. Lunch, served daily except Saturday from 11:30 a.m. to 2:30 p.m., is also à la carte, with cheese soufflés at $10, salads from $5, omelets and other entrees averaging $7 to $14. Or try the Sunday champagne brunch, served from 11 a.m. to 2:30 p.m., and a lovely treat.

Right up there with the greats is **Bagwells 2424,** at the Hyatt Regency Waikiki, 2424 Kalakaua Ave., sumptuous in decor, elegant in service, outstanding for its French and American gourmet specialties. The room is done in warm earth tones, with cocoa velvet banquettes and big cocoa velvet armchairs to sink into, and there is original art and sculpture throughout the room. The Franciscan place settings and crystal are works of art too, and all this, along with background guitar music, sets the mood for the feasting to come.

Start your meal by a consultation with the wine steward, and then proceed to cold or hot appetizers like sashimi, smoked salmon, or lobster-and-scallop casserole; then on to, perhaps, a chilled bisque of shrimp and scampi, plus salad. Appetizers run $7.50 to $12. Now for the entrees, which average about $18 to $25. Highlights are a superb spit-roasted breast of duckling with black currants and orange, Hawaii trout with salmon mousse and crayfish sauce, and whole roast spring chicken with rosemary. Should you possibly have room for dessert, fresh strawberries would be perfect, as would a serving of cheese, port, and grapes, topped off by a cognac, of course—and you're ready for *l'addition, s'il vous plaît.*

Bagwells serves dinner only, nightly from 6:30 to 10:30 p.m. There's entertainment in the adjoining lounge—whose windows overlook the pool or the moonlit ocean—before and after dinner. Make advance reservations by phoning 922-9292 and you'll be given personalized matches.

When **John Dominis** opened its doors a few years back, it became an instant success. Reservations were being taken for weeks in advance. It's not hard to figure out why: a combination of location, decor, and food has made it one of the more enjoyable restaurants in Honolulu. Sitting astride the channel leading to Kewalo Basin, at 43 Ahui St., John Dominis is close enough to the water so that you can hear the laughter and music from the sailboats, charter fishing boats, and tour boats that pass by. Low-ceilinged dining rooms extending some 30 feet over the water create the sensation of being on a cruise ship yourself. Inside, lava rock and koa wood continue the feeling of old Hawaii. And an interior waterway swarming with tropical fish and even sharks provides constant visual excitement.

The menu too is dominated by the sea. You could start your meal with fish bisque, thick with seafood, or with such appetizers as steamed clams, oysters Rockefeller, or escargots, from $5.95 to $7.95. You can select your entree from a large center table, where the catch of the day is displayed on a bed of ice. This is your chance to try Hawaii's game fish, caught in local waters. It could be ahi or tuna (our favorite), local marlin, rock cod, uku, mahi-mahi, or opakapaka. Catch of the day is priced from $18.95 to $26.50, and your entree is accompanied by home-baked sourdough bread.

John Dominis is open for dinner every day from 5:30 to 10:30 p.m., with the bar in action from noon, and a pupu menu available from 3 p.m. to midnight. Reservations are advised, phone 523-0955.

A world-class dining experience can be had at the **Kamaaina Suite,** a restaurant within a restaurant, its host restaurant being the famous Willows (see below), 901 Hausten St. As soon as you mention the Kamaaina Suite at the reception desk, you are escorted through the Willow's Polynesian-style dining rooms to the rear and up a stairway. Then you enter another world. It could be the dining room of a missionary family or a plantation owner. The finery is matched by the impeccable service. Each month there is a different "Discovery of Taste" menu, in which each guest is offered "tasting portions" of a number of superb selections created by the noted chef de cuisine Kusuma Cooray. A native of Sri Lanka and a graduate of Cordon Bleu, Kusuma is a recognized chef and teacher of the Eastern world's distinctive cuisine, with a worldwide reputation.

Our meal began with an appetizer: shrimp salad in poached pear. Then came three entrees separated by an intermezzo of lemon sherbet. First, opakapaka with herbs and orange glaze; second, veal paupiettes with leek purée and truffle sauce; and third, moghul chicken with saffron rice and condiments. After this, dessert was wheeled over; it's hard not to succumb to such delights as fruit tarts or chocolate gâteau with Chantilly cream or creamed chestnuts in meringue with chocolate sauce. The price is fixed at $42.50 per person, without drinks, tax, or tip. But how can you put a dollar value on an experience like this?

The Kamaaina Suite is open for dinner only, starting at 6 p.m., with the latest reservations at 8:30 p.m. Reservations are a must: phone 946-4808. Closed Sunday.

One of the famous oldtimers of Honolulu is **The Willows,** 901 Hausten St. The Willows was converted from a private estate into a restaurant more than 43 years ago, and has since enjoyed an enormous following. It's such a beautiful spot, situated on a pond filled with Japanese carp and surrounded by gorgeous trees and flowers, that it's practically a must, especially if you're not going to visit the neighbor islands, where this kind of unspoiled atmosphere is much more prevalent. After being owned for many years by the McGuire-Perry family (whose good friend Arthur Godfrey made its name famous), the Willows was taken over by Randy Lee, formerly of the Halekulani Hotel; and the new menu is full of delightful island treats. Lunch is gracious and relaxed here, and the prices are moderate. In the evening, when à la carte entrees range from about $14 to $21, you can dine on a variety of seafood and meal entrees, including scallops royale sautéed in butter and sherry, their famous curry, baked lobster with honey butter, and a lavish Hawaiian Poi Supper (the latter repeated on "Poi" Thursdays, from 11 a.m. on, with impromptu entertainment hosted by Auntie Irmgaard Aluli; cost is $12.95). Whenever you dine, though, be sure to save room for dessert. Traditionalists should not miss the legendary sky-high coconut cream pie; but there are also a dreamy chocolate haupia cake and a guava glue sundae, which tastes better than it sounds. While you're enjoying the natural beauty and the good food (The Willows is one of *Travel/Holiday's* six recommended restaurants in Hawaii and the only one in a garden setting), strolling singers will serenade you with the old Hawaiian songs. At lunch, à la carte dishes are available from $5.50.

The Willows serves dinner daily from 6 to 9 p.m., lunch Monday through Saturday from 11:30 a.m. to 1:30 p.m., and on Sunday there's a splendid garden buffet brunch from 10:30 a.m. to 1 p.m. offering a vast array of delicacies, at $15.95 per person.

Reservations are suggested, especially if you want to sit on the lanai. Phone 946-4808.

Visitors to Honolulu and local residents can only be grateful that Guy Banal, the young chef/owner of **Bon Appétit,** 1778 Ala Moana Blvd., in Discovery Bay, decided to leave his native France a few years ago and try his luck here on these far Pacific shores. For Banal is a true master, and his superb cuisine has already won him a large and enthusiastic following, not to mention a *Travel/Holiday* Award. A visit to his charming bistro, so pretty with its mirrors and red banquettes, potted palms and white curtains, is a must for those who are really serious about French food. A group of four of us dined here recently, and after beginning with apéritifs like Kir Marie (champagne with raspberry-and-pear liqueur) and Lillet Blonde, and making a selection from the excellent wine list, we got on to the business of sampling a variety of Guy's specialties, all of which we can heartily recommend. Among the warm appetizers ($6.50 to $8), our group gave the highest rating to the mousse of scallops and smoked salmon with lemon butter sauce and red caviar; and almost equal bravos for the escargots and wild mushrooms in puff pastry and the dainty lobster ravioli with lobster bisque. The onion soup was richer, thicker, and more delicious than any we'd tasted before, made as it was with Brie and Swiss cheese. Among the fish and meat entrees ($16.50 to $27), the fresh filet of the day broiled in a simple ginger-and-lobster butter and the lobster tail poached in its own broth with vegetables and lemon grass were both happy choices. Guy Banal is a master pastry chef, too, so try to save some room for his marvelous homemade desserts: our favorite was the clafoutis, a custard of peaches and black cherries sautéed in caramel, and topped with a warm raspberry sauce. Magnifique! In addition to these à la carte dishes, there is a complete dinner, which changes every week, for about $22.50.

Bon Appétit is not only a superb restaurant, it happens to be Honolulu's largest wine and appetizer bar as well, with a choice of 35 French and California wines by the glass. So you can come by anytime after 4:30 p.m., or after the theater or the evening's entertainment, for a glass of wine and light entrees like cheese or pâté platters, onion soup, pasta, and the like.

Dinner is served every day from 5:30 on. Reservations are suggested: phone 942-3837.

Honolulu's food establishment gave **Il Fresco,** at 1200 Ala Moana Blvd., in Ward Centre, its highest ratings when it opened its doors just about two years ago, and no wonder: owners Mary Ann and Mike Nevin have created a marvelous menu combining the best of Italian and Cajun cooking, with many gourmet touches of their own. The restaurant features a kiawe grill and woodburning oven totally visible to diners (it's fun, in fact, to sit at the bar and watch the items going into the oven) and is done in a modern, almost minimalist decor, with nothing to detract from the splendor of the food. A long list of daily specials complements the regular menu, but you can almost always count on such wonderful items as the grilled oysters with ginger-and-shallot butter, the grilled Japanese eggplant with "chili goat cheese," $7.95, among the appetizers. (Garlic, herbs, chili, and cream mixed with the goat cheese create an extraordinary taste sensation.) And the roasted chicken stuffed with herbed goat cheese ($13.95) is too special to pass up. Mary Ann has created a number of wonderful pizzas that are little meals in themselves; the guests in our party raved about the one with barbecue chicken, tomatoes, mozarella and fontina cheeses, $11.50. Pastas, too, are unusual: it could be chicken pasta with lemon grass and ginger, or tortellini with Sonoma ham and snow peas, from $10.95 to $11.50. Among the grilled items, blackened opakapaka Cajun style is quite special: the fish is spiced, charred, served black on the outside, tender and moist within (market priced, usually under $20). There's a limited menu of homemade desserts: our favorites are the ice cream in praline and the French chocolate cake.

Il Fresco is open for lunch from noon to 2 p.m., Monday through Saturday, and for dinner nightly from 6 p.m. Reservations advised: phone 523-5191.

We'd call **J.R.'s Upstairs** at the Kilohana Square shopping center (in the 100 block of Kapahulu Avenue) more a small gourmet dining room than a restaurant. Owners Ron and Jan Martin—he with experience in world-class restaurants in the U.S. and Europe; she with a flair for making you feel at home with Tiffany plates, damask table linens, and silk flower arrangements—have created a very special dining experience. Tables are located in two separate rooms, creating an intimate, at-home feeling. Only 30 guests at a time can enjoy their fine continental food.

Dinner prices run from $14.75 to $18 for the entree. You can start with appetizers for $3 to $5 more: pasta, perhaps, or that special pâté, soup du jour (cream of avocado the day we were there), or salade maison. Entrees include a roast of the day—for us, leg of lamb, as succulent as you can imagine—or filet mignon at the higher range. Chicken parmesan (wrapped in cream, parsley, and breadcrumbs) is in the middle of the range. And pastas are at the lower price. For dessert, how about a celestial brownie or a macadamia-and-pecan tart?

J.R.'s is open for dinner only from Wednesday through Saturday from 7 p.m. Bring your own wine. Free parking. Reservations are a must: call 735-2204.

The European Touch

The sophistication of a fine meal in one of the great European capitals is what awaits you at **Alfred's,** at Century Center, 1750 Kalakaua Ave., corner Kapiolani Boulevard. The cozy, romantic restaurant is a "celebration" of the Swiss chef/proprietor Alfred Vollen-weider, who serves his gourmet fare in a serene ambience: blue velvet-like armchairs and dropped-parasol chandeliers, pink tablecloths, locally made hurricane lamps, elegant European china, fine wines from a well-stocked cellar. Service is friendly and professional.

With your dinner entree, priced mostly between $15 and $20, comes freshly prepared soup, a combination of salads—the last time we were there these included cucumbers in sour cream, shrimp-and-apple salad, egg salad and tomatoes with dill—and fresh vegetables. Fresh island fish is served every day and done remarkably well. Other good choices include veal Cordon Bleu, entrecôte Café de Paris, coquilles St-Jacques, Chateaubriand—and many more. Desserts are too good to miss, so ignore the calories and find some room for perhaps, the soufflé glacé Grand Marnier, strawberries Romanoff, or Black Forest cake. Then again, there's German cheesecake with pineapple and apple strudel to tempt you.

Weekday lunches offer good value: salads, pastas, steak tartare, escargots, fresh fish, and omelets run from $6 to $10, and a daily lunch special at $7.50 includes vegetables, soup or salad, and rice or potatoes.

Reservations are advised: phone 523-1602. Lunch is served Monday to Friday from 11 a.m. to 2 p.m.; dinner, Tuesday to Saturday from 6 to 10 p.m.

If there were such a thing as a list of the Top Ten—or Top Five —restaurants favored by Honoluluans, then **Nick's Fishmarket,** tucked away behind a door in the Waikiki Gateway Hotel, 2070 Kalakaua Ave., would surely be near the top of that list. Owner Patrick Bowlen is also owner of the Denver Broncos, so diners often get a chance to see famous sports figures who make a bee-

line for the restaurant when they're in town. Everyone appreci-
ates the super service, the cheerful red-carpet and dark-leather
ambience, the fish tanks and, intimate booths, and the scrupu-
lously fresh and delicious fish, the finest from Hawaiian waters,
including mahimahi, swordfish, and ono, as well as mainland
catches like sole, trout, catfish, salmon, and sea scallops. A recent United Airlines poll voted Nick's one of the 100 best restaurants in the United States.

It's fun to begin with a few drinks at the animated bar and
move on to your table for the main event. You can have a complete dinner for $24.95 that includes Fishmarket chowder or
Nick's special salad, vegetable and beverage, with entrees such as
fresh island ono, catfish, Pacific sea scallops, or U.S. prime top
sirloin. Or go à la carte with great appetizers like feta cheese and
Greek olives, sashimi, or smoked Nova Scotia salmon; the plate
of assorted appetizers at $8.95 is a particular treat. Main course
specialties, ranging from $13.95 to $24.95 (more for Maine lobster, flown in from New England every day), include a memorable bouillabaisse and chicken oregano (Greek style). Nick's also
offers some wonderful desserts, presented for selection on a silver tray; favorites include a chocolate mousse cake, coconut
cream cake, and cheese with fresh fruit toppings. There's live entertainment in the lounge from 9:30 p.m., perfect for after-
dinner dancing. Nick's Fishmarket serves dinner from 6 to 11
p.m. seven days a week; naturally, reservations are a must—
phone 955-6333.

Despite its name, **The Bali Room** at the Hilton Hawaiian Village does not have Balinese food. What it does have is a romantic, gardeny setting that suggests one might be dining somewhere
in the mysterious islands of the East, plus a menu to rival the best
continental restaurants in town. Yves Menoret, once the chef at
the famed Bagwell's Restaurant, is now in command of the kitch-
en here, and his marvelous fresh seafood and rôtisserie duck specialties are building an appreciative following. Everything about
this place—from the complimentary valet parking to the excellent wine list to the deft service—suggests an evening of gracious,
romantic, and exemplary dining. And that's just what you'll experience here. Sit down, munch on the tray of baby vegetables
and liver mousse that the waiter brings you, and study the menu.
You might want to make the wonderful salad bar your appetizer.
It's $6, and stocked with island delicacies like Maui onions, fid-
dlehead ferns, enoki mushrooms, Manoa lettuce; you could easily make a meal on this alone. Or, have an order of sashimi and

one of smoked salmon and smoked ahi as we did at a recent meal (appetizers are $7.25 to $8.50). Memorable main dishes ($16 to $25) include opakapaka grilled with lemon butter and a fresh basil sauce; sautéed scallops, wrapped in smoked salmon and baked in a puff pastry; grilled fresh island chicken with garlic and sage; and rôtisserie duck, cooked for long hours to drain out the fat, leaving an altogether succulent creation (it can be prepared with a sauce of green peppercorns, zesty orange, or a purée of papaya and macadamia-nut liqueur). If you're a dessert freak, plan ahead and, at the same time as you order your entree, order whatever wonderful soufflé of the day is available. It could be fudgy chocolate! Or choose as we did from the tray, a flavorful Bing cherry tart with marzipan. Finish with espresso—the end of a perfect meal.

The Bali Room is open every night, from 6 to 10 p.m., with entertainment six nights a week. On Sunday, from 10 a.m. to 2 p.m., there's a $14.50 brunch. Reservations advised: phone 949-4321.

Certainly one of the most beautiful restaurants in Hawaii, **Nicholas Nickolas The Restaurant,** 410 Atkinson Dr., occupies the top floor of the Ala Moana Hotel, the tallest building in the State of Hawaii. The view, as one can well imagine, is spectacular, as is the restaurant. The interior has been designed so that every table has a view of the city: the tables and booths are placed around the perimeter; the bar, kitchen, and dance floor are in the middle. Circling the outside wall are tables; against the inner wall, a few steps up, are booths—so private that the occupants control their own lighting! Dinner and late suppers only are served here. The appetizers are special; they include scampi Fishmarket style (owner Nick Nickolas was the original owner of another fine restaurant, Nick's Fishmarket; see above), Korean ribs Susan, crêpes Madagascar, fresh oysters with seaweed, to name just a few. An inspired lobster bisque and a spicy gazpacho represent the soup department. Complete dinners are an excellent buy at $26.95; they include a choice of Nick's classic salad or New Orleans gumbo and beverage, plus entrees such as Greek chicken, calamari steak, and lamb shanks Papou's style. Many of the dishes here have a Greek flavor: on the à la carte menu ($17.95 to $27.50), you could have swordfish Stavros, single-bone lamb chops "Nick the Greek" style, or Greek chicken. Wonderful salads and "Hash Browns for Jeff" (flavored with sour cream, chives, and bacon) are good extras.

Dinner is served from 5:30 to 11:30 daily. Dance music is

provided by the Connie Kissinger Band on Sunday and Monday and by Cecilio and Friends the rest of the week, from 9:30 p.m. to 4 a.m. The Late Night Menu—in effect from 11:30 p.m.—offers some of the dinner appetizers and side dishes: Greek salad, prawn cocktail, scampi, Korean ribs, smoked salmon or trout, and those famous hash browns, priced from $3.50 to $8.95. Reservations are a must: phone 955-4466.

It's no wonder that **Top of Waikiki,** on the 21st floor of the Waikiki Business Plaza at 2270 Kalakaua Ave., has long been a favorite with visitors and residents alike. As it slowly revolves, it affords one of the most spectacular views in the islands: a 360° panorama of Waikiki Beach and its surfers, Diamond Head, downtown Honolulu, and the Koolau mountains. The restaurant is like a gigantic wedding cake, the innermost tier a cocktail lounge, the succeeding layers lined with tables and diners who sometimes find themselves torn between photographing the view and attending to the very good food. Nighttime is the time for romantic candlelight dining with a view of the stars and the lights winking over the city. You feast on appetizers like Bengal crêpes (thin vanilla crêpes stuffed with crabmeat and a touch of curry), on entrees like veal Cordon Bleu, fresh catch of the day, seafood curry, roast duckling à la cantonese, and specialties from the char-broiler, in a range of about $15 to $20. The house dessert specialty is a red velvet or coconut layer cake. Lunch is quite reasonable—you can get good sandwiches, salads, and entrees like grilled filet of mahimahi, boneless barbecued chicken with Oriental sauce and shrimp, all served with garden vegetables and rice or fries, plus gelatin dessert, between $5.50 and $6. The iced tea, served with a spear of pineapple, is the perfect touch to go with your dessert of homemade pie or coconut parfait.

Top of Waikiki serves dinner daily from 5 to 10:30 p.m. (cocktails till midnight); lunch, Monday to Saturday from 11 a.m. to 2 p.m. Reservations: 923-3877.

In a hotel with the unlikely name of Waikiki Park Heights is a famous steakhouse called **Hy's,** with the unlikely—for Honolulu —decor of the British Victorian era. Located at 2440 Kuhio, Canadian-based Hy's (you may recognize it from Toronto, Winnipeg, Calgary, or Vancouver) looks like somebody's elegant living room—bookshelves, family portraits, upholstered chairs, turn-of-the-century chandeliers, and mahogany-like walls. Here steak is king: prime meat, charcoal-broiled and served on wooden planks with potatoes of your choice done to your specifications. New York strip steak is $16.95 to $22.95, depending on the size of the portion; filet mignon is $17.50 to $19.95, and sirloin goes from $14.95 to $19.50—for all of 20 ounces. All entrees come with soup or salad and delicious hot, fresh garlic-cheese toast. Yes, you can also get baby back ribs or rack of lamb or several fish entrees (from $13.50 up), but we wouldn't miss Hy's masterful steaks.

Appetizers are wide ranging, including lox, linguine with a delicious clam sauce, and pâté maison, and for dessert there's a variety of gourmet cheesecakes as well as parfaits doused with liqueurs. There is, of course, a large wine list in the British tradition. Valet parking. Dinner only, seven days a week, 6 to 11 p.m., closing a bit earlier on Sunday. For reservations, phone 922-5555.

At what Waikiki restaurant can you find blue-point oysters flown in twice weekly from Washington or fresh Dungeness crab legs or San Francisco Bay shrimp? The answer is the famed **Canlis Charcoal Broiler Restaurant,** opposite Fort DeRussy at 2100 Kalakaua Ave. If you've ever dined at a Canlis in San Francisco or Seattle, you'll know that a meal here is expensive but worth every extravagantly tasty moment. Canlis has been a pacesetter for gracious dining in Honolulu for many years. It's an intimate, romantic place, and so handsome is the subdued modern decor that the restaurant has won several decorating awards.

Now for the food, the delicious food. The appetizers mentioned above run from $5.50 to $7.25. Someday, someone will get the idea that they can have dinner at Canlis for under $6 just by ordering the Canlis Special Salad. This tremendous salad, as delicious as it is filling, is made with romaine lettuce tossed with croutons, minced bacon, and fresh-grated romano cheese, and blended with a dressing of lemon juice, imported olive oil, coddled eggs, freshly ground pepper, and herbs. But don't miss the rest of the menu. Canlis does great things with steak and seafood. Fried jumbo shrimp are of the whopping New Orleans variety; steak Pierre consists of thin slices of filet sautéed in a piquant sauce; Canlis shrimp is pan-fried just right; these and other entrees are priced from $12 to $20, à la carte. For dessert, try the house favorite, chilled Grand Marnier soufflé.

Canlis is open every night for dinner from 6 to 11 p.m. and for lunch Monday to Friday from 11:30 a.m. to 2 p.m. There's piano music at dinner every evening from 6 p.m. on; Wednesday through Saturday, from 9:30 p.m., it presents the very popular, award-winning songwriter and pianist, Jay Larrin.

Reservations advised: phone 923-2324.

For one of the ultimate dining experiences in Honolulu, don't miss the **Maile Restaurant** at the Kahala Hilton Hotel. The Maile keeps on winning *Travel/Holiday* Awards and it's no wonder!

From the moment you walk down the winding staircase to the restaurant, set against a lava wall covered with orchids, you'll know you're in a special, rarified atmosphere. Although the room is large, the feeling is an intimate one; you dine by candlelight, amid a background of sparkling fountains, beautiful flowers, and truly gracious island hospitality. But the true marvels come from Chef Andreas Knapp's kitchen. He has taken classic dishes from around the world, given them his own island variations, and come up with a magnificent result. Dinner is $36, table d'hôte, or you may order à la carte. You may have your appetizers either hot or cold, and it's not easy to decide between the likes of a scampi and green asparagus turnover with a lobster cream sauce ($9) or fresh island sashimi ($9). Salads are also quite special: we like the fresh spinach salad, prepared with egg whites and crisp bacon. Then on to the soups—perhaps cream of escargots ($5.50) or lobster bisque ($5.50). The entrees get even more elaborate: that old island standby, mahimahi, comes served on a bed of creamed fresh mushrooms, topped with sautéed banana ($22.50); roast duckling Waialae is flamed in Grand Marnier and brandy, and presented on wild rice along with bananas, lichees, and mandarin oranges ($23.50).

For a good sampling of the Kahala cuisine at a slightly lower price, you might try the **Hala Terrace** on a Sunday night for the $25 Royal Hala buffet. It's probably the most lavish buffet table in town, and here you'll get a chance to try such island delicacies as lomilomi, limu (seaweed), sashimi (raw fish), and octopus, as well as more familiar fare like prime ribs of beef, mahimahi, and beef Stroganoff. A Hawaiian trio plays for entertainment. Reservations are a must (tel. 734-2211).

Medium-Range Meals ($10 to $25)

We've got quite a selection here, divided into categories depending on type of cuisine.

AMERICAN—MOSTLY STEAK AND SEAFOOD: Upstairs at Ward Warehouse, with its unobstructed view of Kewalo Basin and those beautiful Hawaiian sunsets, **Horatio's** is a longtime favorite with local residents. It's pleasantly light and airy, decorated in a modern nautical theme. The bar is a comfortable meeting place, and you might want to start here to sample such pupus as nachos, deep-fried calamari, or kal-bi ribs to go along with your drinks. Dinner entrees run from about $6.75 to $15.95, and include favorites like kiawe-grilled teriyaki, mahimahi, snapper in ginger-and-lime butter, and the very popular slow-cooked prime ribs.

Seafoods, which come from Alaska, the Pacific Northwest, and Hawaii, can be steamed, baked, or kiawe grilled. Lunch prices, from $3.95 to $7.95, are reasonable, and there's a lot of variety: homemade deep-dish quiche, spinach and romaine salads, clams in butter-wine sauce are a few possibilities. The crème brûlée is an unbelievable dessert, a super-rich and creamy caramel custard with a crackly sugar crust; and for something even more decadent, try the Blums Toffee Coffee Pie, a semisweet, chocolate-coffee delight. And there are more desserts where these came from. Horatio's is extremely popular, but you can walk in with or without a reservation (tel. 521-5002), since only half of the dining room is held for reservations. Lunch is served from 11 a.m. to 4 p.m., Monday through Saturday; dinner, from 5 to 10 p.m., Sunday through Thursday, until 10:30 p.m. Friday and Saturday.

Rudyard Kipling would have felt right at home at **The Colony, A Steak House,** in the Hyatt Regency Waikiki, 2424 Kalakaua Ave. It's a bit of the British Colonial past in India come to life, with its rattan furniture, palm trees, revolving ceiling fans, and Indian accents in both food and decor. The plush India print carpet, the gazebo-like tables in the center of the room, and the brilliant use of live greenery all create a warm ambience. Select your own piece of meat—filet mignon, rib eye, New York cut, T-bone, or teriyaki steak, pork or lamb, each individually priced by the ounce (beef, for example, is $1.75 per ounce). Then proceed to the glorious salad bar, included in the price of your entree, while your meat selection is being cooked to your order. House wine comes along with your steak. Dishes like chicken and shrimp curries are also available, as well as a few side dishes like the luscious sourdough bread with melted cheese, jumbo mushroom caps broiled in herb butter, or crisp Maui onion rings. Pupus are great too, and for dessert, we like the raspberry cheesecake. The room is open nightly from 6 to 11 p.m., and the lovely adjoining cocktail lounge, in a harmonizing decor, serves from 6 to midnight. You'll catch a sophisticated performer, perhaps even ukulele virtuoso Herb Ohta as we were lucky enough to do on our last visit. Reservations: 922-9292.

Call a meal at **Bobby McGee's Conglomeration,** in the Colony Surf Hotel at 2885 Kalakaua Ave., an experience, a happening. The eight dining rooms are illuminated just enough so you can barely make out the incredible conglomeration of antiques and oddities that fill up every inch of unused space. The costumed waiters (we were once served by Dudly Do Right and by Dracula) keep up an amusing line of banter that can turn the meal into a comedy routine if you'll play along. But the food is also good, and so decently priced that the place is always packed with locals and visitors alike; you sometimes have to wait a day or so just to get a reservation.

Bobby McGee's specialties include their famous deep-fried zucchini served as an appetizer and, for entrees, fresh catch of the day sautéed in a véronique or other sauce, plus an excellent prime rib of beef for $10.95 to $15.95. The menu offers a wide variety of items such as mahimahi for $10.95, and chicken Cordon Bleu (boneless breast of chicken stuffed with slices of ham, swiss cheese, and mushrooms, and topped off with sauce maltaise) for $12.95. Hand-cut steaks go for $11.95 to $15.95. Along with your entree come Bobby McGee's extras: all the salad you can eat served from an old-fashioned bathtub. (Soup and salad alone are $7.95.) Your meal also includes cooked vegetables or potato, and "special" bread (be sure to ask for it). After all that, and what with keeping up the repartee with the waiters, you probably won't have energy for dessert; if you do, try the chocolate truffle mousse cake or the guava gelato. After dinner, the waiter will ask you to tell your favorite joke (be prepared), and then offer to seat you in the disco part of the operation.

The goofy goings-on go on from 5:30 to 10 (Sunday), 10:30 (Monday through Thursday), and 11 p.m. (Friday and Saturday). The lounge and disco are open nightly until 2 a.m. Valet parking. Be sure to make your reservations early: phone 922-1282.

Among the third-floor row of restaurants at Ward Centre, 1200 Ala Moana, **Ryan's Parkplace** (tel. 523-9132) is a standout. Their draft beers are temperature controlled and their huge stock of liquors and liqueurs lines a whole wall behind the long bar from floor to ceiling. With that kind of look, would you expect a lunch dish like spinach salad with bacon, almonds, and mushrooms? Or a dinner dish like crudités of fresh vegetables with a yogurt dip? It just proves that many different appetites can be soothed here, all in an attractive setting, sparkling with wood and brass, high ceilings, slowly revolving fans, plants everywhere. Service is excellent; tell them you're in a hurry and they'll make sure you finish lunch in 40 minutes. Even the soups are special— fresh broccoli, borscht, Moroccan lentil, among others. The large salads are in the $5.95 to $6.95 range at lunch or dinner; sandwiches and burgers, from about $5 to $6. Snacks and starters at dinner run between $3.25 and $5.50. Seafood, pasta and pizza dishes, sirloin steaks, even specialty dishes run about $7 to $12. Go see for yourself. Lunch starts at 11 a.m., runs smack into dinner at 4:30 p.m., until closing at 11 p.m. daily.

A three-story glass-enclosed aquarium alive with fish dominates the **Oceanarium Restaurant** in the Pacific Beach Hotel at 2490 Kalakaua Ave., corner of Liliuokalani. The Oceanarium is on the ground floor, and there are more restaurants and a disco higher up; but this one affords the best view, and an almost-all-day menu (from 6:30 a.m. till 10 p.m.). It's fun to come at fish-feeding times: 9 a.m., 11:30 a.m., and 6:30 p.m.; on Friday, there are additional feedings at noon and 7:30 p.m.

Dinner here is an especially good bargain, since even à la carte items come with rice or potato, vegetable, rolls and butter. The complete dinner adds soup or salad, ice cream, and beverage. Prices for entrees range from $10.95 for mahimahi Islander to $20.95 for steak and lobster. We sampled a tasty Gulf shrimp curry: large shrimps fried with bananas and onions, simmered in a curry sauce, and served with all the condiments; and our roast beef was the finest prime rib, served with yummy Yorkshire pudding and separate juice for dipping.

At lunch, Monday through Saturday, a buffet is offered that includes a salad bar, two hot entrees, and beverage, at $5.50. On Sunday, it's buffet for all three meals. The phone is 922-1233.

Long a favorite in this Diamond Head part of Waikiki, the **Captain's Table** in the Holiday Inn, 2570 Kalakaua Ave., is your classic Waikiki nautical dining room: ships' lanterns, photographs of Honolulu Harbor in days long past, burgundy velvet booths and draperies. And if you get a table on the right side of the room, you can revel in an unobstructed view of the ocean just across the street. We like to start a meal here with the stuffed grape leaves (the stuffing is rice pilaf, lamb, and herbs glazed with lemon sauce) or the Boston clam chowder, and then proceed on to one of the house specialties like the Captain's Feast for Two, and a feast is just what it is: rock lobster tail, King crab legs, oysters, clams, and scallops, each with its own sauce, $46. Other good choices include mahimahi, seafood Newburg, prime rib, filet mignon, and beef Stroganoff; prices go from about $12.95 to $19.95. Entrees are served with potatoes or rice and vegetables. For dessert, be daring and try the deep-fried ice cream with Melba sauce. Breakfast is served daily from 6:30 to 9:30 a.m.; no lunch; dinner from 6 to 10 p.m. On Sunday, 9:30 a.m. to 1:30 p.m., try their famous Champagne Buffet Brunch, a darn good buy at $11.75 for adults, $6.75 for children under ten, what with its enormous salad bar including many local specialties, its tempura and omelet bars—not to mention that free champagne.

The **Pottery Steak and Seafood Restaurant**, 3574 Waialae

Ave., is both a pottery and a steakhouse—a happy combination that results in good food served in distinctive ceramic ware. All the pottery made by the talented craftspeople—who give exhibitions at the wheel every night—is for sale. A personal favorite is a loaf of bread that is really a big covered dish for serving—you guessed it—bread. It's priced at $24.95.

The food here is also good, with most of the selections from the steak kiln "fired to the desired cone." That means you can have your meat as rare or medium or well done as you choose, and the chef means what he says. The average price of entrees is about $14. The steak and prawns, served on a bed of fried rice, is a particular treat. Another of our favorites is the boned Cornish game hen, cooked in its own clay vessel and stuffed with wild rice. Maybe it's the cooking in clay that makes it so juicy and tender. And the pot is yours to take home. All entrees are served with soup or salad, baked potato or rice, vegetable, and garlic bread presented in that cute ceramic loaf. Smoked salmon or shrimp cocktails served in a hand-thrown dish make excellent starters; apple pie, cheesecake, or chocolate mousse make the perfect finish.

Alas, the Pottery is open for dinner only, but it is open seven days a week (for reservations, phone 735-5594). And if you're planning to visit the Big Island, you can stop in at the Pottery in Kailua-Kona.

One of the most atmospheric (and long-established) seafood restaurants in Honolulu is **Fisherman's Wharf,** 1009 Ala Moana (at Fisherman's Wharf), where you can sit by a huge picture window and watch the sampan fishing boats moored just outside. The indoor decor is jauntily nautical too, even down to the sailor-suit uniforms of its waitresses. You can eat well here in the Seafood Grotto, where there are some 20 to 30 items between $6.75 and $24, including lobster tail, and steak and lobster. The complete dinner includes a choice of fruit or chowder (but we always opt for the Fisherman's Wharf soup with sherry at 30¢ more), vegetables, and coffee. Luncheon entrees run from $5.25 to $16.25, and sandwiches like mahimahi burger on toasted bun run about $4.95. There are special *keiki* menus, drinks available from the bar, and a generally carefree mood. Upstairs is the Captain's Bridge, where fish is broiled to your order. You won't go wrong at either dining room: Fisherman's Wharf rates high, with both visitors and *kamaainas*. For reservations, phone 538-3808.

Take the escalator to the second floor of the Ward Centre, just Diamond Head of the Ward Warehouse shopping center on Ala

Moana Boulevard, and enter the **Monterey Bay Canners Restaurant.** You'll feel as if you are back at the turn of the century, stepping into a Barbary Coast saloon. Ceiling fans, brass-ringed curtains, and hanging plants subdue the sounds of this big, busy restaurant which offers fresh seafood and fish at refreshing prices. A large blackboard announces the fish catch of the day; the day we dined there, it was tropical fish, ono wahoo, and opakapaka (pink snapper). These specials run $12 to $15 and include San Francisco sourdough rolls, New England or Manhattan clam chowder or salad. At lunch, the prices are $3 to $5 lower, but salad or clam chowder is an extra 95¢ with your entree.

Other entrees go from $7.45 to $18.95, beginning with a "light eaters plate" of fish filets, on up to Pacific lobster tails. Vegetarians may have a steamed vegetable plate for under $5. The oyster bar has such delicacies as sashimi, mushrooms stuffed with crabmeat, steamed clams, clams casino, and the like, from $4 to $7. Desserts include a frozen chocolate mousse and a delicious cheesecake.

Monterey Bay Canners serves lunch Monday through Saturday from 11 a.m. to 4 p.m. with basically the same menu as dinner, served 4 to 11 p.m. all week (until midnight on Friday and Saturday.) There's a popular Happy Hour everyday from 4 to 7 p.m., with discounts on food and drinks, and entertainment nightly from 9 p.m. to 1:30 a.m. There's plenty of parking. Phone: 536-6197.

One of the rare good restaurants open 24 hours a day, seven days a week, is **Mango & Miso,** located in the Ala Moana Americana Hotel and entered through a monarchy-style portico at 410 Atkinson Dr. True to its name, Mango & Miso offers a choice of American and Japanese dishes, and quite an extensive choice it is. Make yourself comfortable in the curved-back chairs and plantation-style decor, as the menu takes a lot of reading.

The first lunch or dinner category is fruit or juice. Yes, they serve mango (in season), and always papaya and pineapple. Next, soups—yes, miso, the tasty Japanese vegetable soup, served here with beans. Japanese saimin, French onion soup, and American standards are also available. There are many salads— fruit, health, seafood, garden. The garden salad includes greens, sprouts, mushrooms, daikon, pepper, carrots—a meal. Salads range from $3 to $7.50.

The choice of entrees range from spaghetti with meat sauce at $4.75 to the Land and Sea brochette at $9.75. In between are mouthwatering selections for every taste: Hungarian goulash, Korean barbecued short ribs, grilled chicken American, and Hawaiian hukilau (fish of the day). There are lots of Japanese dishes, of course, including sukiyakis, teriyakis, and tempuras. And there are sandwiches, desserts, and beverages galore.

Breakfasts, again for every taste and pocketbook, are served from 6:30 to 11 a.m. You can park at Ala Moana Center or at the hotel. Phone: 955-4811.

Richard Shimizu, the talented chef/owner of **Richard's Stuffed Potato** at 2109 Kuhio Ave., does a lot more than stuff potatoes at his popular little restaurant, which consists of just a few tables, mostly outdoors, in the courtyard of the "Kuhio District." Richard is a highly talented chef who, on any given night, may cook up dishes like fresh sea bass with chive butter sauce, or giant scallops Dijon with mushrooms, or jumbo scampi Pernod with scallions and garlic (all priced around $10 to $12). A special treat is the fresh New York–cut steak blackened in the Cajun style, $13.95. He also does different pasta dinners every night, and these are great bargains, at just $6.50 to $6.95, including salad and garlic bread. You might have fettuccine Alfredo, pasta marinara, pasta primavera, clam linguine. Have a dessert for $2.50: it could be chocolate mousse or guava whipped cheesecake, fresh lilikoi sorbet or fresh gelati. No alcohol is served, so BYOB. Open 6 p.m. to midnight, every day but Sunday. Credit cards are not accepted. Phone: 922-0102.

Can't choose between steak and lobster? You don't have to. **Buzz's Steak 'n Lobster House,** 225 Saratoga Rd. (tel. 923-6762) in the Reef Lanais Hotel, makes a specialty of both, and it does a terrific job. Enjoy your candlelight dinner surrounded by many antiques, nautical compasses, old maps of the islands, lamps, and plaques. A full glass outside wall lets you watch the flaming torches and street life as you enjoy drinks and dinner. The prices of the entrees include a choice of baked potato, french fries or rice, and generous helpings of French or rye bread. Dinners are hearty meals with prices ranging from $5.95 for ground beefsteak to $20.95 for a steak-and-lobster dinner. The salad bar is $2 extra. Fresh fish from Hawaiian waters (when available) is a very popular entree. Buzz's specialties include chicken, Alaskan king crab, sautéed shrimp, New York–cut steak, and many other varieties of seafood. The bar opens at noon, so you can relax on your way back from beach or shopping with specially priced Happy Hour drinks. Dinner is served from 5 to 11 p.m.

The **Waikiki Broiler** at 200 Lewers St. (tel. 923-8836), in the

Waikiki Tower of the Reef Hotel, provides both indoor and outdoor tables for those who don't want to lose one moment of sunshine. Start soaking it up at breakfast time (from 6 to 2 p.m.), along with a pancake sandwich with bacon and egg, or french toast from $2.45 to $5.65. Special breakfasts, like all the pancakes you can eat and beverage for $1.99, or two pancakes with one egg, bacon or sausage at $1.99, are served through 11 a.m. Lunches run from $2.45 to $5.25; try the hibachi chicken sandwich. Come dinner, we vote for the scampi or the rich and juicy Captain's cut of prime ribs. Along with your entree, priced from $3.45 to $16, comes salad or homemade soup from the kettle, bread, and steamed rice. Note that lunch is on from 11 a.m. to 2 p.m., dinner from 5:30 until 10 p.m., seven days a week. From 8 in the evening until about 1:30 in the morning there is usually a group playing Hawaiian and contemporary music—all of which adds to the fun in this neat nautical spot, a big hit with the visiting crowd.

If you love dining with a view of the ocean—and if you love buffet dining too—make a note of the **Ocean Terrace,** poolside at the Sheraton Waikiki Hotel. The buffet table really shines at night: juicy prime ribs, mahimahi, fried chicken, plus a hot surprise or two. And there's always plenty of salads, vegetables, desserts, and beverages. Considering that it's priced at $15.50, it's not bad for Waikiki. There's a buffet lunch too—roast beef, stews, chop suey, cold cuts, salads, desserts (we counted some 20 choices recently)—and that's $10.95. The breakfast buffet is $9.95, and it's recommended for the big morning eaters; all you want of fruits, cereals, eggs, breakfast meats, pastry, pancakes. At lunch, there are also salads and delicious special items priced from $5.95. Like all of the Sheraton Waikiki, this is a strikingly alive spot, with brilliant green-and-apricot colors from floor to ceiling, even on the uniforms of the helpful staff. Dinner is from 5:30 to 9:30 p.m.; lunch, from 11:30 a.m. to 3 p.m.; breakfast, from 6 to 11:30 a.m.

One of the prettiest medium-priced restaurants in town is **Trellises,** in the beautiful Outrigger Prince Kuhio Hotel up Diamond Head way at 2500 Kuhio Ave. Artfully decorated with greenery, overlooking a waterfall and gardens, Trellises serves all three meals plus a Friday-night seafood buffet and a Saturday-night family buffet, each $12.50. On the regular menu, dinner entrees, which are accompanied by soup or salad, rice or potatoes, fresh vegetables, and rolls, are mostly priced from $5.75 to $11, and include roast beef, sautéed mahimahi, honey-dipped chicken, and a seafood platter. There's a prime rib special on Sunday. Trellises also offers Oriental specialties at lunch and dinner ($2.75 to $8.50), plus chilled salads like tostada salad and salad niçoise, burgers, and hot and cold sandwiches. A big lunch favorite here is the Portuguese bean soup, which works well with a salad or sandwich. Home-baked pastries and luscious ice-cream sundaes are dessert specialties. You can go with traditional favorites at breakfast or, even better, feast on the all-you-care-to-eat breakfast buffet at $7.95.

Trellises serves breakfast from 6 a.m., lunch from 11 a.m., dinner from 5 p.m., daily. For reservations, phone 922-0811, ext. 5151.

AUSTRIAN/HUNGARIAN: Palffy, at 745 Amana St., is Hawaii's only Austrian/Hungarian restaurant. It's named in honor of Ferdinand Palffy, a Hungarian count, who was a patron of the arts and lived in Vienna and Budapest in the early 1900s. Count Palffy would feel right at home in this lovely dining room, with its crystal chandeliers, tufted booths, velvet portières, original paintings, and superb food and service. Hot appetizers, such as escargots in mushroom caps and mushrooms à la Robert (Robert is Palffy's superlative chef), look interesting, as do the cold ones, including Piritott Paprikika (roasted bell peppers with strips of smoked salmon). At a recent dinner, we opted for the Palffy platter for two, with a tantalizing array of meats, imported cheeses, and vegetables. Choosing an entree is difficult, as these are classics of Hungarian and Austrian cookery that you can sample nowhere else nearabout; all are served with a noodle or potato dish and vegetables, and range in price from $14 to $16.50. Well recommended are Hortobagy palacsinta (diced breast of chicken in a crêpe); Zigany borjuborda (medallion of veal gypsy-style sautéed and crowned with a zesty bell pepper sauce); wienerschnitzel; prawns Budapest (simmered in a light wine sauce with parsley and garlic). Or go dramatic with a Flaming Sword for two, a mixed grill of beef, lamb, and veal, flamed right at your table. Desserts are also divine at Palffy: save room for such delights as freshly made crêpes flamed and prepared at your table in an apricot-and-orange sauce; Peach Melba; an outrageously delicious ice-cream liqueur cake; or—if you dare the calories—Gundel palacsinta (crêpes filled with ground walnuts, rum, and raisins and glazed with chocolate sauce and fresh whipped cream). A young Honolulu friend of ours chose to celebrate his 18th birthday here recently; he confided that it was a dinner he will always remember.

Dinner is served from 6 to 11 p.m. nightly; the cocktail lounge opens at 4 p.m. during the week and at 6 p.m. on weekends. A pianist plays haunting gypsy music and sprightly Viennese waltzes during dinner. Reservations, of course: phone 942-8181.

CHINESE: Yen King, that popular northern Chinese restaurant in the plush Kahala Mall shopping center, just keeps getting better all the time, gaining new fans among kamaainas and malihinis alike. It's an attractive place, with beige colors highlighting the filigreed teak screen dividers, tile ceiling, and murals. The menu is vast, at both lunch and dinner, but there's no way to go wrong here, as everything is prepared with master-chef expertise. You might want to try one of their family dinner menus: a favorite, at $9.25 per person, includes the house's famous sizzling rice soup, spring roll, deep-fried shrimp, cashew chicken, sweet-and-sour pork, and Chinese cabbage with mushrooms. Or choose among some 30 vegetarian entrees from $2.75 to $5.50 (the local vegetarians swear by this place), and about two dozen seafood choices from $6.95 to $8.50, mostly featuring squid, clams, and shrimp in various styles. Of course there are plenty of beef, pork, and fowl dishes (garlic chicken and roast duck are especially good), and a wide variety of Peking-style, as well a Hong Kong–style dim sum (dumplings and noodles). Hot Mongolian beef is available anytime, but give them half a day's notice if you want to try their beggar's chicken baked in clay—quite unusual. Newest dish on the menu is the "Firepot," which a group cooks themselves at the table; it is priced from $6 to $9 per diner.

Seafood is delicious. Chinese food is delicious. Add the two together and you have a unique specialty restaurant: **Won Kee Sea Food,** a standout among the restaurants in the Cultural Plaza, at 100 North Beretania St. (tel. 524-6877). This is a gourmet seafood place, where specialties like fresh island fish, island prawns, jumbo shrimp, king crab legs, or Maine lobster are prepared artfully: perhaps steamed with ginger-and-soy sauce, braised with ginger-and-garlic sauce, or stir-fried with black bean sauce. Specialties go from $7.50 to $13.50 or more, depending on market price, but most of the dishes are very reasonable: dishes like fresh clams with black bean sauce, sautéed shrimp with vegetables and mushrooms, mixed seafood casseroles, roast duck with plum sauce, cold ginger chicken, run from about $6 to $8.50. Soup of the day (ours was turnip), rice, and tea are included in the entree price. We ordered five courses for four people, and the cost of this banquet totaled under $50 before the tip.

Won Kee is open daily for lunch and dinner. Don't expect an

ornate place; here you have white tablecloths, simple wood paneling, and Chinese-style wrought-iron fixtures. It's the food that's ornate. Lunch is 11 a.m. to 2:30 p.m.; dinner, 5 to 10 p.m.

Note: There's another Won Kee at 444 Kanakapolei, in Waikiki.

FRENCH: There's a bit of the Riviera in Waikiki. **Chez Michel,** long one of Waikiki's best French restaurants, is now in a garden-like setting in Eaton Square, at 444 Hobron Lane in the Ala Moana area. The restaurant is roofed and walled in by lattices hung with tropical plants, furnished with highbacked and comfortably cushioned wicker chairs, and graced with splashing fountains that create a cool, romantic atmosphere. Michel himself may greet you, if he's not on his annual wine-buying trip to Paris. This is a popular lunch rendezvous (Monday to Saturday, 11:30 a.m. to 2:15 p.m.), so join the members of the business community dining over the likes of poached eggs Benedict, fresh mountain trout, tournedos béarnaise, or a superb chicken sautéed with mushrooms and artichoke. Everything is à la carte, from about $8 to $11, but the dishes are well endowed with Michel's gourmet potato and vegetable creations.

At dinner, the French onion soup is a must. Michel's sauces and gravies are exquisite, so that even chicken livers become a dining experience—not to mention the more exotic selections like carré d'agneau jardinière, fresh opakapaka sauté grenobloise, or the memorable côte de veau au citron. Entrees range from $19 to $23, including fresh vegetables and potatoes. Desserts are quite special: you can choose from chilled orange soufflé, crêpes Suzette, or Grand Marnier soufflé. (Remember to order your soufflé when ordering dinner.) Espresso and cappuccino are offered.

Dinner is served daily from 6 to 11 p.m. Reservations are always advised: phone 955-7866.

Chez Jacques, a *très jolie* little French restaurant at the beginning of Waikiki—1614 Kalakaua Ave.—has an outdoorsy feeling, with its trellises and abundant greenery. Dinner only is served here, every evening with the exception of Monday. For starters, there are the usual escargots and pâté, plus a lovely shrimp creation: crevettes sautées provençales (large shrimp sautéed in a wine and garlic-butter sauce). Complete dinners include the chef's soup of the day, salad, vegetables, starch of the day, and beverage; we'd call the tab of $14.95 to $17.95 bon marché, considering the quality of the cuisine, the pleasant atmosphere, and the competent and courteous service. (You may also order à la carte for about $3 less.) The French Provincial specialties are all excellent, but some special favorites are the coq au vin, the coquilles St.-Jacques, the rack of lamb baked with herbs and served in a light Dijon mustard sauce. For dessert: crêpes Suzette, or Brie with raisins and sliced apples. Diners may bring their own wine or liquor; Chez Jacques does not have a liquor license. Reservations advised: phone 943-1573.

GREEK: A touch of Greece—its charm, music, dances, and cuisine —can be enjoyed at the **Greek Island Taverna,** 2570 Beretania St. near University Avenue. One flight up in a small building with its own parking lot, this authentic Greek restaurant features not only souvlaki, moussaka, and other classic Greek dishes, but also better-known items like gyros, souvlaki, or pita cheeseburgers. We passed up the octopus sandwich for a delicious spanakotivopita (spinach, feta cheese, herbs, and spices in pita bread). Sandwiches run from $3.75 to $4.75. Lunch plates of stuffed cabbage, sautéed mahimahi, or marinated chicken Greek style are $5.25 to $6.50. There's Greek beer to accompany your lunch, baklava to top it off. Dinners are a festive occasion: the Greek music becomes dance music, rich blue cloths cover the tables, and a Greek belly dancer adds a bit of spice to the meal. Tasty hot and cold appetizers—taramosalata, marinated baby squid, or saganaki (green Kasseri cheese flambéed in brandy)—are your starters. Then it's on to moussaka, chicken sautéed in wine sauce, stuffed grape leaves, or souvlaki, among a number of entrees all reasonably priced between $7.95 and $12.50. Well recommended is the spring lamb baked in the traditional manner (arni psito, $10.50). A full combination dinner, consisting of a sampling of entrees plus soup, salad, dessert, and coffee, is a favorite choice at $12.95.

Greek Island Taverna serves lunch Monday to Friday from 11:30 a.m. to 2 p.m., and dinner nightly from 5:30 to 11 p.m. Reservations: 943-0052.

ITALIAN: At 2168 Kalia Rd., opposite the Cinerama Reef and on the grounds of the Edgewater Hotel, is **Trattoria,** home of some of the finest Italian cuisine in the islands. This is a dinner-only establishment, serving from 5:30 to 11:30 p.m. seven days a week. Allow plenty of time to savor your dinner, because everything here is prepared to order by the skilled chefs. Full dinners begin at $14.95, and you may also order à la carte. You might start with one of our favorites, clams casino (fresh clams baked with chopped bacon and shallots) or the escargots. Pastas are well done here, and are modestly priced. Among the fish dishes, we recommend the scampi alla Trattoria, giant prawns broiled and served with a zesty wine sauce; and from the meat choices, the bistecca all' aglio—sirloin sautéed in olive oil—is unforgettable. The meat and fish entrees run from $12.50 to $18.95, à la carte. Phone: 923-8415. From 7 to 10 p.m., there's music by the Italian troubador, Luigi Fumagalli.

Rudy's, a bright little bistro in the Outrigger Surf Hotel, 2280 Kuhio Ave. (corner of Nohonani), is warm and pretty, with its plushy red carpet and deep-red tablecloths. You'll want to luxuriate in one of the comfy tufted booths, bask in the soft light from the red tulip-shaped art-nouveau hanging lamps, and watch the swimmers in the pool through the big picture window. And if you tire of that, you can watch the chef do his thing (part of the spotless kitchen is in full view of the dining room).

The complete family-style Italian dinners are a bargain, priced from $6.95 to $13.95, and served with a hearty homemade minestrone soup, tossed green salad, spaghetti or ravioli, vegetable, and hot French bread. Owner-manager Rudy Biale recommends Rudolpho suprême, his favorite dish, invented by his grandmother back in Genoa. It's shrimp in batter sautéed in wine and butter, served with spaghetti and butter sauce—very rich and filling. We also like the Italian-style scampi and the tender filets of veal piccante with lemon slices. Spaghetti and ravioli dinners are even more reasonable, starting at $2.95 for spaghetti with tomato sauce. There's also an excellent dish of linguine with pesto, that delicious sauce made with basil, at $8.95. Rudy's serves dinner only, from 5:30 to 10 p.m. daily. For reservations, phone 923-5949. A good place to take the kids.

Sergio's in the Ilima Hotel, 445 Nohonani St., was recently described by a Honolulu acquaintance of ours as "the best-kept secret in Waikiki." They do no advertising; they don't need to. Honolulu residents who enjoy really fine Italian food keep the place busy every day. It's a lovely room, of good size, with low lights, paneled walls, and booths separated by panels and quite private. Wine bottles and casks and many plants create a warm atmosphere. At lunchtime (11:30 to 2 p.m., Monday through Thursday), the crowd comes for the seafood combination and cold pasta salads (from $6.25), the veal marengo and piccata style, beef bourguignon, and venison, all $9.50 to $10.50. Entrees are served with vegetables and spaghetti marinara. At dinner (6 to 11:30 p.m. nightly), the favorites are such house specialties as the superb saltimbocca alla romana (veal and prosciutto in a light wine sauce); the pollo all' abruzzese (tender pieces of chicken cooked with tomatoes and bell peppers in sauce); and fagiano "en plumage" (boneless breast of pheasant in a cream sauce with wild mushrooms, served with potato soufflé and vegetables; they run from $14 to $24. After all of this superb gourmet fare, one must literally force oneself to manage dessert, but with specialties such as *Biancave e i sette nani* (literal translation: "Snow White and the Seven Dwarfs")—seven fresh strawberries on a bed of lemon sherbet, topped with a shot of Stolichnaya vodka—it is well worth the effort. Espresso, cappuccino, and Irish coffee are there for the asking, $2 to $4. Reservations: phone 926-3388.

Local friends have been singing the praises of **Phillip Paolo's, a** new restaurant at 2312 S. Beretania St. that has won an instant and enthusiastic kamaaina following. Connie Ortiz, the owner and manager of this charming spot, will greet you at the door (be sure you've made reservations—phone 946-1163—as it's very popular), and seat you in one of the several dining rooms, so pretty with Victorian decor, lace curtains, and fresh flowers. You're in for a very pleasant dining experience here: the waiters are knowledgeable and helpful, the crowd is attractive, the wine is delicious. Pasta, seafood, and salad are featured on the small, but choice menu, with various specialties every day. Portions are very generous, so you may want to share. Two of you should start with the mixed antipasto at $6.95. For your main course, priced from $8.50 to $12.95, you might want to try the delicious fettuccine al pesto, or the frutti di mare (seafood combination). Or, sample one of the kitchen's more unusual specialties, like the fettuccine Dominique (pasta topped with sautéed smoked salmon, tomatoes, onions, mushrooms, and broccoli), or the fettuccine Paolo, these noodles bathed in a sauce of scallops, garlic, onions, and tomatoes. Only fresh herbs are used in all dishes, and all are served with salad and French bread. Everything is cooked to order, so have a drink from the bar while you're waiting. The only dessert—but who needs more?—is cheesecake served with the house's own fresh fruit sauce, $3.75. Have some Italian coffee and relax with a sigh of great contentment.

Phillip Paolo's serves dinner only, Monday through Saturday. Closed Sunday.

A speakeasy to outclass any speakeasy that ever was, **Spats,** in the Hyatt Regency Waikiki at 2424 Kalakaua (tel. 922-9292), is a marvelous bit of the Roaring '20s reborn. Part restaurant, part disco, it's got to be the kickiest place in town, with its knockout gaslight and Tiffany-lamp lighting, flowered carpeting, and a look right out of *The Godfather*. Spats specializes in "pasta with passion"—freshly made pastas in a variety of delectable sauces.

You can program your own gourmet Italian trip from such à la carte choices as fettuccine Alfredo and shrimp aglio, cannelloni, or chicken cacciatore; prices run from about $7.50 for pasta to $15 for the meat dishes. The disco comes to life at 8 p.m. and swings until 4 a.m. Dinner is from 6 to 10 p.m. From 10 p.m. until 2 a.m., a delightful Pasta Bar serves snacks, including a delicious, cheesy small pizza that might be dinner for one or a snack for two. No reservations necessary. Complimentary valet parking.

JAPANESE: You're in for a unique experience at the **Restaurant Izakaya Zen,** on the second floor of the Waikiki Grand Hotel, 134 Kapahulu Ave. The interior was created by a Japanese designer, and its fixtures and furnishings reflect contemporary Japanese understated good taste. At the entrance you remove your shoes and place them in a "getsaboko"—a shoe cabinet with separate cubby holes to which you hold the key. Now you can choose to be seated on *zabutons* (Japanese cushions) on the floor in the traditional manner, or at regular tables and chairs. You could have some regular drinks while ordering, but to keep the Japanese experience intact, try some saké, dry or sweet, heated or iced, as a cocktail. Now decide if you will have sashimi, a delicate soup like salmon rabe (salmon and vegetable), and such traditional Japanese delicacies as beef kushiyaki and yakitori, mahimahi teriyaki, shrimp tempura, pickled vegetables, and grilled rice sticks. Whatever you have will be delicate and delicious. Entrees run from $10.95 to $19.95. Or you may choose a chef's special—perhaps beef sashimi at $6.50 or chicken or roast pork crêpes at $6—and watch them being prepared by the chef in the open kitchen in the center of the dining area. There are a variety of side dishes that run from $1.50 to $7.95.

Izakaya Zen is open daily for lunch from 11:30 a.m. to 2 p.m., and for dinner from 5 p.m. to 2 a.m. Phone: 923-8878.

One of the loveliest Japanese restaurants in town is the sophisticated **Tanaka of Tokyo,** on the fourth floor of the Waikiki Shopping Plaza, at the corner of Seaside and Kalakaua Avenues. Although dinners are on the expensive side, from $12.50 to $26.75, this is one Japanese restaurant that serves Western-size portions, and you walk out well satisfied. You'll be seated at a table for eight, centered around a table-range combo, watching the chef do amusing antics with paring knives and spatulas as he prepares your meal. Three main dinners to choose from are chicken teriyaki, salmon (fresh Pacific) teppanyaki, and Tanaka sirloin. But there is also lobster, mahimahi, and lobster and sirloin. All dinners include delicious soup, grilled shrimp appetizer, cold and crisp salad, teppanyaki vegetable, ice-cream and sherbert desserts, and green tea. You could easily believe you're in Tokyo, with the Japanese music in the background, the waitresses in kimonos (actually, they are all local girls of Japanese ancestry who speak perfect English and radiate island warmth rather than Japanese formality), the low lights, and the understated Japanese decor.

Dinner is served daily from 5:30 to 10:30 p.m., until 10 p.m. on Sunday; lunch is Monday through Friday, 11:30 to 2 p.m. The lunch menu, priced from $5.75 to $8.25, includes the same main entrees mentioned above, but without all the extra courses and trimmings. And a late-night menu (10:30 p.m. to midnight) is now served in the new Kokoro Lounge. Phone: 922-4702.

Note: Tanaka of Tokyo will send one $5 discount coupon, to be applied to the cost of your meal, to anyone living on the Canadian or United States mainland who sends a stamped, self-addressed envelope to: Tanaka of Tokyo, Waikiki Shopping Plaza, no. 406, 2250 Kalakaua Ave., Honolulu, HI 96815.

The same Tanaka of Tokyo management is also in charge at the charming little **Chez Sushi** at Ward Centre, 1200 Ala Moana Blvd., a cross between a Japanese sushi bar and a French bistro. You sit either at the small sushi bar or in the tiny dining room adjacent and are waited upon by servers in kimonos and hapi coats, who will explain the intricacies of sushi to you, should you care to ask. It's fun to order à la carte, mixing and matching such diversities as tempura and truffles, escargots and sashimi, pâté and yakitori ($4.25 to $6.25). Or have a complete Teishoku Japanese lunch for about $6.50 to $10.50, other specialties for less. French wine, saké, and a full bar list are available. Open Monday through Saturday from 11 a.m. to midnight, Sunday to 11 p.m.

MEXICAN: The mood, the food, the drinks, the lights, and the festive feeling all add up to a resounding cheer for **Compadres,** with two locations in town: one at the Outrigger Prince Kuhio Hotel, 2500 Kuhio Ave., in Waikiki; the other at Ward Centre, at 1200 Ala Moana Blvd. At both, prices are moderate and the food is expertly prepared—so much so that the readers of *Honolulu* magazine have named Compadres the "Best Mexican Restaurant" in Hawaii for two years in a row. Among the house specialties, which run from $7.95 to $12.95, favorites include the classic arroz con pollo and chicken mole; the avocado stuffed with crabmeat and topped with green chili and cheeses; the huajolote, marinated and char-broiled turkey breast; and fajitas de camarones, marinated, sliced, and sautéed gulf shrimp rolled in soft warm tortillas and served up with frijoles and salsa fresca. Delicioso! Unusual appetizers (ever hear of Tijuana won tons?), good salads and sandwiches, smoke-oven baby back ribs and chicken, and a large selection of egg dishes and combination plates ($6.95 to $9.25) offer plentiful choices. For dessert, try the mud pie or the taco split or the apple chimichanga! Of course there are terrific margaritas, daiquiris, sangria by the glass and pitcher, Mexican and other imported beers, and other potions that mix well with these Tex-Mex treats.

Both Compadres are open late every day, from 11 a.m. on. The Waikiki restaurant also has a fabulous all-you-can eat Sunday brunch for $9.95 for adults and $5.95 for children, noteworthy for the bread pudding and the omelet station, where everything is made to order. There are special margarita prices from 4 to 7 p.m. daily. In Waikiki, phone 924-4007; at Ward Centre, 523-1307.

NATURAL FOODS: Being on a special diet doesn't mean you can't dine like a gourmet in Honolulu. Just take yourself to **Sherrie's White Flower Inn**, at 2117 Kuhio Ave., up the stairs at no. 215 and tell proprietress Sherrie Orr your needs. She'll come up with something just right. But you needn't be on a special program, or on a vegetarian or natural foods kick to enjoy Sherrie's. Her food is delicious, gourmet cuisine, and there's always a fish and a chicken dish on the menu as well as the vegetarian fare. The restaurant is ensconced in an old Waikiki house, charmingly decorated with antiques; you dine either indoors or out on the pretty lanai which overlooks the lively "Kuhio District." The menu is varied and inexpensive, running from delicious frittatas (not limited to breakfast time) to a variety of sandwiches (the most popular is the "natural" Reuben, with Swiss cheese, sauerkraut, and mustard on home-baked pumpernickel) to salads, homemade soups, wonderful desserts, and unique recipes like Indonesian broccoli tofu, Greek cheese pie, and Thai Evil Jungle Prince made with fresh fish. Sandwiches and salads are about $4 to $6; main entrees, about $7 to $13. Daily creations will reflect whatever is fresh in the market and whatever inspires Sherrie that day: a friend has remarked that "Sherrie takes any common recipe and vegetates it." And she does it very well, at that. You'll probably want to come back for breakfast on the weekend to sample the buckwheat waffles with hot pure maple syrup and walnuts. Liquor is not served, but there is a de-alcoholized wine available, or you may bring your own wine.

Sherrie's White Flower Inn is open every day, from 11:30 a.m.

on weekdays, 10 a.m. on Saturdays, 12 noon on Sundays. Phone: 923-2664.

THAI: Be sure to arrive early if you want to dine at **Rama Thai Restaurant,** 847 Kapahulu Ave., as this cozy, 11-table spot is very popular; get there by 6:30 p.m., and you're not likely to have a problem, but later it fills up and then some. The food is delicious and reasonably priced: most dishes are in the $4 to $6 price range, but serve two or three people easily, and this applies to appetizers, soups, salads, Thai curries, main entrees, and noodle or rice dishes. Vegetarians will be happy here, with a complete menu, from spring rolls to soups to entrees like Thai curry mixed with tofu. We started a recent meal here with the classic sa-teh barbecue sticks—your choice of beef, pork, chicken, or shrimp— to dip in a tangy cucumber-and-peanut sauce, $4.95. Our ginger chicken soup was a winner: the chicken is simmered in coconut milk with parsley, green onions, and Thai ginger. There is a choice of six curries, which can be ordered mild, medium, or hot (we recommend mild), and a score of entrees like fried shrimp with assorted vegetables, beef with Thai red-gravy sauce, and cashew-nut chicken. We topped off our meal with cool and sweet Thai apple banana coconut; next time it will be the Thai corn-and-tapioca pudding.

At this writing, Rama Thai is open only for dinner, from 5:30 to 10:30 p.m. daily. Phone: 735-2789.

Informal and Inexpensive ($10 and Under)

If you're wandering through the Royal Hawaiian Shopping Center, wander over to **It's Greek to Me,** on the street level of Building A, at the Lewers Street end, for a delicious snack or meal. Place your order at the counter, sit down and watch the crowds go by, and pick up your delicious meal when they call your number. Lunch is an especially good bargain, for it's then that you can have entrees like a souvlaki or gyro or moussaka or falafel plate, from around $6 to $8. Delicious pita sandwiches, $5.95 to $6.25, are accompanied by a special salad of the day. At dinner, you could eat lightly on appetizers like taramosalata, olive and cheese plate, or hummus alone ($4.25 to $6.50). Under-$10 dinners include spanakopita (spinach pie with three kinds of cheese in a flaky phillo dough), gyros, and falafel, with all the tasty accompaniments. Don't miss this one if you love Greek food! Open 8 a.m. to 9 p.m. Phone: 922-2733.

It looks like a "hole in the wall," but it's a delightful discovery. **Eggs 'n Things,** at 436 Ena Rd., about halfway between Kalakaua and Ala Moana, is a cozy nook where lovers of omelets, crêpes, and pancakes are habitués. The dozen or so tables are neat and trim. The walls are decorated with wood plaques bearing interesting news items. But it is the kitchen range that is the most interesting. From it are served eggs any style, plus any side meats—from Spam at $4.25 to steak and eggs at $6.75—all accompanied by three of the lightest buttermilk pancakes we've tasted.

A dozen omelets are available from plain to a spinach-cheese-bacon combo, priced from $4.50 to $6. There are a half a dozen ways to order crêpes Suzette, $4.25 to $5.50, with or without sour cream and with lemon, banana, blueberry, or strawberry filling. Pancakes come in six kinds and range from $2.25 to $5.50. This charming spot is open daily but the hours are strange: 11 p.m. to 2 p.m. That means it's open all night, and open for breakfast and lunch, but not for dinner. Phone: 949-0820.

A coffeeshop that is way out of the ordinary is the **Waikiki Circle Coffeeshop** in the Waikiki Circle Hotel. Directly across from Kuhio Beach, this comfortable place with its red carpet on the floor offers a fine sunset view—through the traffic and exhaust fumes, of course! The food is very good and the prices even better: the $5.95 dinner special offers half a pound of U.S. Choice New York steak, and includes salad and rice or mashed potatoes. Priced from $5.15 to $9.95 are ground beefsteak, teriyaki steak, mahimahi filet, fried chicken, and lamb chops. Lunch is similarly inexpensive, and a special $1.99 breakfast offers two golden buttermilk hot cakes, an egg, and a choice of ham, bacon, or sausage. Banana hotcakes are $2.40. An excellent lunch special was being offered at the time of our last visit: a "croissantwich" with ham and cheese, turkey salad or tuna salad, plus soup, is $2.95, between 11 a.m. and 2 p.m.

There's nothing very glamorous about the **Minute Chef** in the Princess Kaiulani Hotel, all vinyl and Formica at its counter and tables, but this place has one of the best reputations in town for good, inexpensive food, and how it packs the people in! At lunch or dinner (same menu, same prices), you can have entrees like roast stuffed turkey with cranberries, mahimahi, and teriyaki steak, served with french fries or rice, roll, and butter, from $4.50 to $5.95. Fried chicken, chili, hamburgers, and a very popular breakfast special—Canadian bacon, scrambled eggs, toast, marmalade, fruit or juice, and coffee, at $4.95—round out the menu.

If you choose to dine at a **Jolly Roger** in Waikiki, you have your choice of two locations: one is in the heart of Waikiki, right on

Kalakaua Avenue at no. 2244, and another, Jolly Roger East, at 150 Kaiulani Ave. Both seem to be packed most of the time, since the food is always tasty and reasonably priced. On Kalakaua there are a few sidewalk tables and a cooler and quieter mood inside. At Jolly Roger East, there are comfortable booths, a step-down bar, and entertainment nightly at 9. At both you can eat a good dinner for $7.95 to $8.50: perhaps beef liver with sautéed onions or bacon, honey-fried chicken, breaded veal cutlet. There are also changing daily specials, from $3.95. Dinners are served with soup or salad, rice or potato, and a dinner roll. There are also plenty of salads, sandwiches, and burgers to choose from. Doors open around 6 a.m., and breakfast, lunch, and dinner are served until midnight, dinner starting at 4 p.m.

The **Original Pancake House** is for lovers of those breakfast delights who would like to eat them morning, noon, afternoon, or night. You'll find three Original Pancake Houses in town, one in the Waikiki Marina Hotel, 1965 Ala Moana Blvd. (tel. 955-0714), another at Suite 103 at the rear of 1221 Kapiolani Blvd. (corner Pensacola St., one block past the Ala Moana Shopping Center; tel. 533-3005), and a third at 1414 Dillingham Blvd. (tel. 847-1496). All are offspring of Portland's Original Pancake House, which later spread around the world and has been given a *McCall's* Citation and a James Beard Award. More than 20 varieties of pancake are at the ready, plus five types of waffle and sourdough french toast; the tab is from $1.75 to $6.50. They're known for their German Dutch baby and German apple pancakes, both baked in the oven. Other tempting possibilities might be Swedish pancakes, coconut pancakes, Kijafa cherry crêpes (a Danish treat), and Palestine pancakes (rolled with sour cream and Cointreau). There's a wide variety of oven-baked omelets (potato, Portuguese, ham jubilee, etc.), plus eggs any style, but the star of this show is pancakes—Mandarin pancakes, potato pancakes, pecan-and-apple pancakes. Open daily from 6 a.m. to 2 p.m. The Waikiki restaurant is open for dinner and offers validated parking.

It's easy to catch **Crêpe Fever** if you're shopping at Ward Centre, 1200 Ala Moana Blvd. Because the tables are open to strollers and because it has an inviting counter, you may find yourself ordering a crêpe before you realize it. Go ahead; the crêpes are light, the fillings are delicious, and the price is right. Lunch or dinner crêpes like lemon spinach, Mexican chicken, and tuna or ham "melts" are mostly $3.95 to $4.95; dessert crêpes, on the order of strawberry and cream, or banana splits are about $4.25.

Crêpes are served on disposable plates, cradled in a wicker holder; most are accompanied by salad and a scoop of brown rice. Soups and salads are available too, at $3 to $4. Shopping early? Breakfast on crêpes with fruits and berries or french toast. Breakfast starts at 8 a.m. and is served all day. Crêpe Fever closes at 9 p.m. daily; on Sunday at 4 p.m. Phone: 521-9023.

If you're downtown during the day, pop into **Croissanterie** at 222 Merchant St. near Alakea. Croissants are as popular here now as they are on the mainland. The place is plain, and the service is cafeteria style, but, oh, those croissants! Breakfast croissants, served until 11 a.m., have flavorings like cherry and chocolate, fillings like cream cheese with tomato or fresh spinach. From 11 a.m. to the 8 p.m. closing, the fillings become more elaborate—perhaps broccoli and cheese sauce, ham or turkey, cheese—and are priced at $2.50. There are several salads, and excellent coffee, which you can have either plain, espresso, or in some elaborate variations. Downstairs, a Lion Shop sells the coffees to take home.

Use your noodle when you're downtown; save money and have a tasty meal for under $4 by visiting the **Hong Kong Noodle House.** This small, plain restaurant on the *mauka-Ewa* corner of the Chinese Cultural Center, 100 North Beretania, facing the river, is one of about seven in a row that feature Chinese, Japanese, Korean, and Mongolian cooking. Even those who are not noodle fans could be converted. There are 12 different noodle soups, and any one of these, priced at about $2.75, is a full meal, like fishball noodle soup or roast duck noodle soup. There are almost as many tossed noodle dishes with soup served separately, priced around $3.25; the noodles with shrimp are delicious. Brave souls might want to try the noodles with pigs' feet. A dozen rice soups in the same price bracket include such fascinating combos as abalone with chicken or preserved eggs with unsalted pork. A few specials like stewed beef and crispy roast duck are offered in the same under-$4 price range. Prices are the same at both lunch (10 a.m. to 2:30 p.m.) and dinner (5 to 9 p.m.). Closed Sunday. Phone: 536-5409.

The Hotel Street area of downtown Honolulu, "Sin City" since World War II, contains some bargain surprises and some finds in dining. **Sau Duong,** a Vietnamese restaurant at 58 North Hotel St., near Smith Street, is such a discovery. It is sparkling clean and its mirrors, high ceilings, and multicolored plastic-topped tables lift it above its rather sleazy neighborhood. House specialties include vegetable with shrimp and papaya with dried beef at $3.50; plus a long list of noodle, long rice, and rice-paper dishes that run mostly between $3 to $5. Our sour shrimp soup with pineapple was unusual at $4.50. You won't break the budget here; you will get a chance to taste the unusual spices and flavorings of Vietnamese cooking. Open Monday to Saturday from 8:30 a.m. to 9 p.m., Sunday to 4 p.m. Phone: 538-7656.

Chapter V

ADVENTURES IN THE COSMOPOLITAN CITY

EVEN THOUGH there is more than enough to keep you busy in Waikiki, we don't think you should pass up the rest of Honolulu. For this is a city with more than the usual share of diversity and excitement, with a rich cultural past and a stimulating, cosmopolitan present. And how to see it need present no problem at all. If time is short or if you want to get an overall, bird's-eye view before you begin in-depth exploring, simply take one of the excellent commercial sightseeing tours that hit all the major points. Or you can rent a car and drive to all the things you want to see (details on car rentals can be found in Chapter II). But even without benefit of a car or guided tour, you can get around very well indeed. Honolulu is, after all, a major United States metropolis, and it has an excellent public transportation system: the MTL buses, popularly known as TheBUS. For 60¢ a ride, 25¢ for children, plus a little bit of ingenuity and determination, you can get almost anywhere in Honolulu you want to go.

IN DEFENSE OF BUSES: Besides saving you money, riding the buses gives you an added advantage: you go at your own pace, heading where your interests take you, lingering as long as you like in any given spot. On a guided tour, everybody has to see everything. While the ladies in front of you may just adore 'Iolani Palace, you might be much happier poking through the rickety little streets and alleys of Chinatown. Or you might want to skip all the historical sights and just come up for air once in a while as you peruse the splendors of the Honolulu Academy of Art or the Bishop Museum. On TheBUS, you're your own person; you decide when and where to go and how long to stay there. For Honolulu is such a varied city, with such a diversity of things to see, that it should be seen at your own pace.

Renting a car, of course, is the easiest way to do the town. But cars and taxis can get to be expensive, and bus travel is quite congenial. The buses run all over the city, they maintain good schedules, and the drivers are friendly and genuinely helpful. If you need information about TheBUS, phone 531-1611. Visiting senior citizens are eligible for free passes after three to four weeks (tel. 524-4626). Remember that most major thoroughfares in Honolulu are one-way: most buses going in a Diamond Head direction should be boarded on Kalakaua Avenue; those going toward downtown Honolulu or Ala Moana, on Kuhio Avenue.

THE ORDER OF THINGS: In the pages ahead, we outline for you the major sights of Honolulu. The first section will trace, in more-or-less chronological order, the sights that will show you what Hawaiian life was and is like, from the Stone Age days of the Polynesian settlers, through the missionary period and the era of Hawaiian royalty, to the Space Age Hawaii of the '80s. At the end of this section, we'll show you how to take some walking, bus, and boat tours.

In the next section, we'll tell you a little about the ethnic life of the city, about the important ethnic festivals always going on in Honolulu. Should you be lucky enough to catch the yearly Japanese Bon Dances or the Chinese New Year, for example, these could be the highlights of your trip. We'll also take you on a tour of the Hong Kong of Honolulu, the city's engaging Chinese neighborhood.

The last section of this chapter gives you a look at the museums, galleries, concerts, theaters, experimental films, and educational centers that make Honolulu just about the most exciting combination of beach resort and urban metropolis anywhere. Put on a comfortable pair of walking shoes, arm yourself with some good maps, and off you go to savor the excitement of this cosmopolitan city.

Hawaii, from Stone Age to Space Age

BISHOP MUSEUM: One of the most important natural and cultural history museums of the Pacific, the Bishop Museum makes the world of the early Polynesian settlers come alive, through such exhibits as outrigger canoes, a model *heiau,* feather cloaks of the *alii,* rare Hawaiian artifacts. There's an exciting collection of

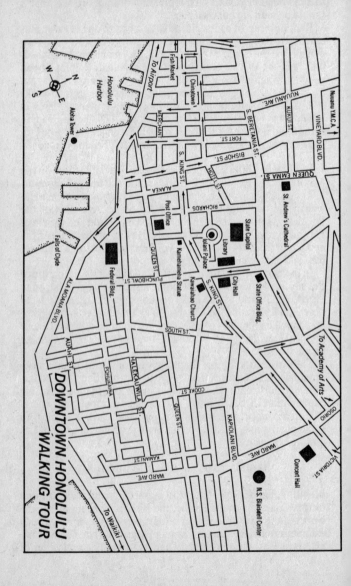

primitive art of Polynesia, Micronesia, and Melanesia. A visit here will give you a basis for understanding much of what you will see later throughout the islands. And the Shop Pacifica is laden with attractive items, everything from $2 kukui-nut pendants to a $1,000 Niihau shell necklace. The Bishop Museum is located at 1525 Bernice St. (tel. 847-3511); open daily from 9 a.m. to 5 p.m. Admission is $4.75 for those over 18.

QUEEN EMMA SUMMER PALACE: "Hanaiakamalama," the country estate of Kamehameha IV and his consort, Queen Emma, has been restored by the Daughters of Hawaii to its mid-19th-century Victorian splendor. The address is 2913 Pali Hwy.; open daily from 9 a.m. to 4 p.m., closed holidays. Guided tours. Admission: $4 for adults, $2 for ages 12 to 18, 50¢ for those under 12.

ROYAL MAUSOLEUM: This is where the *alii* of the Kamehameha and Kalakaua Dynasties are buried. The address is 2261 Nuuanu Ave.; open Monday to Friday, 8 a.m. to 4:30 p.m.; closed Saturday, Sunday, and most holidays (open March 26, Kuhio Day, and June 11, Kamehameha Day).

PEARL HARBOR: It would be unthinkable to leave Hawaii without making a pilgrimage to the U.S.S. *Arizona* Memorial at Pearl Harbor. This tomb of more than 1,000 American servicemen who died on December 7, 1941, the day bombs fell on Hawaii, is a silent, stark reminder of the continued folly of war. You can drive to Pearl Harbor or simply take TheBUS no. 20 direct from the Waikiki area to the Pearl Harbor Visitors Center, administered by the National Park Service. If you prefer to take a commercial shuttle bus rather than TheBUS, phone Terminal Transportation at 926-4747; the cost is $3 each way.

Try to arrive early in the morning at the Visitors Center to avoid huge crowds. While you're waiting for the U.S. Navy boat to take you out to the U.S.S. *Arizona* itself—you'll be given a number and an approximate time of departure—you can busy yourself with the absorbing exhibits at the Visitors Center and museum. Many of these show the personal mementos of the attack victims, plus photographs, paintings, and historical documents. A 20-minute film precedes your actual trip to the ship itself. Children under 45 inches in height will be permitted in the Visitor Center/museum and in the theaters, there, but they are not permitted on the U.S. Navy shuttle boats. Children 6 to 12 must be accompanied by adults. Full programs (films and boat ride to the Memorial) operate Tuesday through Sunday from 8 a.m. to 3 p.m. On Monday, the film is shown, but no boats operate.

MISSION HOUSES MUSEUM: These three 19th-century buildings are still the way they were when the New England missionaries lived in them, full of antique furniture, mementos, clothing of the missionary ladies, and aging trinkets, plus contemporary exhibits documenting the lives of the families who lived and worked here. A fascinating look into the past, it's at 553 South King St. Open daily, 9 a.m. to 4 p.m.; admission (including a guided tour) is $3.50 for adults, $1 for those under 16, free for children 6 years and under. On Saturdays, costumed players from the Museum staff portray the missionaries in a program entitled "A Social Gathering at the Binghams." The Museum staff is occasionally joined by actors from the community who depict other historical characters. A walking tour of historic downtown Honolulu leaves the museum every weekday at 9:30 a.m. The $7 fee includes admission. Special events here are of a high quality; check the local papers for information. There's a charming gift shop, full of Hawaiiana. Behind the Mission Houses is a library containing the collections of the Hawaiian Mission Children's Society and the Hawaiian Historical Society. Researchers are welcome. Phone 531-0481.

KAWAIAHAO CHURCH: The church that the king, his subjects, and missionaries built has been, since its dedication in 1841, the "Westminster Abbey of Hawaii." Even if you don't get to Sunday services (10:30 a.m., conducted partially in Hawaiian; free guided tours afterward), take a look around any day from 9 a.m. to 4 p.m. Note the fine portraits of Hawaiian royalty that hang in the church. The address is 957 Punchbowl St., across Kawaiahao Street from the Mission Houses.

'IOLANI PALACE: The official residence of Hawaii's last reigning monarchs, 'Iolani Palace was designed in the European manner for King Kalakaua, "The Merry Monarch." Royalty resided here for 11 years (1882 to 1893) until the monarchy was overthrown. From 1893 to 1968 'Iolani Palace was the site of the provisional government, the Republic, Territory, and State of Hawaii. Since 1978 it has been a museum, opened to the public after a $7-million restoration-reconstruction program. Although some areas are unfurnished, the Throne Room, State Dining Room, King's Library, and Privy Council Chamber are complete. Other rooms and areas are partially furnished. A tour of the building is well worth your time to see the intricate woodwork, the highly polished fir floors, the shining banisters and mirrors, and to be taken into the lovely rooms as guides fill you in on the furnishings that were and are there and the history that went on in each room. Tours are conducted by the Friends of 'Iolani Palace from 9 a.m. to 2:15 p.m. Wednesday through Saturday; they last 45 minutes and cost $4 for adults and $1 for children 5 through 12 (children under 5 not permitted on tours). Reservations are recommended: phone 523-0141.

On the same grounds are the **Archives of Hawaii,** the largest collection of Hawaiiana extant. The location is at King and Likelike Streets; open Monday through Friday from 7:45 a.m. to 4:30 p.m.

DOWNTOWN HONOLULU: The highlight of a little walk downtown will be the **Aloha Tower,** Hawaii's Empire State Building. Even though it's now dwarfed by the two 21-story AmFac towers and other modern buildings, it's still the symbol of the city, overlooking the harbor and affording spectacular views of the metropolis. It is open 8 a.m. to 9 p.m., seven days a week. The Aloha Tower is part of the Aloha Maritime Center. For an admission fee of $3 ($1 for children 6 to 12, under 6 free), you can see the museum, tour the *Falls of Clyde* (the world's only fully rigged, four masted ship, she plied the waters between Hilo and San Francisco for many years, beginning in 1898), and also tour the *Hokule'a* when she's in port. The *Hokule'a* is a replica of a double-hulled canoe, the kind that brought the first settlers from Tahiti years ago; the boat repeats that voyage frequently, navigated only by the stars, as in ancient times. Open daily, 9:30 a.m. to 4 p.m. Information: 536-6373.

You can come down to earth now and head for Hawaii's Wall Street, Merchant Street, where the major corporate empires of Hawaii, the "Big Five," still have their offices. The architecture of Alexander and Baldwin, Castle and Cook, Theo. H. Davies, among others, is 19th-century elegant. Then you can head toward **Fort Street** and a pleasant shopping mall closed to traffic where you can browse among some of the big downtown department stores.

STATE CAPITOL BUILDING: The first unit and the crowning jewel of the growing Civic Center is undoubtedly one of the grandest capitols in the world. Using Hawaiian materials and motifs, the colors of sand and sea, the building soars upward from expansive pools to an open-air crown suggesting the peak of a volcano. There is a

"Welcome, Enter" sign on both the governor's and lieutenant-governor's offices during regular working hours, and they are worth at least peaking into. Outside the building, a huge medallion bears the state seal and motto, *Ua Mau ke ea o ka aina I ka pono* ("The life of the land is perpetuated in righteousness"). Note Marisol's controversial statue of Father Damien out front, as well as the statue of Queen Liliuokalani and the reproduction of the Liberty Bell on the King Street side.

FOSTER BOTANIC GARDEN: On view are 15 acres of rare tropical plants from around the world plus orchid displays. A cool interlude, it's at 180 North Vineyard Blvd. Phone 531-1939 for information on excellent free guided tours held Monday, Tuesday, and Wednesday. Open daily from 9 a.m. to 4 p.m. Admission is $1.

PARADISE PARK: Walk back into the Hawaiian jungle, emerge into a charming park where trained birds go through their antics in regular shows. This 15-acre stretch of tamed jungle is delightful for everyone, a must for the kids, who will get a kick out of walking through a giant aviary. Features include five multiethnic villages and gardens representing Hawaii's people; "Animal Quackers Duck Show," an outdoor show featuring ducks and chickens; puppet shows; and educational exhibits on the history of Hawaii. Tour guides are available at a nominal charge. With or without entering the park, you can lunch at the beautiful Henri Hawaii Restaurant, with its view of gardens and waterfalls. The park is located at 3737 Mano Rd. in Manoa Valley (tel. 988-2141), open daily except Christmas, from 9:30 a.m. to 5 p.m. Admission for adults is $7.50; children 13 to 17, $6.50; 4 to 12, $3.75; under 4, free.

LYON ARBORETUM: Just above Paradise Park, at 3860 Manoa Rd. in lush upper Manoa Valley, this superb arboretum is open to the public from 9 a.m. to 3 p.m. Monday through Friday. A free 1½-hour guided tour, held at 1 p.m. on the first Friday of each month from January to December and on the third Wednesday from June to December, will tell you all you'll ever need to know about exotic, economic, and tropical plants, as well as the flora of Hawaii. Reservations for the tour area a must: call 988-7378 between 9 a.m. and 3 p.m. weekdays, and inquire too about a wide variety of classes, outings, and programs. Write for schedules or information.

PLANETARIUM: Daily sky shows delight all ages. Learn how the ancient Polynesians found the Hawaiian Islands and used the stars for navigation. Take a trip to Tahiti's skies. It's part of the Bishop Museum, 1525 Bernice St. (see above). Admission is $2 for adults, $1 for children; phone 847-3511 for show times and information.

CASTLE PARK: Hawaii's one and only amusement park is fun for all ages. Some of its attractions include Water Country (a four-acre water park), Grand Prix racing cars, Bumper Boats, three 18-hole miniature golf courses, Merlin's Magical Midway carnival rides, a video arcade, and a batting cage loaded with big-league softball and hardball pitching machines. You can pay for each individual attraction as you go, or, better yet, take advantage of Castle Park's Super Saver Pass at $8.50 for adults or $6.50 for ages 3 to 11. Castle Park opens daily at 10 a.m. Prices and hours subject to change; call 488-7771 for current information. Castle Park is about 20 minutes from Waikiki by car. Take Rte. H-1 West and follow the Aloha Stadium signs.

DOLE PINEAPPLE CANNERY: Watch those pineapples get into those cans in an absorbing $2 walking tour through the world's largest fruit cannery. Canning season is usually May through August. Other months there's a film tour, and always a free drink from the pineapple-juice fountain. Combine this with a visit to Hilo Hattie's Fashion Center at 700 Nimitz Hwy. and you get free bus pickup from Waikiki hotels or the Kodak Hula Show (tel. 537-2796). Or take TheBUS no. 8 direct to the cannery (tel. 536-3411).

HISTORY AND ARCHITECTURE BUFF'S WALKING TOUR: Begin this morning or afternoon walking excursion at the **Mission Houses Museum,** described above. If you're driving downtown you may, depending on space available, find metered on-street parking. After you've steeped yourself in the atmosphere of the past at the Mission Houses Museum and browsed through the gift shop, walk Ewa on King Street. You will come to historic **Kawaiahao Church,** described above. Continuing in an Ewa direction, you will pass the **War Memorial** in front of the Territorial Office Building. Beyond is the imposing **Statue of King Kamehameha I,** dressed in golden helmet and feathered cape. He stands at the entrance to the **State Judiciary Building, Aliiolani Hale,** built by

Kamehameha V for the legislature, courts, and cabinet officers of
the king's domain. It was formally opened by King Kalakaua for
the legislative session of 1874. Just beyond is the **Post Office,** done
in Spanish style with a large courtyard entrance garden.

Cross King Street now, and have a look at **Honolulu Hale—
City Hall.** It's the off-white stucco Spanish-looking building on
the corner. There is usually an art exhibit in the courtyard. Continuing in a Diamond Head direction (back the other way; we're
strolling in an S-shaped route) on the mauka side of King, you
will pass some very attractive white-trimmed brick buildings that
house various city agencies. The thing just beyond them that ap-
pears to be numerous sections of castoff black stovepipe gone
mad is really an "art object": **"Sky Gate,"** commissioned by the
city and county at a six-figure fee, has caused a bit of artistic con-
troversy in Honolulu. There are often free noontime concerts in
its vicinity during the summer; check the newspapers for details.

The tall, gray concrete slab just beyond *Sky Gate* is the **Honolulu Municipal Building** (the rationale behind putting a gigantic
structure in the midst of all the low-rises seems to have been making a choice between losing a lot of rolling green lawn or spoiling
the view—and the latter won). Diagonally across from it, you will
see a monarchy-style building with a terracotta roof; that's the
News Building, home of the *Honolulu Advertiser and Star-
Bulletin.* Now walk straight through—or around—the Municipal
Building, and you'll be on Beretania Street, preparing to walk the
third leg of our "S." The soft green building just mauka is the
main **Board of Water Supply** office complex. Walk Ewa (turn left)
on Beretania Street and note the very lovely building across from
City Hall. This is **Kalanimoku,** one of the new state buildings.
Have a look at the abundant tropical plantings that surround it.
Just across Punchbowl from Kalanimoku is the **State Capitol**
building, described above, where we end our walk.

GUIDED TOURS: Certainly the easiest way to see the sights of Honolulu and the island of Oahu is to take a guided tour—especially if
your time is limited. Of the major tour operators, **Gray Line**
(P.O. Box 30046, Honolulu, HI 96820; tel. 834-1033) is well recommended; basic city tours begin around $13. Check with the
Gray Line Travel Desk at the Royal Hawaiian Shopping Mall, or
call them, toll free, at 800/367-2420. They also run tours on all the
major islands. If you don't mind spending a few dollars more, it's
usually more fun to go on one of the smaller tours. **E Noa Tours**
(110 University Ave., Room 306, Honolulu, HI 96826; tel. 941-
6608), for one, takes you out in a 13-passenger van and provides

delightful, personalized looks at the island sights. You can't go wrong either way. Travel agents and hotel desks can arrange tours with both companies.

Sightseeing on the Sea

Although they do not let passengers off at the U.S.S. *Arizona* Memorial or the Visitors Center & museum, the sightseeing boat cruises to Pearl Harbor are both informative and enjoyable. The *Adventure V* leaves Kewalo Basin daily at 9:15 a.m. and 1:15 p.m. for a narrated cruise to Pearl Harbor, viewing the U.S.S. *Arizona* Memorial and Battleship Row. The cost is $8.50 for adults, $4.25 for children; call 923-2061 for reservations. A very pleasant dinner cruise aboard the *Adventure V* departs from Kewalo Basin at 5:45 p.m. and cruises along the shoreline to Diamond Head, returning at 8 p.m. The cost of $25 per person includes open bar and a sit-down dinner.

Another popular dinner cruise takes place on a catamaran, a double-hulled sailing vessel. This is the *Rainbow I,* which leaves the Hilton Hawaiian Village dock every day at 5:30 p.m. The Twilight Buffet Dinner Sail lasts two hours; there's an open bar and a sumptuous buffet dinner, as well as entertainment and dancing. The price is $34 for adults, $18 for children. For reservations, phone 955-3348.

To see the world under the water, you could go snorkeling, or more lazily, take the *Ani Ani,* a glass-bottom boat, which offers six one-hour narrated cruises every day, beginning at 9:30 a.m. The price is $8 for adults, $4 for children under 12. Call 537-1958 for information and reservations.

Hawaii, the Melting Pot

Perhaps the most intriguing thing about Hawaiian life is the fact that everybody here came from somewhere else. First the Polynesians; then, centuries later, the English, the Americans, the Chinese, the Japanese, the Filipinos, the Koreans, the Puerto Ricans, the French, the Irish, and so on, ad infinitum. Since so many of the races intermarried, the result is a colorful mèlange, a tapestry of hues and textures unmatched anywhere else. But, fortunately, many of the races have still maintained their own traditions and cultures, and these are particularly evident in their yearly festivals and celebrations. Visitors are warmly welcomed to these events, and we suggest that you take in as many as may be going on when you are in the islands. Some people even plan their vacations around the festival calendar; for them, the Chinese New Year or the celebration of Philippine Independence or the Japanese Bon Dances of the summer season are the highlights of their trip. Below is a seasonal calendar of events to watch for.

Chinese New Year: Help the local people welcome in the Year of the Dragon or the Year of the Horse or the year of the whatever. Chinese New Year is usually at the beginning of February, and for three weeks before and five days after there's the Festival. There are cultural shows, banquets, the crowning of a Narcissus Queen, parades with lanterns and lions, and dancing in the streets.

Japanese Girls' Day: Look in the windows of the big Japanese department stores at Ala Moana Center and in downtown Honolulu for displays of regally costumed dolls, all in honor of this holiday—March 3—when all Japanese girls receive dolls as presents.

Prince Kuhio Day: March 26 is the day on which the native Hawaiians celebrate the birthday of the "People's Prince," Jonah Kuhio Kalanianaole. Catch the ceremonies at 'Iolani Palace, at the tomb in the Royal Mausoleum, and at the site of his home at Kuhio Beach.

Cherry Blossom Festival: Since the Japanese are now Hawaii's largest ethnic group, it seems as if everyone gets in on this spring event. In March or April, for about six weeks, you can see displays of flower arranging, judo, the tea ceremony, parades in the streets, and an "International Revue" straight from Japan.

Wesak Day: April 8, the birthday of Gautama Buddha, is the signal for the islands' Buddhists (mostly Japanese) to gather in Kapiolani Park for a sunrise ceremony. You can join the day-long celebration of music and dance.

Lei Day: May 1 is dear to the Hawaiians. Join the islanders in wearing a lei and be sure to see the Cazimero Brothers' show at night at the Waikiki Shell. In the afternoon there's a lei competition and exhibit.

Japanese Boys' Day: May 5 is the day ancient tradition specifies to decorate the family residence with colorful paper and fabric carp in honor of the eldest boy in the family. On the first Boys' Day after his birth, all of his grandparents and aunts and uncles, etc., would send a carp to be flown in his honor. These days carp are flown for all the family's male offspring, and you'd be surprised how many families of other nationalities also fly the bright fish for their boys.

Kamehameha Day: June 11 is one of the biggest celebrations of the year—a huge parade, luaus, fancy-dress balls, all in honor of the conqueror and uniter of the islands. The statue of Kamehameha in front of 'Iolani Palace is draped with hundreds of enormous flower leis, and the Mission Houses Museums runs a charming "Fancy Fair" on the grounds, where local craftspeople show their work.

Filipino Festival: Philippine Independence Day and Rizal Day fall in mid-June, and it's then the local Filipino population goes mad with a 17-day, Spanish-accented fiesta including dancing, singing, and a big-name show at the Waikiki Shell.

Bon Dances: Watch the papers for the dates of the Bon Odori Dances, which are given throughout the islands in July and August. These ancient religious dances, honoring the spirits of the ancestors who have reached paradise, are probably the most colorful affairs of the summer. The dances are performed outdoors, both by adults and the especially adorable Japanese keikis dressed in their native costumes. Visitors can observe or even take a few lessons in Bon dancing (classes are announced in the papers).

Aloha Week: Once a year, in late October, all the varied racial and ethnic groups get together for one big blow-out, and Aloha Week explodes. Kalahaua Avenue is blocked off, stages are set up along the entire stretch for almost nonstop entertainment, and the whole celebration begins with an enormous parade. The other islands also hold celebrations during different weeks in October—it's a good reason to come to Hawaii in October.

The rest of the big holidays—Thanksgiving, Christmas, New Year—are observed just as they are back on the mainland. Except that the faces around the Thanksgiving table gazing at the turkey may be Hawaiian-Chinese and people sing Christmas carols in the sand rather than the snow. That's the fun of Hawaii.

A WALK AROUND CHINATOWN: Whether or not there is anything special going on among the various ethnic groups when you are in Honolulu, you can always have an Oriental adventure of your own. An hour or two spent walking around Chinatown, either by yourself or on a guided tour, is a fascinating experience. A pleasant Chinese gentleman conducts an excellent shopping-and-temple tour sponsored by the Chinese Chamber of Commerce every Tuesday morning at 9:30 a.m. from 42 North King St. The tour costs $3, and there is an optional lunch at $4. Phone 533-3181 for reservations.

If, however, you don't have the time for an organized tour or just want to walk about on your own, it's easy enough (although you miss the engaging running commentary that is provided). You should start at the **Cultural Plaza** (in the block bordered by Beretania, Maunakea, Kukui, and River Streets). Pause to look at some of the shops, if you like, then continue your walk along Maunakea Street. Here you could poke your head into a bakery and munch on those irresistible Chinese pastries, candies, and buns (don't miss the moon cookies if the Chinese Moon Festival happens to be going on; otherwise almond or wedding cake will do nicely). Then on to a food market across the street where you can pick up the bladder of an eel or sharks' fins. Or get some bird's-nest soup. It used to take the Chinese cooks days to prepare this, since they had to carefully extricate the feathers from the birds' saliva. Now it's all conveniently packaged, and no traditional nine-course Chinese banquet would be complete without it.

If you've got a cold or tummy-ache, you might stop in at the herbalist's shop next—there are several on Maunakea Street. Lots of *haoles* as well as the local people consult the herbalist (who studies for four years, then undergoes an internship and is licensed by the state to practice). He makes a diagnosis by examining your pulse in several different spots, to determine the condition of different organs, then prescribes a concoction to be brewed and sipped; his office is usually behind the pharmacy. The brew may be made out of sea horses and sea dragons, antelope horns, or snakes (they're good for arthritis) and what not. Don't say you weren't warned.

There are literally dozens of gift shops in the neighborhood, where you can buy anything from a $1 sandalwood fan (very useful in the hot Hawaiian sun) to a piece of rare jade or an antique Oriental screen. And don't miss **Cindy's Lei Shoppe** at 1034 Maunakea St. Somehow or other, Cindy manages to keep her prices lower than just about any other place in town, her work is beautiful, and the quality of the flowers is the best.

Probably the single most interesting place in Chinatown, and one you should visit whether or not you make the rest of the trip, is the **Kuan Yin Temple** at 170 North Vineyard St. near the Foster Gardens. It's straight out of the Orient, complete to its huge gold-leafed statues of Kuan Yin, the goddess of mercy, and various other gods, burning incense and joss sticks, offerings of fruits and flowers on the altars, and the people rustling about lighting candles. It's an authentic bit of Oriental life that should be seen and experienced.

Hawaii, the Cultural Center

Too many tourists think there is no entertainment in Hawaii besides hula shows and slack-key music. That's all well and good, but what they don't realize is that there's plenty going on in the arts-entertainment-cultural scene and that they're missing a good bet if they don't join the local people in enjoying it. Most of the shows and events are inexpensive, compared to mainland prices, and the quality is high. For the imagination of the people of Hawaii, the result of the blending of great ideas from many divergent cultures, has produced some ingenious results. To wit:

A Japanese Adventure

The Japanese neighborhood of downtown Honolulu is all but gone now, its rickety hotels and pool halls and saimin stands torn down for shiny new office buildings. You could visit the wholesale fish market auction early, early in the morning, at Kewalo Basin. But there's an easier way to catch the flavor of the old neighborhood-that-was, and that's to take a trip to **Tamashiro Market,** 802 North King St. (at the corner of Palama). This is the Kalihi neighborhood, near the Bishop Museum, and it's easiest to drive here. It's nominally just a fish store, but so unusual that peo-ple come from all over Honolulu, and school groups regularly make visits. The place is huge, crowded, pungent with the odors of the weirdest varieties of fresh seafood you can imagine. Like to try octo-pus? or Kona crab? raw aku? or sea cucumber? They're all here. There's also a huge table of fresh seaweed, barrels of snails, live clams, live crabs, live lobsters, and live Hawaiian prawns in running water. So fresh is the fish and so excellent the quality that many of the leading restaurants buy here. Besides the fish, there are fascinating local dishes to buy and take out, like Filipino rice cakes made with coconut milk and mochi rice, Puerto Rican pasteles made with pork and bananas, Korean cucumber kim chee, and dozens of types of "poke" (prepared seafoods, island style). You may need a native to help you pick and choose the dishes, but even if you just look, it's lots of fun. Tamashiro Market is open every day of the week.

THEATER: It's 5,000 miles from Broadway, but it's pretty good and it's getting better all the time. The top local group is the **Honolulu Community Theater,** housed in the Ruger Theater, just behind Diamond Head. Major Broadway shows are the fare here, and you see them sooner than you'd expect, since the rights are easier to secure 2,500 miles out in the Pacific than on the roadshow touring circuit. Sometimes name performers come out to join the local acting company. Check the local papers or phone 734-0274 for specific attractions and prices.

Up at the University of Hawaii at Manoa, serious theater endeavors continue all year long. The **John F. Kennedy Theater** here showcases University of Hawaii productions, as well as lectures and performances by students attending its East-West Center.

The **Windward Theatre Guild** brings contemporary theater to the windward side of Oahu. Performances by this talented group are held in the Kailua Elementary School Auditorium. Phone 261-4885 for information on current performances.

The **Hawaii Performing Arts Company** (known as **HPAC**) is another of the top-notch theater groups in town. This nonprofit resident theater company, sponsored by the State Foundation on Culture and the Arts and supported by the National Endowment for the Arts, was established in 1969, and has since earned a reputation for presenting exciting new playwrights as well as reviving the classics. Recent productions have included *Amadeus, Joseph and the Amazing Technicolor Dreamcoat,* and *Vanities*. Performances are held at the Manoa Valley Theater, 2833 East Manoa Rd. For information, call 988-6131 or check the entertainment section of the newspapers.

The nationally acclaimed **Honolulu Theater for Youth** puts on excellent productions for children, but adults enjoy them too. We recently saw a neat production of *Frankenstein*! Most shows are aimed at age 6 and up. For information, call 521-3487.

ART: Hawaii's citizens, so attuned to the glories of nature, are also attuned to the glories of art. The islands are producing some talented young artists, and the local citizenry eagerly seeks out their works at a number of galleries. Art is constantly being commissioned for public buildings, and one of the great prides of the city is the **Honolulu Academy of Arts,** a must-see.

The academy is a supremely graceful building, a model of what an art museum should look like. Small galleries look out on serene courtyards through which you can wander after getting your fill of the treasures within. While both island artists and the masters of Western art—Picasso, Braque, Van Gogh, etc.—are well represented, the real glory of the museum is in its collections of Oriental scrolls, paintings, tapestries, screens, and sculptures from Korea, China, Japan. Be sure to see the awe-inspiring statue of Kuan Yin, a 12th-century representation of the Chinese goddess of mercy, which is far more beautiful than the one in the Kuan Yin temple in Honolulu. Newly opened at the academy is a gallery devoted to late-19th- and early-20th-century Japanese art, notably the works of Shibata Zeshin. A sculpture garden contains masterpieces from the academy collection, including some Noguchis and Henry Moores. The academy is located at 900 South Beretania St. (across Thomas Square from the Neal S. Blaisdell Center), and is open Tuesday to Saturday from 10 a.m. to 4:30 p.m., and on Sunday from 1 to 5 p.m.; closed Monday. The academy shop is first-rate. TheBUS no. 2 going downtown from Waikiki takes you to the academy's front door in about ten minutes. A delightful lunch is served in the Garden Café from September to May. Phone 531-8865 for reservations. Outstanding primitive art of the Polynesian peoples can be viewed at the Bishop Museum, which we've discussed above.

There are a number of private galleries that deserve a look-see, like the beautiful **Following Sea** at Kahala Mall Shopping Center, which represents outstanding work by craftspeople from all over the United States. You'll find many beautiful works in wood, fiber, ceramics, glass, jewelry, and more . . . **Rare Discoveries** at Ward Warehouse is a winner for outstanding craft work, and **Artists Guild** at the same Ward Warehouse is also full of beautiful treasures . . . There's a small showroom displaying pottery, sculpture, paintings, and miniatures done by artists who have their studios at **The Foundry**, 899 Waimanu St. Surrounding studios include pottery, stained glass, metal sculpture, leather-work, handmade knives and miniatures, and even topiaries. Visitors are invited to watch the craftsmen at work. . . . **Center Art galleries** are to be found in many locations (at the Waikiki Shopping Center and the Hyatt Regency Hotel, among others), and feature works by such island artists as William de Shazo and Margaret Keane, as well as originals and graphics by such masters as Chagall, Picasso, and Dali . . . Up at the Kahala Hilton Hotel is Bernard Hurtig's **Oriental Treasures and Points West,** a collector's haven for fine antiques and contemporary works of art and jewelry . . . Well worth a stop as you travel around the island of Oahu is Punalu'u Art Center, 53-352 Kamehameha Hwy, in Punalu'u. Owners Joy Goodenow and Hauoli Martin, talented artists themselves, show only original works by top island artists of the caliber of Peter Hayward, as well as lesser known talents, with prices beginning at very little and going way up.

MUSIC: There's more to Hawaiian music than the ukulele and the old island songs. Much more, for Hawaii is a music-minded community. The local people flock to the concerts of the great orchestras and soloists who play engagements here en route to the Orient (or vice versa), and take great pride in their own splendid **Honolulu Symphony Orchestra.** Since it plays over 100 concerts a year throughout the island chain, including summer concerts under the stars at the Waikiki Shell, you will probably get a chance to hear it.

If you're in Honolulu in February or March, you may get to see the yearly **Opera Festival** at Neil S. Blaisdell Concert Hall. World renowned opera stars sing with local choruses, under the auspices of the Hawaii Opera Theater.

DANCE: Hawaii's unique contribution to the art of the dance is, of course, the hula, and it is much more than just an entertainment for tourists. At one time it was a dance of spiritual significance. As you travel through the islands you will become aware of the importance of the natives placed on the dance of Laka, the goddess of hula and the sister of the volcano goddess, Pele. You can still see the remains of a *heiau* on the Na Pali Cliffs of Kauai, to which devotees from all over Hawaii—men (who were the original hula dancers) as well as women—came to be trained in the *meles,* chants, and dances sacred to Laka.

Seeing the hula danced in Hawaii is always pleasant, if not always completely authentic. You should plan to see the **Kodak Hula Show,** which is a good, solid presentation of Hawaiian dance and which, besides, is free. It is presented Tuesday, Wednesday, Thursday, and Friday mornings in Kapiolani Park (after the show you can board the Dole Pineapple Cannery/Hilo Hattie's free bus to visit the fashion center and cannery). . . . An entertaining free hula show, a combination of dance, music, and images, is held at the **Waikiki Shopping Plaza** every day at 6 and again at 7:15 p.m. . . . On Tuesday, Thursday, and Saturday from 9 to 11 a.m., performers from the Polynesian Cultural Center are usually on hand, presenting their native dances and songs at the **Royal Hawaiian Shopping Center.** . . . Another free hula show is presented every Sunday morning at 9:30 at the Ala Moana Shopping Center. That's the **Young People's Hula Show,** and the adorable performers start at the age of about 5. When school's out, there are also shows on Tuesday and Thursday at 2 p.m. Check the tourist papers for exact times of all shows, as they change frequently. The free show on the beach in front of the **Reef Hotel** every Sunday night at 8 is always fun.

If you have a yen to learn the dance yourself, that can usually be arranged. Perhaps your own hotel will be giving hula classes, and there are often series of classes given by the city's Department of Parks and Recreation. Check the local papers for exact dates. There's usually a small admission charge.

But if you haven't got time for concentrated learning, at least observe the hula dancer carefully. You're supposed to keep your eyes on the hands, which tell the story, but you might be distracted by the wind-blown grass skirts (actually made of ti leaves), the flashing slit-bamboo rods used to beat out a tattoo, the featured gourds *(uliuli)* that sounds like maracas, the clatter of koa-wood sticks against each other, or the click of smooth stones *(iliili)*. And remember, if you see any really violent hula dancing, it's probably Tahitian, definitely not Hawaiian. For the Hawaiian hula is smooth as the trade winds, graceful as the swaying palms.

MOVIES: The latest Hollywood movies and the top films by international directors both draw big crowds in Honolulu. You can see them at various theaters in Waikiki and elsewhere in Honolulu, but you can also catch a Japanese movie, a Chinese, or maybe even a Filipino or Korean one—and you probably can't do *that* back home. The entertainment pages of the Honolulu newspapers will provide the data. Experimental filmmaking is on the rise in Honolulu, especially at the University of Hawaii, and small, informal film screenings are announced periodically.

THE UNIVERSITY OF HAWAII: Pride of Hawaii's nine-campus public system of higher education, the University of Hawaii at Manoa is well worth your visit—not only for a theatrical presentation or a concert or an experimental film or a presentation of Asian folk dancing, but to see the campus itself.

Located in the lush, tropical Manoa Valley, with the mountains as a backdrop, the campus is just a short drive or bus ride from Waikiki, where a number of university students live. Originally a small, land-grant agricultural college, the university has grown the way everything in Hawaii has since statehood. It's now become an important center of higher learning for some 20,000 students, many from far beyond the islands. The campus itself is a flower garden, art is prevalent everywhere, and the buildings are beautiful.

There are no guided tours of the university, but visitors are welcome to explore the campus. Maps and directions for self-guided tours are available at the University Relations Office (Hawaii Hall, Room 2). If you're an art enthusiast, be sure to see

Jean Charlot's two-story murals of the history of the island in Bachman Hall and Juliette May Fraser's *Makahiki Ho'okupu* in Hamilton Library. There are other important murals by island artists at Bilger and Keller Halls and in the Music Building: good changing art exhibitions are on view at the Campus Center and the gallery in the Art Building; there are occasional exhibits at Burns Hall. For nature lovers, rare varieties of tropical plants and trees are everywhere. But for us, the most interesting sights of the university are the students, especially the ones in native costume who are studying at the East-West Center. This important institute accepts graduate students from both East (Asia and the Pacific Islands) and West (the mainland), trains them in each other's cultures, and then sends them on fieldwork to those areas.

Chapter VI

HONOLULU AFTER DARK

WE HAVE HEARD IT rumored that there really are visitors to Honolulu who have dinner early, watch TV in their hotel rooms, and go to bed at 10 p.m. But we strongly suspect these are only rumors. For the streets of Waikiki are thronged at night, the bars and clubs are jammed to the gills, and there's so much to do once the lights go on over the city that it seems a shame to waste time resting (you can always do that during the daytime on the beach). On a night out in Honolulu you might catch anyone from Danny Kaleikini to Don Ho to Sammy Davis, Jr. You could see a hula show or a Tahitian revue, hear some "Hawaiian mod" sounds, drink beer with the kids at the university while the stereo rocks the tables, look in on the disco scene, or sit at a quiet ocean-side garden with someone you love and watch the sun set over the Pacific. You may spend a few dollars, or you may have to go all out and blow the budget for the big-time shows. Happily, though, the cost of nightlife is much cheaper here than, say, in New York or Las Vegas. And there's plenty of it.

The Name Entertainers

Note: Because nightclub entertainers have a way of moving around a bit, it's always wise to check the local tourist papers and phone ahead to get details on prices before going to a show. Be sure to check the papers for coupons and discount deals. On a recent off-month, we found $35 shows being advertised for as low as $15.

The **Danny Kaleikini** show is practically an institution in Hawaii, as much a part of the scene as Diamond Head or Waikiki Beach. Danny is the star attraction up at the **Hala Terrace** of the Kahala Hilton Hotel. A one-man show in himself (he sings, dances, and plays drums, ukulele, and nose flute), Danny presides over a talented company of Hawaiian musicians and singers. He exudes charm, warmth, and genuine old-fashioned aloha. The Hala Terrace is set against a backdrop of particularly romantic sea and sky, and it's great for those hand-holding evenings. Cost of the dinner show is $48, inclusive of tax and tip. The show only is $8 cover plus a two-drink minimum. For reservations, phone 734-2211.

After (or during) dinner, one of the best spots in town is the elegant **Monarch Room** of the Royal Hawaiian Hotel, where the islands' leading entertainers perform. You might catch the Cazimero Brothers and their excellent all-Hawaiian revue. The dinner show is $42 for adults, $31.50 for children 12 and under, all inclusive; at the same show, you can have two cocktails and see the performance for $18.50 inclusive; or take in the 11 p.m. cocktail show, which includes one cocktail only, $11 inclusive. (Prices are subject to change.) To make reservations for the Monarch Room, call 923-7311.

It will cost you $37.50 for adults, $26.50 for children, to see **Don Ho,** Hawaii's best known entertainer, at the **Hilton Dome Showroom** of the Hilton Hawaiian Village Hotel. That price, for the 8:30 p.m. show (seating at 6, Sunday through Friday) includes a steak-and-mahimahi dinner, plus a drink, tax, and gratuities. For cocktails only (seating at 8), the tab is $19.75 for adults, $14.25 for children. Don heads up a gala Polynesian extravaganza and has less opportunity for making not-so-subtle innuendos to the adoring grandmothers in the audience than he used to. Don is very, very popular, and some people wouldn't consider their trip to Hawaii complete without seeing him. The phone number for reservations is 949-4321, ext. 70105.

The **Polynesian Palace** of the Reef Towers, 227 Lewers St., is the lavish home of one of Hawaii's best loved entertainers, **Al Harrington,** who used to play Ben Kokua on "Hawaii 5-O." The "South Pacific Man" leads a smartly paced review that is always entertaining. The price is $35 for the Sunday through Friday dinner shows, which includes a prime-rib buffet dinner, a drink, tax, and tips; for those under 12, it's $20. Lower prices of $20 and $15 prevail for the cocktail shows, and include all tips and taxes. Reservations: 923-9861.

Marge Akana and **Pauline Kumalaa,** two native Hawaiians otherwise known as the Kuhina Serenaders, keep the crowds happy every night except Monday at the **Kumu Lounge** of the Pacific Beach Hotel. They have an extraordinary rapport with their audiences, exude that old-fashioned aloha spirit, and are splendid musicians. No cover or minimum.

Another big favorite with the local folks is **Frank DeLima,** a singing comedian whose outlandish parodies and skits can usually be counted upon to keep the patrons of the **Noodle Shop** more or less rolling in the aisles. Cover is $2.50, and there is a two-drink minimum.

The virtuoso of the ukulele—in his hands it truly sounds like a classical instrument—is **Herb Ohta,** also known as Ohta San. He's currently at the **Colony Lounge** of the Hyatt Regency Hotel. No cover, no minimum.

Hawaiian and Polynesian Revues

Want to catch a great Polynesian show and a great buffet dinner at the same time? The Moana Hotel's "Polynesian Revue," one of the most professional in the islands, lets out all the stops. The sensational Tahitian shimmy, the gentle Maori slap dances, the heart-stopping Samoan fire dance, and of course the languid Hawaiian hulas are performed by top artists. They're on twice nightly in the lovely **Banyan Court** of the Moana Hotel, and while you're watching the fireworks on stage you can feast on a bountiful buffet for an all-inclusive tab of $36 per person, $25 for children under 12. Cocktails and show only runs $18.25 for adults, $13.50 for children under 12. For reservations, phone 926-4474.

Another top Polynesian show can be found at the **Hawaiian Hut** of the Ala Moana Hotel. That's "Kalo's South Seas Revue," featuring, again, the dances of Tahiti, Samoa, and the Maori, all done with great style by highly skilled artists. Also featured is an elaborate prime-ribs buffet, which includes an exotic drink along with the prime ribs and southern fried chicken. There are two shows a night, 6:30 and 9:30 p.m., for an all-inclusive tab of $29.50. Or just have a drink and watch the show for $17. For reservations, call 941-5205.

Free Shows

If you'd like a free show for a change—and who wouldn't?—we can recommend several. Most Sundays, beginning about 8 p.m., there's an informal hula show on the beach in front of the **Reef Hotel.** The performers are all talented amateurs and the show never winds down until about 9:30 or 10 p.m. There's a darn good hula show every night at the **Waikiki Shopping Plaza** called "Waikiki Calls." It uses both live dancers and an audiovisual program, skillfully intertwined. Show times are 6 and 7:15

p.m. The Royal Aloha Extravaganza is presented every night at **Kuhio Mall** at 8. You can frequently watch singers and dancers perform at the Lewers/Kalakaua corner of the **Royal Hawaiian Shopping Center;** most events take place from 6:30 to 8:30 p.m. The **Young People's Hula Show,** held every Sunday morning at 9:30 p.m. on the Lanai Stage of the **Ala Moana** Shopping Center, is a perennial Hawaii charmer.

For Romance

It's hard to imagine a more romantic spot in Waikiki than the spectacular **Hanohano Room** in the Sheraton Waikiki Hotel. The view is nonstop from Diamond Head to Pearl Harbor, the sunset is unforgettable, and from 8 p.m. on, you can listen and dance to good music while you're having dinner. Afterwards, there's music till 1 a.m.

The **House Without a Key,** one of Hawaii's traditional sunset spots, is back at the rebuilt and better-than-ever Halekulani Hotel. This open-air, waterfront cocktail lounge affords a fabulous view of the sun sinking over the water, and while you're enjoying that spectacle, you'll also enjoy relaxing music by either Sonny Kamahele and his group or the Jerry Byrd Trio, plus hulas by Kanoe Miller, a former Miss Hawaii. The music begins at 5 p.m. on Sunday, Monday, Tuesday, and Thursday, at 5:30 the rest of the week, and continues until 9 p.m. Loverly.

Windows of Hawaii, the revolving restaurant atop the Ala Moana Building, has glorious views of Honolulu, plus soft background music by which to dine and drink.

From the top of the world to the bottom of the sea you go, and right into **Davy Jones Locker II,** "Under the Pool" at the Outrigger Hotel, where the bar is the underside of the hotel's swimming pool.

And the cozy and rustic **Blue Dolphin Room,** overlooking the pool at the Outrigger Hotel, offers music with no cover or minimum every night of the week. It's known for old-style Hawaiian music, and there's a dinner show every night at 9:30.

Where the Discos Are

The disco craze has spread just about everywhere, and Honolulu has gotten right into the action. To join the local fanatics, you can make the scene at places like **Spats** at the Hyatt Regency Hotel (no cover, no minimum); **D.B.G.'s Dance Menagerie** in the Waikiki Beachcomber Hotel (on Friday and Saturday, two-drink minimum and $2 cover charge); and the **Shore Bird Disco,** beachfront at the Reef Hotel, which offers dancing to nonstop video on two dance floors from 9 p.m. to 2 a.m. Two-drink minimum, no cover. Perhaps the prettiest spot is the semiprivate club **Annabelle's** at the top of the Ilikai, 30 stories up, from which you can see the glittering kaleidoscope of the city lights below. You can dance from 5 p.m. to 4 the next morning; the $4 cover charge does not begin until 9 p.m. During the 5 to 9 p.m. Happy Hour, it's big-band sounds (drinks, $1.50); after 9 p.m., the music is Top 40, accented with big-screen video clips of popular performers.

Chapter VII

A HONOLULU SHOPPING BONANZA

ASK ANYONE WHO'S BEEN THERE: Honolulu is a great place to shop. In fact, if you walk along Kalakaua Avenue any afternoon or evening, it's sometimes seems that the tourists are doing nothing else. For even though there's no favorable exchange rate here or duty-free shopping, and prices are just about what you'd expect to pay back home, there are so many good buys in so many interesting things that everybody gets caught up in the shopping fever. New shopping complexes have blossomed all over Honolulu, with scads of temptations right in or very near Waikiki. Indulge and enjoy yourself—it can't be helped.

Spend an hour or two in the shops that line Kalakaua Avenue, in the Ala Moana Shopping Center, at the Royal Hawaiian Shopping Center, and you'll have a pretty good idea of the things that everybody wants to bring back from the islands. Clothing is undoubtedly the most popular item—island resort wear in bright, bold Hawaiian prints, the colors of the sun and the tropical landscape. And then there are fragrant, flowery island perfumes, the carved tikis (figures of the Hawaiian gods), calabashes, carved woods, tapas (bark cloth printed with primitive religious symbols), dolls with grass skirts, ukuleles, shell necklaces and other fanciful island jewelry. And the food—macadamia nuts, Hawaiian jams, coconut syrup, Kona coffee—not to mention the pineapple and coconuts that you'll want to have or send back home. All these are typical of the islands and they are on sale everywhere.

Souvenirs

You will, of course, have to buy dozens of souvenirs—small, inexpensive gifts for a few dollars, to bring to all the relatives and neighbors back home. We've found the best prices for these items—key chains, letter-openers, money clips, and the like, all decorated with some Hawaiian symbol or figure, as well as Hawaiian perfumes—are at the **ABC** discount stores, which are found everywhere in Waikiki (there's a large one at the corner of Kuhio and Kanekapolei). Other good places where you can pick up scads of these items are the **Woolworth's** on Kalakaua Avenue and Ala Moana Shopping Center, **Long's Drugstore** in Ala Moana, and the Hawaiian gift shop at **Sears** in Ala Moana.

Clothing

Could you possibly come back from Hawaii without at least *one* muumuu or aloha shirt or bathing suit? Unthinkable! Let us first, however, tell the ladies a little bit about the Hawaiian fashion scene. Although every kind of contemporary fashion idea has hit Hawaii, we still think the most beautiful Hawaiian dresses are the graceful full-length muumuus that Hawaiian women have been wearing for centuries. You'll find them perfect for evening, and for daytime there are many lovely "shorty muus" as well as versions of the Chinese cheongsam. Men, of course, will want aloha shirts—boldly printed and cut fuller than men's ordinary sport shirts, since they are designed to be worn outside the trousers. They are, as you well know, the rage of the mainland right now. You can find Hawaiian clothing just about anywhere, but we'll give you a few hints on our own special favorites, where we feel the quality is the best for the money.

After a while, so many of the clothing shops begin to look like repetitions of each other. One place where you won't run into this mass-production syndrome is at the **Carol & Mary** shops (there are seven of them, the largest at Ala Moana Shopping Center); they handle the better Polynesian lines and a large selection of beautiful sportswear from mainland designers. (They also carry European and American couture designer fashions, accessories, children's clothing, and crystal and china giftware.) There's no beating the quality and brilliant styling, for men and women, at **Andrade's** in the Royal Hawaiian and Moana Shopping Centers, among many other locations.

Other names to remember for top resort fashions as you make your way around town: **Liberty House,** one of the city's biggest and nicest department stores, with branches on Kalakaua, at Ala Moana Center, and elsewhere around town and on the other islands; **Watumull's,** with attractive branches in the Ala Moana Shopping Center, the Sheraton Waikiki Hotel, the Holiday Inn, and the Princess Kaiulani Hotel, among others; **Aloha Fashions,** right on Kalakaua (at no. 2368), at 224 Lewers St., and in the Hilton Hawaiian Village Hotel; and **McInerny's,** in the Royal Hawaiian Shopping Center and Kahala Mall. **Sears** at Ala Moana has one of the best-priced Hawaiian-wear sections anywhere; and prices are also quite low at **Holiday Mart,** a discount department store near Ala Moana Center, at 801 Kaheka St.

Some Special Boutiques

The boutique craze has hit Honolulu too, and although most of the shops in the tourist areas feature Hawaiian resort wear, a few are cropping up here and there that could be straight out of New York or London or even Paris. Take, for example, **Fabrications,** at Kahala Mall, where designer-artists Janet and Jeffrey Berman create and sell custom-made clothing along with ready-made lines. Their fashions are timeless, with simple classic lines, and their fabrics, ranging from soft French crêpes to Swiss cotton jerseys, are exquisite. Prices begin at $125 for day wear. They also sell handbags and fashion jewelry and, for those who want a touch of the islands, long caftans in rich colors.

We doubt if there are any cities outside of Japan—except Honolulu—where you might find a shop like **Orizaba,** 1149 South Beretania St., Orizaba has an enormous collection of antique kimonos and obis from Japan, most in pure silk. While many of the shop's customers buy these things to cut and use as fabric, the kimonos are lovely for lounging or as dressing gowns, and the obis can be made into evening belts and handbags—you can get many small items from one obi. The kimonos range in price anywhere from the ones on the bargain rack at $5, to the really quality items, which may go from $40 to hundreds of dollars. Occasional sales will bring prices down around 25%. Obis run from $5 to $40. You may browse and try on to your heart's content without being pressured, and all your questions will be answered in a most friendly manner.

Le Cadeaux, 2354 Kalakaua Ave., is like no other shop in Honolulu: it's very European, and its wares seem to have come right out of Victorian England or perhaps turn-of-the-century France. The treasures here are costly, but so lovely that they warrant at least a look. Here are dolls to collect or just to love: antique dolls in limited editions, porcelain dolls, puppets, Louis Nicole dolls, Vlasta cloth dolls dressed in antique laces. Prices start at about $50. There are many bears and other stuffed animals. You can buy lace dresses for children, beautiful straw hats, Quimper ware from France, and luscious chocolates imported fresh from Belgium every week, at $20 a pound. Elegant.

King's Village

As much fun to browse through as to shop at, King's Village, at the corner of Koa and Kaiulani Avenues, recaptures the flavor of Hawaii's 19th-century monarchy period with its cobblestone streets and classic architecture. You'll sense the European feeling as soon as you pass through the gate. There's a changing-of-the-guard ceremony nightly at 6:15, followed by a 20-minute precision rifle drill. The tiny shops might suggest Victorian London at first glance, but their wares are definitely international, with a smattering of Polynesia. Shop and poke around as much as you like; we'll simply point out a few of our favorites en route.

Stop in at **Kitamura's,** a shop specializing in antique kimonos and obis as well as dolls from Japan. . . . **Liberty House** has a good selection of resort togs, and at **Harriet's Custom Made Ready to Wear,** you can select your material and your style and have garments made to your size in 24 to 48 hours. On their ready-to-wear rack, we've often paid less for garments here than at other stores. . . . **Crazy Shirts** has a large store here. . . . If you like to sew your own clothes, you can get fabrics, patterns, and ideas for accessories at **Cal-Oahu Fabrics** very reasonably. . . . The **Royal Peddler** has scads of gift items, with very large selections of brass and nautical nifties. . . . All kinds of candles in whimsical shapes are available at **Candle Odyssey.**

In keeping with the British atmosphere of King's Village, there's an English pub: the **Rose and Crown** is perfect for a glass of ale and a snack, a sing-along at the piano, or even a game of darts. **Waikiki Light House,** a new restaurant here, features Mongolian-style foods and cooking, and serves all three meals.

Atrium Shops at Hemmeter Center

The exquisite Hyatt Regency Waikiki, that skyscraper hotel on Kalakaua Avenue across from Kuhio Beach, houses a beautiful shopping complex, glistening with fountains, waterfalls, superb metal sculptures, massive plantings—and all in a stunning Hawaiian monarchy setting. Three tiers of shops are reached by staircase or escalator. Many of the names here are designer—Gucci, Paris Shop, Bugatti—but others are in a more competitive price range. **Cotton Cargo** believes you can't improve on nature, and shows a delightful collection of women's clothing in 100% cotton, with styles ranging from traditional to avant-garde.

. . . **Tarbo** hails from Japan and sells beautiful tie-dyed fabrics by the piece, as well as stunning island jewelry. . . . This complex is a good place to buy a fine gem: **House of Opal, Coral Grotto, House of Jade,** all offer handsome selections. . . . Those hard-to-please teenagers can be outfitted at **Happy Fashions,** which will also take care of the rest of the family. . . . **The Royal Peddler** specializes in brass and nautical gifts. . . . If you'd like to make an investment in art, have a look at the work of both island and international artists at **Images International,** the sculpture at **Bennett Sculpture.**

In between shopping chores, catch some of the free events that go on all day—classes in Hawaiian quilt making, lei making, hula dancing, and more. Check the local tourist papers to find out about free programs of Hawaiian entertainment and fashion shows that are often held in the Great Hall. Hemmeter Center is ideal for after-dinner walking and browsing and obligingly stays open from 9 a.m. until 11 p.m.

Waikiki Shopping Plaza

One expects to find open-air, palm-tree-lined shopping plazas in Waikiki, with booths selling grass skirts and coconuts; what one does not expect is a completely enclosed, several-storied building sporting the finest in European and mainland clothing and accessories. Yet that is basically what you'll find at the **Waikiki Shopping Plaza** at 2250 Kalakaua Ave., corner of Seaside. From the ethnic snackshops on the lowest level to the luxurious restaurants on the top floor (Japanese, Chinese, seafood, etc.), this complex is an international adventure.

Some of the outstanding shops here include European fashion favorites like **Courrèges, Roberta di Camerino, Ferragamo, Bally of Switzerland, Paris Shops;** Oriental outposts like **Yokohama Okadaya** for Japanese folk crafts (with many handmade objects), and **Okada** for men's and women's clothing from Japan. . . . We're very impressed with the level of work at **South Shore Gallery,** an artist-cooperative gallery, with changing exhibitions by local artists, always of interest; and with the arts and crafts of great taste that you'll find at **Bazaar.** . . . Eelskin bags and wallets are among the vast array of goods at **Ali Baba,** a wholesale importer-exporter. . . . **JKL Gems** is the place for fine jewelry, antique porcelain, Thai Buddhas, and carvings. . . . Our favorite clothing shops here are **Villa Roma** and **Chocolates for Breakfast,** both designer boutiques. . . . Best bargains are at **Gold 'n' Gifts,** and **Plaza Sundries.** . . . Waikiki's only bookstore—**Waldenbooks**—is here, too.

You can use the elevators here, but it's more fun to ride the escalators all the way to the top, admiring the million-dollar waterfall five stories high with dancing waters and changing colors. "Waikiki Calls," a free hula show with live dancers and a computerized audio-visual program, is located on the 4th floor. Playing nightly at 6 and 7:15 p.m., it's a "must see."

Royal Hawaiian Shopping Center

One of the newer shopping centers in town, this is also one of the biggest and most grandiose: $40 million and 6½ acres of the most valuable real estate in Hawaii went into its making. Located on Kalakaua Avenue, fronting the entrance to the Royal Hawaiian and Sheraton Waikiki Hotels, it is three city blocks full of island shops and restaurants set in a tasteful and still-growing tropical environment. Its courtyard is filled with Hawaiian plants and trailing vines, and new shrubbery, plantings, and palm trees are being added all the time. More than 100 shops and restaurants can provide hours of amusement.

There's so much to see here that you should wander around as fancy leads you. We'll point out a few of our favorites, just to get you started. **McInerny's** is a must; in business in Hawaii since 1850, it has opened its flagship store here, with particular excitement in the island fashion and gift departments on the first floor, the Hermès Boutique (for those famous French scarves and handmade leather bags) on the second, and the special Sports Fashion Boutique. . . . Don't miss the **China Friendship Store;** everything here—from carvings, clothing, carpets, embroidery, jewelry, glass, and much more—is imported directly from the People's Republic of China; prices are affordable, and it's a treat just to browse. Lectures, films, arts and crafts, and cooking demonstrations are held frequently. . . . Almost everything at the **Little Hawaiian Craft Shop** is handmade in Hawaii. Rare Niihau shell necklaces, authentic kukui nuts, feather hatbands, and the like are among the traditional handcrafts of Old Hawaii to be found here. Prices are modest, beginning at $1 or less, and the people couldn't be nicer. . . . The **Hawaiian Wood Shed,** next door, specializing in replicas of Hawaiian artifacts as well as collectors' items, is run by the same management.

"Everyone is born right-handed; only the greatest can overcome it," reads the motto on a T-shirt at **Left is Right, Too,** a left-handers idea of heaven. Left-handed clocks, corkscrews, and can openers are just a few of their helpful and fascinating gadgets. . . . Using only silk, cotton, and other natural fabrics, dying them in the subtlest and softest of colors, designer Marlo Shima creates women's clothing of great beauty. Dresses, long and short, are on the third level at **Marlo's Boutique;** sportswear is at her other store, **Cotton Lover,** one level below. . . . The popular **Andrade's** has a very large store on the second floor, with boutiques for men's and women's clothing, plus a Bargain Attic. . . . **Aki International** has lovely gifts that start at low prices. . . . You'll want all the butter-soft leather items in **Raku Leather:** attaché cases, backgammon sets, and beautiful bags.

If you had to, you could eat all your meals at the Royal Hawaiian Shopping Center and never get bored. We love **It's Greek to Me,** a café for tasty sandwiches and salads and classic Greek favorites; **La Mex,** for delicious Mexican meals (try their avocado salad at lunch), and **The Great Wok of China** for delicious food prepared in flaming woks as you watch. **Copenhagen Cones** is famous for waffle-like cones baked in a Scandinavian oven right on the premises, and good old **McDonald's** has an exciting collection of Hawaiian art and artifacts. Free entertainments, lectures, demonstrations go on all the time; check the local papers for details. The Royal Hawaiian Shopping Center is open from 9 a.m. to 10 p.m. Monday through Saturday, until 9 p.m. on Sunday.

Ala Moana Shopping Center

Ala Moana is a shopping center for those who hate shopping centers. It's 50 acres of island architecture at its best, laced with pools and gardens, plantings and sculptures, fountains and wide shady malls. In between are the shops—and what shops! An international array from East and West, as dazzling a selection of goods as can be found anywhere, in as wide a price range as possible, and a fascinating barometer of how far the 50th state has come into the modern world of merchandising.

All the big Hawaiian names are here: **Sears** has an attractive store with very well-priced selections in souvenirs and resortwear, as does **J.C. Penney.** . . . You'll find excellent clothing selections at **Watumull, Liberty House,** and **Carol & Mary.** . . . Join the throngs of local citizens who flock to the Japanese department stores like **Shirokiya.** . . . And while you're still in the mood for the exotic, look in at **India Imports,** with vast quantities of silken saris, dresses, bedspreads, Indian jewelry. . . . **Musahiya** sells beautiful fabrics by the yard. . . . **Hopaco Stationers** has all sorts of tasteful gifts, Hawaiian specialties, and stationery. . . . At the **Hale Kukui Candle Shop** you'll find tiki gods and pineapples to burn.

The Sharper Image is the catalog store to end all catalog stores. You can actually try all those amazing gadgets—exercise machines and electronic massage tables—as well as say hello to a robot or experience the latest in biofeedback equipment. A must! . . . You'll find something at the **Slipper Shop** to soothe your feet, something to read at **Honolulu Bookstore,** something to wear at **Laura Ashley** or at **Waltah Clarke,** where a sign that we like advises: "Walk in, hula out."

As for food, the restaurants on Ala Moana's lower level offer a tasty variety of international goodies, yours to eat indoors or take out and munch on the mall as you watch the crowds go by. **Lyn's Delicatessen** is super for a corned beef on rye, old-fashioned pickles, garlicky hot dogs, and a terrific weeknight steak dinner, with all the trimmings, for around $4. . . . **Patti's Chinese Kitchen,** large and comfy, serves its delicious hot plates (most around $3.30) cafeteria-style to hungry and happy throngs. Its manapua (dumplings) selection is irresistible. . . . Next door is **Bella Italia,** fragrant with cheeses and salamis, and low-priced meals of spaghetti, meatballs, and the like. . . . **La Cocina,** the only Mexican restaurant at Ala Moana, has a take-out counter for quick servings of tortillas, tostadas, and such, plus an attractive Mexican dining room where the food is fresh and tasty, portions huge, and the prices just right: around $4.95 to $7.25 for a complete dinner. . . . Cheers for **The Haven,** which offers attractive seating, natural-type sandwiches on nine-grain bread, lots of good salads, meat sandwiches, and intriguing desserts. And health-food freaks will be well contented with the huge vegetarian sandwiches—as well as "real" sandwiches and plates—plus juices, smoothies, and low-cal frozen desserts at **Vim and Vigor.** . . . Everybody's crazy about the new al fresco bistro at Ala Moana called **Baguette:** wonderful croissants and coffee, plus omelets, quiches, salads, and soups—light and fast and very French.

To reach Ala Moana from Waikiki, take either TheBUS no. 8 or no. 19 from Kalakaua Avenue; it's about a ten-minute ride. The center is open 9:30 a.m. to 9 p.m. Monday to Friday; it closes at 5:30 p.m. on Saturday; Sunday hours are 10 a.m. to 5 p.m. There are acres of parking.

Not far from Ala Moana Center, at 666 Keeaumoku St., antique lovers will have a field day at **Animal Crackers,** a charming little duplex shop, chockablock with American memorabilia, mainly relating to advertising. There are advertising posters, packages (some wonderful tobacco canisters), postal cards, bottles, and campaign buttons. Old dolls abound, and the shop is starting to feature vintage clothing. Prices go from 50¢ for postal cards up to about $500 for some of the antique dolls.

Ward Warehouse

A shopping center with class and charisma is the Ward Warehouse, 15 minutes from Waikiki at 1050 Ala Moana Blvd., across from Fisherman's Wharf. The artistic level here is surprisingly high, both in the buildings, reminiscent of the dockside warehouses of early Hawaii, and in the shops and boutiques (this is one shopping center equally as popular with sophisticated Honolulu residents as with visitors). Many shops have to do with fine and decorative arts. **Future Arts Collectibles,** for one, deals with Asian arts and crafts, everything from a lacquer shell box at $25 to an ethnic Japanese jacket to a museum-quality carving from China or Thailand. . . . The contemporary ceramics, stained glass, soft sculptures, carvings, hand-wrought jewelry, etc., at **Rare Discovery** are superb examples of the craftsmen's art. A dazzler. . . . **Artist's Guild** is another stunner: many local and Oriental artists show glass, hardwoods, sculpture, jewelry, paintings, prints, and much more. Prices vary, beginning modestly. . . . Posters, prints, original photographs, all at small prices, can be found at **Frame Shack** and **Art Board.** . . . The art of neon comes alive at **Neon Leon:** you're invited to custom-design your own logos, names, frames, or whatever, in this new art medium.

The artistic impulse at Ward Warehouse also translates into clothing at shops like **Blue Ginger Designs,** with its delicate hand-blocked batik fabrics; **Manyo Gallery,** with its superb Japanese wedding kimonos, fabrics by the yard, and attractive "furoshiki" blouses for around $30; **Kinnari,** where beautiful long muumuus are handcrafted by a lovely lady from Thailand. . . . You can create your own Hawaiian clothing from the attractive fabrics sold at **Strawberry Patch,** which also keeps the needlepoint, quilting and appliqué buffs happy with exclusive, hand-painted designs with island themes. . . . You can get a bit of everything at **Pause 'n' Paw,** fit yourself to a pair of comfy sandals at **Birkenstock Footprints,** gather a bouquet of silk flowers or an elegant vase at **Extra Dimension,** or buy some coffee or tea (Hawaiian teas include up-country Maui blends like Makawao Mint) and a big coffee mug at **The Coffee Works.** You can have a cup of coffee or pastry while you're about it.

Ward Warehouse has some highly enjoyable restaurants, like **Upstart Crow and Company,** both restaurant and bookstore, with light dishes, coffees, and pastries; plus all the latest books and the **Old Spaghetti Factory,** laden with outrageous Victorian antiques, and serving meals at mini-prices. **Horatio's** (see Chapter IV) is a great choice for a more elaborate meal.

Shopping hours at Ward Warehouse are 10 a.m. to 9 p.m.
Monday to Friday, to 5 p.m. on Saturday, and 11 a.m. to 4 p.m.
on Sunday. Any no. 8 bus from Waikiki (except those marked
"Waikiki Beach and Hotels") will get you there.

Ward Centre

A sister shopping complex to Ward Warehouse, Ward Centre,
1200 Ala Moana Blvd., offers island shopping with elegance.
Polo/Ralph Lauren is here, and so are women's boutiques like
Susan Marie (so elegant that it has its own white grand piano up
front), and **Lady Judith,** which shows wonderfully romantic fashions for women and girls by designers like Gunne Sax, Jessica
McClintock, and Lanz. . . . **Flamingo Flower** tends toward wild
prints for women, in silk and cotton imports; **Flamingo for Men** is
a bit more sedate, with contemporary and designer clothing. . . .
Harry Haimoff has won a number of international and local designs awards. His works are shown in **Haimoff & Haimoff Creations in Gold,** which also offers specialty watches, pearls, and
jade. . . . For the precious children in your life, beautiful clothing and educational toys abound at **Chocolate Moose.** . . . and
My Favorite Things is the place to get them handmade teddy
bears, fine porcelain dolls, and enchanting dollhouse miniatures.
. . . **Ward Centre Gallery** is a premier showcase for the work of
top island artists. . . . Wonderful breads and fanciful pastries
emerge from the ovens at **Mary Catherine's**—we dare you to
resist! . . . Gourmet food items, wines, and spirits are offered at
R. Field Wine Co.

Ward Centre houses some of our favorite Honolulu restaurants, many of which, like Compadres, Il Fresco, Monterey Bay
Canners, Crêpe Fever, Roxsan Pâtisserie, and Ryan's Park
Place, we've already told you about in Chapter IV. Another winner is the **Yum Yum Tree,** for dining indoors or out on a garden
lanai, with reasonably priced food and the best pies in town. Indeed, Ward Centre has perhaps more terrific restaurants under
one roof than any other place in Hawaii!

Operating hours and directions are the same as those for Ward
Warehouse, above.

Kahala Mall

Islanders love to shop at Kahala Mall, and you very likely will
too. It's an indoor, air-conditioned, fully carpeted suburban
shopping center, with none of the frenetic pace of Ala Moana.
There are many intriguing specialty shops here. It's difficult to

know whether to call **Following Seas** a shop or a crafts gallery, but this striking place is such a beautiful visual experience that it should not be missed. You'll see no mass-produced tourist junk here: everything is one-of-a-kind, created by outstanding American craftspeople, and truly unusual. Jewelry, woodwork, paperweights, stained-glass items, carvings, ceramics, etc., are priced from a little to a lot. . . . **Fabrications** is a lovely shop with yarns of all types for those who knit, crochet, macramé, or weave. In the adjoining boutique, described earlier, you'll find Jeffrey Barr resort wear for international resort dressing, in cottons, priced from $100 to $185. . . . **Carol and Mary** is the tops in sophisticated island clothing for both men and women. . . . **Nancy Long Couture Boutique** is a unique shop, with exclusive imports from Mexico, Greece, Malaysia, and accessories from the Philippines and the Marshall Islands. They also carry the Malia and Princess Kaiulani muumuus, as well as high-fashion, ready-to-wear clothes from mainland designers. . . . For teens and young career girls, there's trendy **Wildflowers.** . . . One of our favorite natural-food stores is here too: **Vim and Vigor,** with a tasty line of healthful goodies. Try their great sandwiches and baked goods, made fresh every day.

When it's time for a coffeebreak—or something more substantial—there's **Yum Yum Tree** (known for its fabulous pies and moderately priced meals), **Yen King** for tasty Northern Chinese food, **Woolworth's Coffee Shop** and **Farrell's Ice Cream Parlour.** Across the street is a new branch of the always enjoyable **Tony Roma's,** for ribs and fun.

Note: major construction was underway at Kahala Mall at this writing; by the time you read this, it should have 5 movie theatres, 17 new stores and 3 new restaurants—better than ever!

To reach Kahala Mall by car, take the Waialae exit from the Lunalillo Freeway East; it's about a 15-minute drive from Waikiki. Most of the shops are open from 9:30 a.m. until 9 p.m. Monday through Friday, until 5 p.m. on Saturday, and from 11 a.m. until 4 p.m. on Sunday.

Chapter VIII

CIRCLING OAHU

THE BEACH WAS BEAUTIFUL, the urban sights of Honolulu were exciting, but there's still more, much more, to see before you leave the island of Oahu. For on the other side of the mountains that border Waikiki is a verdant landscape almost as diverse as the city itself. Here are quiet country towns jostling bustling suburbs that feed commuters into the central city; ruins of old religious *heiaus* where sacrifices were made to the ancient gods near the modern meccas of the surfing set; cliffs thrusting skyward along the shores of velvety beaches where children play and campers set up their tents, not far from an enormous concentration of military muscle; acres of pineapple plantations using the most modern agricultural methods, and places where the taro is still cultivated the way it was in the old days. Hotels here are as peaceful as they should be, picnic spots are around every bend, and the restaurants are scenic attractions in themselves. And, of course, there are the sightseeing centers here, some of the most unique and interesting in the state. You'll have to see **Windward Oahu.**

Travel Choices

Should your time be short, you might want to pick out just one or two of the important sightseeing attractions windward and make a short, direct trip to them; you can take the tunnels carved through the mountains (the Pali or the Wilson Tunnel) to get you to places like the Polynesian Cultural Center or the Byodo-In Temple in less than an hour. But if you have the time, it is eminently rewarding to head out Diamond Head way and circle the island slowly, basking in the omnipresent natural beauty, stopping en route at the places that interest you the most. You must plan on a full day's trip, and it helps enormously if you have a car. Even without one, however, you can make this trip, thanks to Wahiawa-Kaneohe Bus 52, which departs from Ala Moana Center every 15 minutes during most of the day (from 6:15 a.m. to 6 p.m.). It can get you around the island, albeit quite slowly; fare is 60¢, payable each time you board or reboard the bus. You might also take a sightseeing limousine, which is easy and comfortable, but if you're on a group tour, you're not free to stay as long as you want in any one place or jump out of the car for a swim whenever you feel like it. Your own wheels promise the most fun; so get yourself a good road map, take the flat rate, and prepare for the memorable adventure that follows.

The Major Sights

We'll begin at Diamond Head Road. Circle around the beautiful residential area here and then get onto Rte. 72, which will lead you past Koko Head to **Hanauma Bay,** a turquoise beach at the bottom of a volcanic crater. Snorkelers rate this as one of the most beautiful spots on the island. Fish are so tame here that they will eat right out of your hand. Unless you stop here for a swim (or for the day), you'll soon be speeding along a stunningly dramatic coastline where ancient lava cliffs drop down to the surging sea below. But don't speed; slow down to enjoy the beauty. The colors are spectacular, and just ahead is a geyser in the lava called the **Blow Hole.** This is the place to stop the car and lose yourself in the wind and the spray, before you get back to the business of living in the 1980s. Just ahead of you, the island's daring—and expert—body surfers are forgetting their problems in the giant waves of **Sandy Beach,** and a few miles down the road below the lighthouse, at **Makapuu Beach.** You probably won't want to join them, but drive on and join, instead, what will seem like half the island's families at Sea Life Park.

Sea Life Park is a great place to take the keikis, and also yourself, for it's a thoroughly entertaining enterprise. Marine mammal research goes on here, but what you come for is the fun: you can travel three fathoms down a cavernous ramp and see some 2,000 species of fish swim gracefully by large glass windows in the 300,000-gallon Hawaiian Reef Tank. Comical penguins and daring dolphins perform at the Ocean Science Theatre, and the Whalers Cove show, with its cetacean stars and Hawaiian folklore theme, is always entertaining. The emphasis here is on a truly Hawaiian ocean experience. Mini-lectures are held throughout the day. Food and beverages are served at the Galley Restaurant and Spouter Bar. Admission (subject to change) is $7.75 for adults, $6 for juniors 7 to 12, and $2.50 for children 4 to 6. Special behind-the-scenes tours are also offered at low prices. Open daily from 9:30 a.m. to 5 p.m.

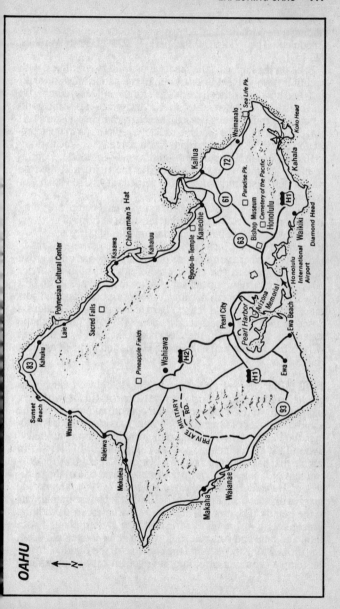

OAHU

←N→

Several special excursion tours are available from Waikiki, including transportation and admission. Sunday evenings a luau is scheduled. The phone at the park is 259-7933; in Waikiki, 923-1531.

Back on the highway, the spectacular scenery continues, with beautiful **Bellows Field Beach** (open to the public only on weekends and holidays; other times it's just for the military) coming up on your right. If you want to see Kailua, which has some good restaurants and a lovely, peaceful beach, turn right on Rte. 61. If not, continue until the road meets Rte. 61, drive left to the intersection of Rte. 83, and turn right. If you're ready for lunch, a stop at **Haiku Gardens** is a peaceful—and scenic—interlude. Continue along 83 until you see Safeway on the right, and then go mauka (left) a short distance to the gardens at 46-336 Haiku Rd. in Kaneohe.

Haiku Gardens, in fact, is worth a stop even if you're not going to have lunch, since it is situated in ten acres of tropical gardens, some of which the public is free to roam through. If you do have lunch or a drink, ask for a table out on the porch, where it's shady and cool and where you can look out over a lily pond and a grove of bamboo trees as you enjoy a buffet lunch ($8.50) or dinner ($12.95), or medium-priced sandwiches, salads, etc. With soft Hawaiian music (taped) playing in the background and the gorgeous scenery all around you, it's hard to leave. Haiku Gardens is closed Monday; for reservations, phone 247-6671. (To reach the restaurant directly from the city, take Likelike Hwy. through Wilson Tunnel, turn left at Kahekili Hwy., and turn left again at Haiku Road.)

ON TO BYODO-IN: Now drive back to Kahekili Hwy. (which runs parallel to Rte. 83 for a short distance), drive north for two miles, and prepare yourself for one of the most enthralling sights in the islands. No lover of Orientalia will want to miss a visit to **Byodo-In** in the Valley of the Temples, in the verdant Ahuimanu Valley. Byodo-In is a $2.6-million replica of the 900-year-old Byodo-In temple that has been proclaimed a National Treasure by the government of Japan. There is no doubt that this is one of the treasures of Hawaii. It was dedicated on June 7, 1968, almost 100 years to the day from the arrival of the first Japanese immigrants to the islands. The grounds are beautifully landscaped, with the temple sitting in the midst of a Japanese garden planted with plum and pine and bamboo. Before you enter the temple itself, ring the bell for good luck and the blessings of the Buddha. Inside the temple is an immense, imposing golden carving of Amida, the Buddha of the Western Paradise, an important work of sacred art, as are the filigree screens and panels. When you finish gazing at the treasures within, you can buy some fish food to feed the carp in the two-acre reflecting lake. You can also shop for Oriental souvenirs, walk through the tranquil gardens, and recharge yourself with the almost palpable serenity of the Orient. There is a small admission charge of $1.50 for adults, 75¢ for children under 12. (To reach the temple directly from Honolulu, take the Likelike Hwy., and turn left at Kahekili Hwy. until you see the signs for the Valley of the Temples.)

Get back on Hwy. 83 now, and backtrack a couple of miles until you come to Kaneohe Bay and the little village of **Heeia.** Here you may want to drive out to the Heeia Kea pier and board one of the glass-bottom boats to see the coral gardens under the sea. The charge is $7.50 for adults, $3.50 for children under 12, for an hour's trip. (For advance reservations, which are suggested, phone 239-9955 before you leave Honolulu.)

ON THE WAY TO LAIE: The next important destination on your trip is Laie, the site of the Polynesian Cultural Center, but relax—you still have a way to go. And what a beautiful way it is, with gardens curving around to the green sea at every turn of the road. On the left are the remnants of the old **Waiahole Poi Factory,** which no longer is in operation. **Chinaman's Hat,** an island that looks just like its name, is the next point to notice on the right, and the ruins of an old sugar mill are on the left. Then, a few miles farther, you'll notice the rock formation called the **Crouching Lion,** which, with a little effort, you could imagine springing at you. But it's not at all menacing; it houses, in fact, a pleasant restaurant where you sit out on the lanai and have lunch. Go along a little farther now, and you'll find yourself at **Pat's at Punaluu,** a marvelously scenic beachside restaurant hidden behind a tall condominium building. Stop here for lunch, or have a picnic and a swim at **Kaaawa Beach Park** or **Swanzy Beach Park,** or stop off to admire the original artworks at the **Punaluu Gallery,** 53-353 Kamehameha Hwy. (Don't spend too long swimming and picnicking, however, if you want to pack all of this trip into one day.)

THE POLYNESIAN CULTURAL CENTER: Laie is a Mormon town. Mormon missionaries have been in Hawaii for over a hundred years, and the island's largest Mormon population makes its home in Laie. Here you can see the beautiful Hawaiian Temple and explore its gardens (enter from Halelaa Boulevard), see the Hawaiian campus of Brigham Young University and, most

interestingly, the **Polynesian Cultural Center.** Built over 20 years
ago to provide work and scholarships for Polynesian students and
to revitalize the ancient Polynesian cultures, the Polynesian Cultural Center is one of the top tourist attractions in the islands.

Seven authentic Polynesian villages have been created at the
center—Hawaiian, Tongan, Fijian, Samoan, Maori, Marquesan,
and Tahitian—and they are staffed by Polynesians who have been
brought here from their respective islands for just this purpose.
They demonstrate their crafts, perform their ancient songs and
dances, explain their culture to you. Under a new policy, it is no
longer possible simply to visit the villages, which would put a stop
here easily on the itinerary of a one-day round-the-island trip.
Now you must buy a complete package ($36 for adults, $27 for
children ages 5 to 11, free under 5), which includes a visit to the
villages and its various attractions and events, plus a lunch or dinner buffet, plus a performance of the spectacular production of
"This is Polynesia." All of this means three or four hours (you
should arrive before noon for the daytime package, around 3
p.m. for the evening package), so plan accordingly, perhaps saving this as a special trip for another day.

Tickets can be purchased in advance at the Center's ticket office on the ground floor of the Royal Hawaiian Shopping Center
in Waikiki.

THE NORTH SHORE: Since you've now covered the major sightseeing points on the Oahu trip, and since it may be getting late, you
could drive back to Honolulu through the tunnels and be back at
your hotel in about an hour. If, however, you're still game for
more, and especially for some beautiful scenery, keep going. A
few miles ahead, after the road dips inward and then comes back
to the shore, you're in surfer's country. This is Oahu's North
Shore, and here, along **Sunset Beach** and **Waimea Bay,** where in
winter the waves can come thundering in as high as 30 feet, you
may see some of the best surfing in the islands. In summer, the
water is usually quite gentle here and idyllic for swimming. **Waimea Falls Park,** which is just across the road from Waimea Bay,
could be a refreshing stop now; situated in an 1,800-acre lush valley rich in the history of old Hawaii, the park includes one of the
world's finest arboretums and botanical gardens, a wildlife preserve and bird sanctuary, miles of hiking trails, magnificent
plants and flowers—many of them rare and endangered. Photog-
raphers, take note. You can play the ancient sports of old Hawaii
—spear throwing, lawn bowling, Hawaiian checkers—at the Hawaiian Games site, and watch the park's resident hula troupe

present ancient hulas several times daily. You may also catch the Acapulco-style diving from the cliffs at Waimea Falls. The Country Kitchen provides lunchtime snacks and the Proud Peacock Restaurant offers fine dining and a spectacular view of the valley. Twice each month the park opens its gates for free Moon Walks under the full moon. Incidentally, this is one of the most popular spots for Hawaiian weddings! (For information on planning such an event, write Tinker Bloomfeld, Waimea Falls Park, 59-864 Kamehameha Hwy., Haleiwa, HI 96712.) Admission is $6.95 for adults, $4.50 for juniors (ages 7 to 12), and $1.50 for children (ages 4 to 6). Open daily, including holidays, from 10 a.m. to 5:30 p.m. Phone: 638-8511 or 923-8448.

Should you like to indulge in a bit of *la dolce vita* now, stop at the **Turtle Bay Hilton Hotel and Country Club,** just before you reach Sunset Beach. This luxury caravanserai, where the president of the United States and the premier of Japan once met for summit talks, is fun to walk around and explore. You can have a buffet lunch ($9.50) in the attractive Palm Terrace overlooking the pool and ocean, or dinner plus entertainment in one of the two dining rooms. (They have a fabulous Sunday brunch from 10 a.m. to 2 p.m. at $14.95 for adults, $7.50 for children.) Or plan your visit for the sunset hour and take yourself to the cocktail lounge overlooking the ocean at the Bay View Lounge in Kahuku, where you can watch the sun slip into the horizon and disappear behind that giant North Shore surf.

You may be interested in stopping off at Sunset Beach and Haleiwa and joining some of the young people who've found a relaxed, close-to-nature way to live here, far from the urban pace of Honolulu. Many of them work in or run attractive craft shops and galleries in the area.

You have two more chances for a swim now, at **Pupukea Beach Park** and **Haleiwa Beach Park** on Wailua Bay, before the road will turn inland. You cannot completely circle the island of Oahu since there is no paved road around rugged Kaena Point. You've got to go inland and start out from Honolulu again if you want to see the other coast. Now you pick up Rte. 82, Kamehameha Hwy. make your left, and soon you're in the midst of the largest pineapple plantation in the world, **Leilehua Plateau.** At the top of the road is a stand where you can buy what will undoubtedly be the finest Hawaiian pineapple you've ever tasted. Delicious.

The next town coming up on the map is **Wahiawa,** an area noted mainly as the home of the U.S. Army's **Schofield Barracks.** The army has opened a new museum right inside the main gate and you are welcome to visit it. Across from the main gate of

Schofield is **Kemoo Farm,** a favorite restaurant with the locals since 1927, known for excellent food (its dining room overlooks Lake Wilson), old-fashioned prices, and gracious, welcoming service. If you're in town on a Wednesday or Sunday, it's worth a special drive just to take in their noontime lunch show, hosted by one of Hawaii's favorite talents, Charles K. L. Davis, with a varied roster of guest artists. The address is 1718 Wilikina Dr. on Hwy. 99 (tel. 621-8481).

Also in Wahiawa are the **Wahiawa Botanical Gardens,** 1396 California Ave., where you can wander free of charge through four acres of lovely trees, flowers, and shrubs, including a garden of native Hawaiian plants.

Soon Kamehameha Hwy. becomes a four-lane freeway, and you can speed along home. Take Hwy. 99 to the left when it intersects with Kamehameha or Interstate Hwy. H-2 and proceed onto Rte. 90, which goes by Pearl Harbor. If it's dinnertime, **Pearl City Tavern** (at the intersection of Kam Hwy. and Pearl City) is a top choice for seafood and/or Japanese cuisine. At Middle Street, cross to the right side on Rte. 92 (Nimitz Hwy.) and it's nonstop past Honolulu Harbor and home to Waikiki.

Chapter IX

THE BIG ISLAND: HAWAII

WHEN YOU LIVE on an island, where do you go for a vacation? To another island, of course. The residents of Honolulu usually take their vacations on what they call the neighbor or outer islands—the Big Island of Hawaii, the Garden Island of Kauai, the Valley Island of Maui, the Friendly Island of Molokai. And so should you. Take a vacation-within-a-vacation to one or two or, better yet, all four of the neighbor islands. For while Oahu is the most important place to see in Hawaii, there is a great deal more beyond its shores. Although the outside world is fast catching up with the neighbor islands, they are still much more relaxed than Honolulu. And they offer a panorama of natural wonders unmatched just about anywhere. It's not expensive to visit the islands; inter-island plane fares are reasonable. As for living expenses, expect about the same mileage from your travel dollar as you get in Honolulu.

No matter which way you choose to see the neighbor islands, see them you must. The lush mountains and glorious beaches of Kauai, the golden languors of Maui await you. But now, the Big Island of Hawaii beckons.

Hawaii: Hotels, Restaurants, and Nightlife

On Hawaii the earth is red, the sand is black, and a goddess named Pele still reigns. On Hawaii two jetports boom, the state's second-biggest city grows, and the beautiful people from the mainland arrive to lead *la dolce vita*. The island of Hawaii is a fascinating mix of legend and reality, of old beliefs and new ambitions. It probably contains more variety per square mile than any other part of the 50th state. It encompasses tropical beaches and snow-clad mountains; a very-much-alive volcano that spouts jet fountains of fire into the air quite often; lush, lush vegetation and

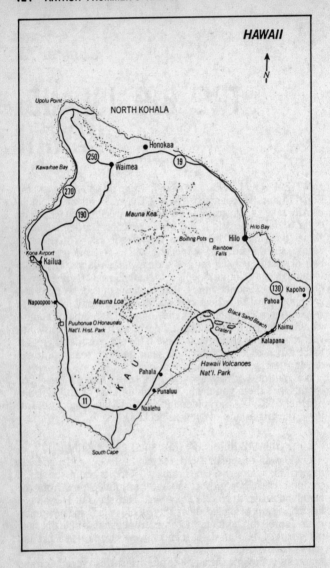

rainfall, which make the orchids bloom as easily as weeds any-where else; a cattle ranch as big as they make them in Texas; acres of coffee plantations; some of the best big-game fishing waters in the world; and a population fiercely devoted to their island and its legendary history. For it was from here that Kamehameha the Great went to conquer and unite the independent island king-doms around him, and to the federation that resulted he gave the name of his homeland—Hawaii.

Although some people call it the Orchid Island and some call it the Volcano Island, there is just one name that the islanders real-ly use to refer to Hawaii: the Big Island. And big it is—4,038 square miles, almost twice as big as all the other Hawaiian islands combined, and about the same size as the state of Connecticut. To really see the Big Island, you should plan on at least three or four days, making your headquarters in either Hilo on the east-ern coast or Kona on the western coast. Kona has more in the way of beach, fishing, and resort activity; Hilo is the closest to Volcanoes National Park, which you won't want to miss. A good plan is to spend one night in Hilo, and then move on to Kona. Since United Airline's big jets stop at both Hilo and Kona, you can easily work them into your itinerary, even arriving or depart-ing the islands from Hawaii if you choose.

Seeing the Islands in Style

For a spectacular way to see the neighbor islands, and if money is not a major consideration, book yourself a berth on the S.S. *Independence* or the S.S. *Constitution,* two luxury cruise liners that sail from Honolulu each Saturday, making all-day calls at Hilo and Kona on the Big Island; at Kahului, Maui; and at Nawiliwili, Kauai; before returning to Honolulu one week later. The S.S. *Independence* overnights at Maui, while the S.S. *Constitution* overnights at Kauai. Daily activities, entertainment, accommo-dations, and food are all first-rate on these "floating" Hawaiian resorts. And you only have to check in and unpack once during your seven-day, four-island visit. Passenger activities include pool games, hula lessons, ukulele instruction, aerobics, and more. Rates range from $995 per per-son, double occupancy, to $2,495. American Hawaii Cruises also supple-ments part of the round-trip air fare to Honolulu. Information is available from **American Hawaii Cruises**, 550 Kearny St., San Francisco, CA 94108. The toll-free phone number for reservations is 800/227-3666.

Note: The **telephone area code** for all phones in the state of Hawaii is 808.

HILO HOTELS: Several of the major hotels in Hilo have closed in recent years, but those that are left offer good value for the traveler. Don't expect, however, to find gorgeous ocean beaches at these hotels. The shoreline on this side of the island is mostly volcanic rock. Although local kids do swim in Hilo Bay, it is somewhat rocky and swimming is not really good; the hotel pools offer a better answer to the tropical heat.

The traditional site for luxury hotels in Hilo has long been along the shore of Hilo Bay, and it's here that you'll find the fragrant, flowery **Naniloa**, 93 Banyan Dr., Hilo, HI 96720 (tel. 935-0831), its lobby blending into spacious tropical gardens and overlooking the ocean. There's a gracious air about this place, despite its huge size, and we think you'll like the rooms, especially those from the fourth floor up—the wide-view rooms overlooking Hilo Bay. All of the rooms, from the standard at $50 to the superior at $60, the deluxe at $70, and the Surf deluxe at $80, single or double, $12 more triple, are attractively decorated in Polynesian motifs, and have full tub-shower combination, air conditioning, TV, radio, and coffee-maker; most have a private lanai, and there's courtesy ice on every floor. Children under 18 stay free in the same room with their parents. The elegant suites, some of them with a wrap-around lanai big enough to hold your own luau, range from $135 to $175. The pretty Hutu Terrace coffeeshop overlooking the pool offers moderately priced meals, there's music to dance and listen to in the Hoomalimali Bar, and sometimes cabaret shows in The Crown.

A bit less luxurious than the Naniloa, the **Hilo Hawaiian Hotel**, 71 Banyan Dr. (tel. 935-9361), is nevertheless a first-class choice. This beautifully landscaped, 8-story, 290-room hotel overlooks Hilo Bay, and its spacious open lobby with bamboo sofas is one of the most comfortable around. From its lanai terrace and pool you can walk right over to neighboring Coconut Island; in the distance is mighty Mauna Kea. Rooms are all of a piece, cheerfully furnished in a red, white, and blue color scheme, with twin beds, a table and two chairs, posters of seagulls and figureheads, air conditioning, color TV, separate dressing areas, full baths and showers. Lanais are on the smallish side. Standard rooms, at $52 single and $55 double, are on the lower floors; superior rooms, at $62 and $65, bring you up in the world somewhat; and deluxe rooms, which are more spacious and overlook Hilo Bay, are $72 and $75. Junior Suites are $85; Banyan Suites with kitchenettes go for $140; Ocean Suites, $180. The rates are the same for up to four in a suite. The Queen's Court Dining Room serves up another marvelous view of Hilo Bay along with good food; and the Menehuneland Cocktail Lounge is a whimsical charmer. You can write to Hawaiian Pacific Resorts, 1150 South King St., Honolulu, HI 96814; or for toll-free reservations, phone 800/367-5004 in mainland U.S.A., 800/665-8818 in Canada.

Everybody likes **Uncle Billy's Hilo Bay Hotel,** on the waterfront at 87 Banyan Dr., Hilo, HI 96720 (tel. 925-0861; reservations, toll free 800/367-5102), as well they should, for Uncle Billy Kimi and his large Hawaiian family are in charge here, and they extend plenty of aloha—from the hotel to the restaurant where you get a free Hawaiian show along with your dinner every night. Rooms are comfortably and nicely appointed in the island style, with private lanais, air conditioning, and views of either a tropical garden or the oceanfront. For an extra $8 added to the price of your superior or deluxe room here, you can command a kitchenette. Rates are $41 single and $44 twin for a standard room, $46 and $49 for superior, $51 and $54 for deluxe; add another $10 to that and you've got yourself a room-and-car package.

Just a few blocks from the heart of town, in an area overlooking the bay, is one of the cutest little places to be found anywhere in the city, the **Dolphin Bay Hotel,** 333 Iliahi St., Hilo, HI 96720 (tel. 935-1466). Full kitchens make this place ideal for the budget-conscious, and the hotel is as pretty as it is practical, since the grounds are resplendent with tropical vegetation (which you're welcome to pick and eat). The units are large and very nicely furnished, with big, modern tub-shower combinations; you couldn't ask for a cozier setting. A breeze from the bay provides natural air conditioning, and the price is certainly right—$23 for a single, $29 for a double in the four studio units. The superior studios, a bit larger and fitted out with doubles, corner beds, or a double and a single, cost $29 for one, $39 for two. There are also one-bedroom units at $49 and a two-bedroom giant at $55; an extra person in any of the accommodations is charged $7. No pools or fancy restaurants here, just comfortable living in a place where you'll feel really at home, plus plenty of good suggestions for sightseeing excursions. Write to John Alexander, the delightful manager, way ahead of time.

HILO RESTAURANTS: Ever since **Harrington's,** "An Eating and Drinking Establishment," opened its doors at 135 Kalanianaole St., overlooking the Ice Pond at Reed's Bay, the crowds started coming. Hilo-ites must have been starving for the kind of restaurant that combines sophistication, relaxed elegance, scenic views, and terrific food. Well, they—and visitors, too—need starve no more. Call to make a reservation (961-4966), since this place is always busy. Once seated out in the open-air dining room, you can enjoy delicious appetizers like oysters on the half shell or fresh steamed clams along with your libations. Main courses, which are served with rolls, homemade soup, a choice of salads, and a starch, always include the fresh catch of the day and lobster, market priced. Prawns, scallops, calamari meunière, prime rib (Friday and Saturday), Slavic steak, and chicken teriyaki, priced from $10 to $16.95, are featured on the small menu, and certain items are available in combination (your waiter will explain). If you haven't made a reservation don't fret; you can probably be seated in the lounge area and served from the appetizer and side-dish menu, enjoying the scene at a small price. A jazz pianist plays nightly in the lounge, and there's live entertainment Friday and Saturday night.

Harrington's serves dinner only, nightly from 5:30 p.m. to closing.

Believe it or not, *mes amis,* there's a little bit of New Orleans right here in old Hilo town. **Roussels,** 60 Keawe St., serves authentic French Créole cuisine in a setting of southern charm: potted palms, white curtains at the windows, bentwood chairs, white tablecloths, sparkling wooden floors. Bert Roussel and brothers Spencer and Andrew Olivier from New Orleans, know their gumbo and their shrimp rémoulade, and their blackened fish, to be sure; their menu is authentic and delicious. You'll want to sample the hearty gumbo, thick with bits of shrimp, crab, oyster, and okra ($3.50 for a cup, $11.75 as an entree), then proceed to such main dishes as shrimp Créole (in tomato sauce), shrimp étouffée (a Louisiana classic, with brown seafood sauce), or trout meunière amandine (with slivered almonds and brown-butter sauce). If you've not yet tried that current culinary craze, blackened fish, this is the place to do so: chef Paul Prudhomme's Louisiana style of blackening the outside, keeping the inside moist and tender, is well carried out here, applied to the local catch of the day and market priced. Appetizers run $3.75 to $5.65; entrees from $9.95 to $15.95. At lunch, when most of the same dishes are served, prices run from $7.50 to $9.95. A select assortment of French and California wines is available by the bottle and glass.

Call Roussels an experience in elegant dining. A pianist plays softly on the baby grand to accompany your dinner. The lights are romantic. Roussels serves lunch weekdays from 11:30 a.m. to

2:30 p.m., dinner from 5:30 to 10:30 p.m., Monday through Saturday. Closed Sunday. Reservations advised (tel. 935-5111).

Flickering torches out front, a curtain of gourds, and a carp pond nestled by a waterfall flowing out of lava rock set the scene for **J.D.'s Banyan Broiler** at 111 Banyan Dr. (tel. 961-5802), an old favorite. Tapa-covered Hawaiian drums for lights, bamboo and leather chairs, ceiling fans overhead, and candlelight continue the romantic mood, and the food is always good. Specialties of the house are steak, seafood, a fresh fish of the day, chicken teriyaki, and kal-bi; most entrees are in the $10.25 to $15.95 range and are accompanied by long-branch potatoes or fried rice and a turn or two at the salad bar. Daily specials in the $5 to $7 range are offered at lunch, 11 a.m. to 2 p.m. Open Tuesday through Sunday, with dinner from 5:30 to 10 p.m., and entertainment nightly.

An elegant setting for a well-priced meal, the **Queens Court** of the Hilo Hawaiian Hotel, 71 Banyan Dr. (tel. 935-9361), affords a splendid view of Hilo Bay. Blue banquettes, beige caned seats, golden drapes, anthuriums on the tables, and portraits of Hawaiian royalty set the indoors scene. It's fun to come here for the nightly buffet dinners: an Oriental buffet for $12.95 on Monday, a seafood buffet for $15.95 on Wednesday, a prime rib buffet for $15.25 on Thursday, another $15.95 seafood buffet on Friday, and a steak buffet for $15.25 on Sunday. Wines are included at all buffets, plus saké on Monday and champagne on Sunday; there's a wide selection of delicious desserts. Many local dishes are featured among the daily lunch specials, in the $3.50 to $7 range.

The family that runs the **K. K. Tei Restaurant,** 1500 Kamehameha Ave., between Hilo and the airport (tel. 961-3791), has been serving fine Japanese food for well over 30 years now. The setting is attractive, and dinners, which average about $8 to $9, include sukiyaki, yosenabe (a succulent soup of chicken, seafood, vegetables, and fish), and shrimp tempura (K.K. Tei's specialty). Each dinner comes Japanese style, with all the extras—miso soup, pickled cold vegetables, sashimi, rice, and hot Japanese tea. No matter what you choose, it's a bargain, and lunch is even more inexpensive, with complete Japanese lunches served in lacquer trays starting around $4.75. You can also get American-style food, and luncheon sandwiches from $3.75, including a choice of salad.

Note: If there are at least eight of you, reserve ahead for one of the tea-house rooms in the rear of the restaurants; they afford an all-dinner-long view of a beautiful Japanese garden, complete with graveled walkways and a spouting pool teeming with lilies and orchids, beautifully lit up at night.

At the edge of old-town Hilo at 90 Kamehameha Ave., **Norberto's El Café** is fast becoming the most popular restaurant in the area, with a tasty selection of Mexican dishes in the $8.25 to $9.95 range at dinner. A multitude of potted plants add to the coziness of the medium-size dining area, which seats about 60. There's full bar service (great margaritas by the glass or pitcher), special ingredients for vegetarians, children's menus. A simpatico choice. Norberto's is open Monday through Saturday from 5:30 to 9:30 p.m.

Want some more budget ideas? That's easy. **Ting Hao Mandarin Restaurant,** in the Puainako Town Center, close to the Prince Kuhio Shopping Plaza, enjoys the services of a gourmet chef and the plaudits of its customers, and charges between $3 and $7 for most entrees. Lunch and dinner daily. . . . **Dick's Coffeeshop,** in the Hilo Shopping Center, is a perennial favorite with the local people. Main courses on the à la carte dinner menu, served with soup or salad plus starch, run from $2.90 to $5.65, and include New York–cut steak, ham omelet, grilled fish fillet, and pork cutlet. Cozy booths, a cocktail lounge, and fine food for the money. Open for all three meals. . . . Dessert heaven might be a good way to describe **Bears Coffee,** which adjoins The Most Irresistible Shop in Hilo at 110 Keawe St. You can relax at cheerful marble-topped tables and indulge yourself in yummy pastries plus a dozen kinds of coffees and espresso drinks, as well as salads, cold soups, deli and vegetarian sandwiches, and hearty breakfast items. Open 7 a.m. to 5 p.m. weekdays, 8 a.m. to 4 p.m. Saturday.

HILO AFTER DARK: The Naniloa Hotel's **Hoomalimali Bar** provides Happy Hour prices and complimentary pupus from 5 to 7 p.m. nightly. Then it's listening and dancing the rest of the night, no cover, no minimum. Inquire at the Naniloa's Activities Desk about possible cabaret shows in The Crown. . . . A good hula show is the one put on each night at **Uncle Billy's Restaurant** in the **Hilo Bay Hotel,** at 6:30 and 7:30 p.m. The entertainment is casual island style, and dinners go from about $7.95 to $12.95, including salad bar. No cover, no minimum. . . . Most of the hotels have attractive bars and cocktail lounges, but if you're a Happy Hour devotee, note that the **Menehuneland Lounge** at the **Hilo Hawaiian Hotel** offers dancing from 5 p.m. to closing, free pupus from 4 to 6 p.m., and a clever mural of Menehune antics all the time. On Wednesday, catch the free hula show from 5:15 to

6:15 p.m. . . . . **Rosey's Boathouse,** 760 Piilani St., is known for its menu and service, as well as the "Seven Day Weekend" in the lounge, featuring live entertainment nightly. . . . There's a variety of entertainment at **JD's Banyan Broiler:** everything from slack-key guitar during dinner hours to small groups and big-band sounds. . . . **Harrington's** features a jazz pianist nightly in the lounge, live entertainment weekends.

GETTING TO KONA: You'll want to rent a U-Drive to get from Hilo to Kona or vice versa, so you might keep the following car-rental agencies in mind. Besides the big companies like **Hertz, Avis, National,** and **Budget** in Hilo, you'll find smaller outfits like **Phillip's U-Drive** (tel. 935-1936), **Marquez U-Drive** (tel. 935-2115), and **Liberato's U-Drive** (tel. 935-8089). At most companies standard-shift Datsuns and Toyotas may rent for as little as $21 a day, flat rate, during the off-season. Automatic-shift and larger cars will of course cost more. **Holiday Hawaii Rent-A-Car** (tel. 935-5201) does well with all flat rates, no mileage charge. (They rent cars on the four major islands, and can be reached toll free at 800/367-2631.) If you're flying into Kona first and will rent your car there, you can choose from **Hertz** (tel. 329-3566), **Avis** (tel. 329-1745), **Holiday Hawaii Rent-A-Car** (tel. 329-1752), **Phillips** (tel. 329-1730), and others at Keahole Airport. **Budget** (tel. 329-8511), for one, offers a good deal, in that they provide weekly specials that may be split up between islands, saving the customer the need to pay higher daily rentals on each island (they also have free coupon books on each island). Note that at most companies there may be a ferrying charge (between $15 and $25) if you drop off the car at other than its home base; and since you're most likely driving from Hilo to Kona or vice versa, that will usually be the case.

KOHALA COAST RESORTS: Make no mistake about it: the Kohala Coast is now the number-one upscale resort destination in the state. A combination of magnificent scenery, the best sandy beaches on the Big Island, and the willingness of investors to pour in millions upon millions to turn ancient lava flows into tropical oases (both Hyatt and Westin Mauna Kea are currently planning multimillion-dollar luxury developments here) has created a glorious playground for those who can afford the best.

Among certain members of the jet set the words "Mauna Kea" and "Hawaii" have become practically synonymous, ever since Laurence Rockefeller created the fabulous Mauna Kea

Hotel on the Kohala coast some years ago. It is now known as the
Westin Mauna Kea, P.O. Box 218, Kohala Coast, HI 96743 (tel.
882-7222, 947-3914 in Honolulu; reservations, toll free 800/228-
3000). Presiding over a domain of some thousands of acres of
cool ranchlands and gentle beachside, the hotel offers vacation-
ers the best of many worlds: the bountiful slopes of Mauna Kea
for hunting; deep-sea fishing in nearby Kona where the world re-
cords are set; golf on an 18-hole championship course designed
by Robert Trent Jones, Sr.; water sports, swimming, and the sun-
worshipper's life on a glorious crescent of beach (where friends
report the snorkeling is out of this world). The grounds and buildings are models of landscaping and architecture, with priceless
treasures of art from the Orient and the South Pacific vying with
the natural splendors of trees and flowers. The rooms are spacious, with every modern convenience, Hawaiian and Polynesian
decor, and graceful lanais open to the view everywhere. The food
in the Batik Room ranges from American to continental to Sri
Lankan, and of course there is plenty of island-style entertainment. Harmonious and serene are probably the best words for
Mauna Kea; it is consistently the recipient of such awards as
AAA's Five Diamond Award, the highest honor that can be be-
stowed on a Hawaii resort.

And now, oh yes, the price. All rates (subject to change) are
on the Modified American Plan, and rooms go for $270, double
occupancy, with mountain view; $340, double occupancy, beach-
front; $360, double occupancy, ocean view. Single rooms are $15
less; third person, $75 more, $25 for infants under 3. Golf, tennis,
scuba, and honeymoon packages are often available. And
whether or not you're staying here, it's fun to stop by for the famous buffet lunch priced at $16.50.

The **Sheraton Royal Waikoloa Hotel,** P.O. Box 5000, Waikoloa, HI 96743 (tel. 885-6789; reservations, toll free 800/325-3535
from mainland U.S., 800/537-1504 from Honolulu) is the first
major hotel of the planned Waikoloa Development, and it's a
stunner. Located on 16 acres of former Parker Ranch land 18
miles north of Kona's Keahole Airport, in an area once sacred to
the Hawaiian *alii,* it abounds in Hawaiian history, from the royal
fishponds adjacent to the magnificent lagoon to the most extensive petroglyph fields in Hawaii. The arrow-straight King's Path-
way, a hand-laid lava-rock path once reserved only for the feet of
royalty, now passes two 18-hole championship golf courses
mountain-side of the hotel. Six tennis courts, a freshwater swimming pool, horseback riding nearby, and most important of all,
one of the most perfect white sand beaches in the island, the half-

mile crescent of Anaehoomalu, make this the kind of resort vacation paradise that tempts one to forget all about the world outside.

At Waikoloa, the boundaries between outside and inside are softened: open-air terraces extending over the surrounding pond make a gentle transition to the indoors. The 532 guest rooms in the six-story building and the 20 lagoon cabañas in their own two-story building are all attractive, decorated in island tones and motifs and each with its own lanai. All rooms have color television, in-room movies, AM/FM radios with alarm clock, and air conditioning; fully 65% of them have ocean views. Minimum rooms, at $110, are too small for our taste. Standard, superior, and deluxe rooms, at $130, $160, and $200 ($10 for a third person) are better. And the junior suites, at $225, overlooking the lagoon, are lovely.

Dining facilities are as extensive and lovely as you would expect, from the hotel's main dinner showroom, the Royal Terrace, which offers live entertainment every night, to the more intimate Tiare Room for continental food of a high order, to the open-air coffeeshop beside a meandering stream where guests take dinner and lunch. And for sunset viewing—sunsets are spectacular all along the Kohala Coast—the airy Petroglyph Bar, with its open terraces, is just about perfect.

Visitors are welcome to come and enjoy the beach and the grounds, and explore the archeological sites.

The newest of the grand hotels along this Kohala coast is the **Mauna Lani Bay Hotel,** P.O. Box 4000, Kohala Coast, HI 96743 (tel. 885-6622; reservations, toll free 800/367-2323 in continental U.S., 800/992-7987 in Hawaii), the "Emerald of Kohala" and by far one of the most beautiful resorts in these or any other islands. Built at a cost of about $80 million, this green oasis among the lava flats is an architectural stunner, a sportsman's paradise, and a world-class destination for those who demand—and can afford —the top of the line. The six-story, 351-room hotel is set amid acres of gardens, plantings, ancient royal fishponds, and crystal lagoons: on one side is one of the more scenic golf courses on earth and a ten-court tennis garden, with pro facilities at both; on the other side is a perfect beach, its waves gentled by an offshore reef, and on the sand, deeply relaxing blue-covered cabañas by the palm trees. Blue tile walkways lead to the Grand Atrium, where waterfalls tumble beside the stairways, fish swim in the ponds, the air is fragrant with tropical perfumes. Once you've checked in with the knowledgeable concierge (and been served juice from a silver tray while doing so), a glass elevator takes you to your room. It is spacious, of course, high ceilinged, with every comfort (including a refrigerator and a television set hidden away in an armoire), and its lanai probably overlooks the ocean or beach—92% of the rooms do (others overlook the slopes of Mauna Kea). Guests can choose from among four restaurants and four bars, including a re-creation of the fabulous Third Floor Restaurant of Honolulu (see Chapter IV); the Bay Terrace, scene of a weekend buffet lunch; the Golf Clubhouse, for dining in an informal setting; and the Ocean Grill poolside. There is no end to activities: one needs only enough time to stay here. A sampling of possibilities includes, in addition to golfing, tennis, and swimming in either the ocean or the pool surrounded by tropical gardens, fishing, hunting, catamaran cruises, sails to secluded beaches, instruction in scuba and snorkeling, morning aerobics classes, glass-bottom boat cruises, jogging, Hawaiian cultural activities—even painting classes by the hotel's artist-in-residence.

You may book either European Plan or MAP at Mauna Lani Bay. The cost for the good life, in a single or double on the European Plan, is $185 for mountain or garden view, $210 for partial ocean view, $215 for ocean view, $220 for oceanfront, $275 and up for corner oceanfronts, and $375 and up for suites. Add $45 per person for MAP. Golf, tennis, and honeymoon packages are available.

CLOSE TO KONA: There's a lot of talk about Old Hawaii in the 50th state, but few ever get to really experience it—except those lucky enough to stay at **Kona Village Resort,** an enchanting old Hawaiian village that has been reborn a century and a half after a lava flow destroyed almost everything around it. The small area that was spared is the village of Kaupulehu, an idyllic 65-acre oasis in a 12,000-acre lava desert, the most purely get-away-from-it-all resort/retreat in the islands. At Kona Village, which is only 15 miles from the bright tourist world of Kailua-Kona and five miles from Keahole Airport, there are no lobbies, no elevators, no sidewalks, no cars, clocks, radios, televisions, or room phones to remind you that you are living in the world of the '80s. Instead, there are 95 *hales*—thatched huts—built in the styles of Polynesia, Micronesia, and Melanesia; these luxuriously "primitive" cottages, with beautiful interior accoutrements (king-size or extra-long twin beds, dressing rooms, refrigerators, baths), stand on stilts facing ocean, beach, lagoon, or garden. They are not inexpensive: rates range from $265 to $395 a night for two people, depending on location. But they do include three meals; breakfast and dinner are served in the impressive Hale Moana, a New Hebrides longhouse, and lunch is buffet-style in a garden setting. Weekly luaus, international cuisine nights, and paniolo steak fries provide variety. And there is entertainment every night.

Also included is a wealth of activities: tennis, Sunfish sailboats, snorkeling, fishing, guided historical walks to nearby petroglyph fields. You can also swim in a lava-lined freshwater (from an underground ocean spring) pool. Also available are charters for scuba diving, deep-sea fishing, and catamaran sails, as well as tennis lessons from a Peter Burwash International pro. Kona Village will even make all the arrangements for a Hawaiian wedding at sunset, in conjunction with their four-night honeymoon plan.

But the best thing about Kona Village is the feeling of seclusion, of retreat. Walking beside the almost mystically peaceful fishponds (designated long ago by King Kamehameha I), listening to the song of birds, swimming on a secluded beach, one begins to feel what Hawaii must have been like long before the modern age.

For reservations, write Kona Village Resort, P.O. Box 1299, Kaupulehu-Kona, HI 96745, or phone toll free to the resort: 800/367-5290.

HOTELS IN KONA: Built high up on lava beds that meet the sea at Keauhou Bay, a few miles out of the town of Kailua-Kona, the **Kona Surf**, 78-128 Ehukai St., Kailua-Kona, HI 96740 (tel. 322-3411; reservations, toll free 800/367-8011 from mainland U.S., 800/524-7200 from Oahu) is one of the most purely spectacular hotels in the islands. This $180-million, 537-unit hotel is one of those places where it's hard to tell where the indoors ends and the outdoors begins, spread out as it is on some 14½ acres bursting with tropical vegetation (there are 30,000 plants on the property alone). There are lava cliffs and waterfalls (man-made but beautiful) wherever you look, and magnificent artworks from the Pacific Basin casually interspersed among the public areas and walkways. The loveliness extends to the rooms, even down to the striped sheets, decorator towels, and sunken bathtubs, plus the more usual amentities like air conditioning, color television, private lanais with fine views. (Practical types will appreciate the coin-operated washers and dryers on each floor.) Rooms run $85 for standards, $100 garden view, $115 ocean view, $130 oceanfront single or double, $15 more for a third person. Suites go from $250 way up, and are particularly elegant. Along with the room, guests are offered complimentary champagne and punch from 3 to 5 p.m. in the lobby, and a cup of Kona coffee from 8 to 9 a.m.

We can't imagine, however, spending too much time in one's room since the facilities are exceptional, and the hotel is dedicated to providing many kinds of services and niceties, from the fresh-flower lei on arrival to the orchid on the pillow at night. There are two pools. The huge, saltwater Nalu pool has a fabulous slide that kids—and lots of adults too—spend hours a-whooshing down. Keauhou Bay is fine for snorkelers, but not for casual swimmers. At the freshwater pool you can take free swimming lessons, and snorkels and fins are provided gratis. There are tennis and golf pros on hand, several championship tennis courts, and a golf course that literally hangs over the water. Add to all this frequent shuttles into Kailua for shopping and to White Sands Beach for ocean swimming; shell-collecting trips; lessons in lei-making, hula dancing, coconut-palm weaving, you name it. And when you need to relax from all this activity, there's the Puku Bar for cozy drinks and the Nalu Terrace Bar; Pele's Court with its handsome mural for buffet breakfast and lunch and à la carte dinner, and the handsome S.S. *James Makee* for great seafood and steaks at dinner. A free hula show is held every night at the Nalu Pool. The Kona Surf is a fantastic place, so if you're not staying there, come by anyway Monday, Wednesday, and Friday at 9 a.m. for free tours of the grounds and buildings—it's a sightseeing stop in itself.

Another winner in the Keauhou Bay area is the gracious **Keauhou Beach Hotel**, 78-6740 Alii Dr., Kailua-Kona, HI 96740 (tel. 322-3441), a 318-room, calmly beautiful resort only six miles away from the busy center of town, yet relaxing enough to be a world apart. And that it is, sprawling out on grounds that are rich in both natural beauty and Hawaiian history. It is almost a living Hawaiian museum, with two restored *heiaus*, a reconstructed grass shack, an ancient fishpond or "sacred pool," and petroglyphs carved on a flat lava reef that runs straight out from the hotel, reminding guests of the olden days when this area, from which Kamehameha the Great launched his armies, was a favorite retreat of Hawaiian royalty. An exact replica of King Kalakaua's summer home, **Ka Hale Kahakai** o'Kalakaua, has been reconstructed on its original site, complete with koa floors and exact reproductions of his furniture.

Nature has been generous here too: the hotel has its own private swimming beach (rare for Kona) adjoining Kahuluu Beach Park, and even a volcanic tidal pool facing the sunning beach where one can watch the creatures of the deep swim in. There's an 18-hole championship golf course three minutes away, six tennis courts and a pro shop (lessons are available using the most modern facilities), and a beautiful freshwater swimming pool overlooking the ocean. And when you're hungry, there's the Sunset Rib Lanai for its famous prime ribs or fresh seafood, plus salad bar; and the inexpensive and cheery Kona Koffee Mill for breakfast. A popular buffet brunch is held poolside on Sunday from 10 a.m. to 2 p.m., at $10.95 per person.

But let's not forget the rooms here. They are spacious and handsome, decorated in subtle tones of beige, with every facility for comfort, including a small refrigerator, a spacious bath and dressing area, a radio/alarm clock as well as color TV, air conditioning, of course, and even full-length mirrors on the closets. All rooms are the same; only the locations and views are different. Without much of a view, the standard single or double is $55; with a better view, the superior room is $60; with an excellent view, the deluxe room is $70; and with the best oceanfront locations, $85. A third person in the room is charged $6 more. Rates are subject to change.

Our favorite condominium resort in the Keauhou area is **Kanaloa at Kona,** 78-261 Manukai St., Kailua-Kona, HI 96740 (tel. 322-2272), an 18-acre complex or 37 low-rise, wood-shingled buildings situated on a gentle rise overlooking ocean and bay on one side, fairways on the other. It's perfect heaven for golfers (the 18-hole championship Keauhou Golf Course borders the resort), tennis players (two lighted courts), snorkelers and surfers, and anyone who wants to enjoy the sporting or lazy life in a setting of pure island beauty. The surf is too rough here for casual swimming, but there are three freshwater pools, one reserved only for grown-ups. One-, two-, and three-bedroom ocean and fairway villas are superbly furnished, have koa wood cabinetry, fully equipped kitchens (microwave ovens, washers and dryers), phones, color TV, large lanais with their own private wet bars. Oceanfront suites even have their own private Jacuzzis! There is daily maid service. The Terrace Restaurant is pleasant, and there are more restaurants, and shops, too, at the Keauhou Shopping Village two blocks up the road. Rates are quite affordable for two couples or a large family. From April 1 to December 19, one-bedroom, two-bath fairway villas are $85 for up to four people; ocean villas are $110. Two-bedroom, two-bath fairway villas for up to six people are $120; ocean villas are $130. Three-bedroom, two-bath fairway villas for up to eight people are $140; ocean villas are $150. The rest of the year, each unit is $10 to $20 more. For reservations, call Colony Resorts toll free at 800/367-6046, or write to Kanaloa at Kona.

One of the nicest ways we know to live the lazy Kona life is at the self-contained **Kona Hilton Beach and Tennis Resort,** P.O. Box 1179, Kailua-Kona, HI 96740 (tel. 329-3111), nestled on 12 acres of oceanfront just half a mile from the center of Kailua-Kona Village. The three buildings containing some 450 guest rooms make the most of the natural setting here, and wherever you look there are stunning vistas of mountains and sea. You can dine or have a drink or watch the sunset and nightly entertainment in the surfside restaurant and cocktail lounge; you can swim in a split-level circular pool close enough to the beach to hear the breakers crashing on a lava cliff below. And you can also swim at a sandy lagoon beach, unusual for Kona, where the waves can be rough. Children can swim at the half-moon-shaped shallow area of the pool reserved for them. And tennis players have four championship courts and a pro shop at their disposal.

The rooms are as handsome and spacious as you would expect, with dark-wood paneling and tropical colors setting the mood. Under-the-counter refrigerators, separate dressing areas for him and her, air conditioning, coffee maker, and color TV are standard. A sliding panel leads to your landscaped lanai from which you can view either the garden, mountain, or sea; the view pretty much determines the price tab. Single or double occupancy goes from $65 to $115, with most rooms available at $90; one-bedroom suites are $135, $150, and $185; two-bedroom suites are $350. A third person is $15, but your child, of any age, stays free in your room. The Hele Mai, Windjammer Lounge, and Lanai Coffeeshop are fun for meals, and there's a constant program of dining and entertainment events. Make reservations at any Hilton Reservations Office, or write to the reservations manager at the Kona Hilton Beach and Tennis Resort.

Right in the village of Kailua-Kona, a new **Hotel King Kamehameha** (tel. 329-2911) has been rebuilt on the site of the old landmark hotel, combining the best of Hawaii past and Hawaii present. Adjacent to the hotel is the royal Kama Kahonu ground, where King Kamehameha ruled until his death in 1819; out on the peninsula is the restored Ahuena Heiau, or sacred temple. Two six-story twin towers with 230 air-conditioned guest rooms in each—all of which have color TV, radio, refrigerator, and their own lanai—are separated by a shopping mall laced with museum displays. The rooms are richly decorated, as is the spacious lobby in its handsome sienna and orange hues, accented by three-dimensional koa-wood walls, Polynesian murals, and Hawaiian artifacts. Modern conveniences include four tennis courts (two of them championship), two saunas, good dining rooms like Moby Dick's for seafood and the Kona Veranda Coffeeshop. On Sun-

THE ISLAND OF HAWAII 139

day, from 9 a.m. to 1 p.m., Moby Dick's is the scene of an excellent $13.95 buffet brunch. Not the least of the charms of the Hotel King Kamehameha is the fact that, in addition to its pool and engaging poolside bar, it has its own sandy beach, the only one right in the heart of town. Three nights a week, the Kona Beach luau is held here.

Single or double rooms at the Hotel King Kamehameha go from $65 for a standard to $110 for deluxe oceanfront. A third person is charged $10 extra. One-, two-, and three-bedroom suites run from $185 to $330. For reservations, phone toll free 800/227-4700, or write to Amfac Resorts, 2255 Kuhio Ave., P.O. Box 8520, Honolulu, HI 96815.

Inquire at the hotel for information on free historical, ethnobotanical and "hula experience" tours.

There's a special feeling at a family-run hotel, and that's what you get when you stay at **Uncle Billy's Kona Bay Hotel** on Alii Drive (tel. 329-1393), a sister hotel to Uncle Billy's Hilo Bay Hotel. Right in the center of town, within walking distance of all the shopping-dining-fishing excitement, this is a crescent-shaped, 123-room low-rise, overlooking pools, restaurants, and gardens, with the emphasis on comfortable living at a reasonable price. Rooms are of good size, nicely decorated, with full bathrooms, ample lanais, air conditioning, refrigerators, TV, and some have small kitchenettes as well. Owner-managers Kimo and Jeanne Kimi are family people, and families are made to feel right at home here. And the price is definitely right: rates (subject to change) are $41 single, $44 twin for standard rooms; $46 and $49 for superior rooms; $51 and $54 for deluxe. Add another $8 in the superior and deluxe category and you can have a kitchenette. An extra person is charged $10; children under 12 are free. Room-and-car packages are available for $54, $59, and $64. Cousin Kimo's Steak 'n' Seafood Restaurant provides good family meals and a free hula show every night at 6:30 and 7:30 p.m. Reservations are handled at the central office in Hilo: 87 Banyan Dr., Hilo, HI 96720. For toll-free reservations, you can dial direct to Hawaii: 800/367-5102.

Down the coast, just outside of town and past the **Kona Hilton,** is a neat little budget find. The **Kona Tiki Hotel,** P.O. Box 1567, Kailua-Kona, HI 96740 (tel. 329-1425), seems sleepy enough when you pull off the highway into the parking lot, but once you're up in your room the action begins. This place intrudes upon King Neptune's territory, and he lets you know about it with a nonstop display of rainbow water that crashes against the (thank goodness) sturdy seawall surrounding the hotel. Free breakfast (coffee with doughnuts) is available in the lobby every morning. A freshwater pool competes with the ocean for attention. The rooms are modest but comfortable, with carpeted floors and double or twin beds, small but adequate bathrooms, and sliding doors that lead to a private lanai from which the sunset is spectacular. Every room has a refrigerator. Standard rooms are $29 for a single or double, and rooms with mini-kitchenette

Condominium Vacations

If you'd like to stay in your own apartment in Kona, complete with all the comforts of home, a condominium vacation is the perfect answer. The Kona Coast is liberally sprinkled with these vacation complexes, and all offer apartments with spacious living, sleeping, and eating quarters, full kitchens, and all the amenities. Minimum stays of three days are required; daily maid service is usually not included but is available on request.

To stay right in the heart of town, choose **Kona Plaza,** 75-5719 Alii Dr., Kailua-Kona, HI 96740 (tel. 329-1132), a 77-unit complex tucked behind the Kona Plaza Shopping Arcade on Alii Drive. Apartments are fully carpeted, and have lanais, full electric kitchens (washer-dryer, dishwasher, etc.), pleasant furniture; there are ocean views from the third- and fourth-floor rooms. A beautiful sundeck overlooks Alii Drive and the ocean. Below it is an outdoor dining area where guests gather for potluck dinners and picnic meals. There are also two recreation areas and a pool. Rates vary, but one-bedroom apartments might start at $50 for two; two-bedroom, two-bath apartments at $75 for up to six; weekly rates at $300 and $450. The seventh day is free. For reservations, write to John Klein, Kona Plaza Resident Manager.

If you prefer a location a bit out of town, overlooking the waterfront, then choose **Kona Makai,** 75-6025 Alii Dr., Kailua-Kona, HI 96740 (tel. 329-1151). This sprawling, 102-unit complex has an oceanside swimming pool and Jacuzzi, two tennis courts, and handsomely decorated and spacious modern apartments. Kitchens have everything, including washer-dryers, eat-in bars and instant coffee makers. One-bedroom apartments run from $65 to $75 from April 16 to December 14, from $75 to $90 from December 15 to April 15. Two-bedroom apartments go for $80 to $130.

are $33, with additional persons $5 more. The managers are on duty, it seems, just about always, generous with tips regarding excursions and car trips, restaurants, and island history. There are only 15 units here and they fill up fast, so write for reservations (three-day minimum) in advance.

RESTAURANTS IN KONA: For gourmet dining in the Kona area, **Dorian's,** in the Magic Sands Hotel, has long been a top choice. The room is a study in quiet elegance, with high-backed chairs, white napery, stem crystal on the tables, graceful touches everywhere. Service is impeccable—the waiters are all ruffle-shirted, good-looking, and charming—and the food of a high continental order. Everything is à la carte. Among the appetizers, the stuffed mushrooms with crab are highly recommended, and so is the thick and crusty French onion soup (the vichyssoise is also expertly done). Our main course was the Chef's Silver Seafood Platter, served for two at $22 each, a truly magnificent presentation on a silver tray of ono, crab thermidor, shrimps in sauce, baked potato, cauliflower topped with onion rings, and fresh chunks of drawn butter. And the house salad, laden with shrimp, crabmeat, feta cheese, hard-boiled eggs, and topped with Roquefort dressing, was a wonder, served in a clam-shell bowl, and a meal in itself, at $9.50. Entrees are mostly in the $6.75 to $14.75 range, and are accompanied by tossed lettuce salad and warm white bread, very fresh and moist, with lots of butter. Desserts are something special; save room for the guava cheesecake.

Lunch, which can be taken on the umbrellaed lanai, is lighter, featuring entrees, most under $6, such as crab or shrimp salad, eggs Benedict, and London broil. At the Sunday gourmet champagne brunch, favorite egg dishes average about $8. For reservations, phone 329-3195.

Another longtime Kona favorite is **Huggo's,** beautifully situated on the waterfront not far from the Kona Hilton; from your al fresco dining perch, you can watch the sun set into Kailua Bay. And the food is as good as the view, with lots of fresh seafood and fish dishes, plus a good choice of meat and chicken entrees as well. Entrees like shrimp scampi, steamed clams, mahimahi, Alaskan king crab legs, prime rib, pineapple chicken, and teriyaki steak are priced from $7.50 to $17.95; Hawaiian lobster is a bit more. There is always fresh fish of the day. With all entrees, you can help yourself to all you want at the salad bar. Sashimi is a favorite among the appetizers; side dishes like zucchini fritters and rich desserts like Mud Pie are all temptations. The wine list is well selected and extensive, and several wines are served by the glass; the bar scene is always lively. Huggo's serves lunch weekdays between 11 a.m. and 2:30 p.m. and dinner every night from 5:30 to 10 p.m. There is usually live musical entertainment Thursday to Saturday from 8:30 p.m. For reservations, phone 329-1493.

The setting of the **Kona Inn,** on Alii Drive (tel. 329-4425), can only be described as idyllic: tall wicker chairs and beautifully inlaid koa tables overlook the Pacific, and palm trees sway in the ocean breezes at this popular lanai restaurant. In this storybook setting you dine on superbly fresh and beautifully prepared seafood and steak. Most dishes run $8.95 to $14.95 (although Great Barrier Reef lobster goes up to $18.95), and include a tangy chicken Cordon Bleu, a vegetable-cheese casserole that our vegetarian friends raved about, and a marvelous broiled seafood combination of shrimps, jumbo scallops, and fish. The local fish of the day is outstanding; it should be, what with all the big-game fishing off the Kona Coast! Along with your entree comes a good mixed salad with choice of dressing or hearty New England–style clam chowder, baked potatoes or rice pilaf, vegetables, and warm bread. On no account should you miss their Mud Pie for dessert; the taste of chocolate-cookie crust, coffee ice cream, and chocolate syrup will live in our memory. Children's menus are reasonably priced at $6.95.

Lunch is nice here too, with good sandwiches, fish entrees from about $4.75 to $6.95, and a chowder-and-salad meal at $4.25. And Sunday brunch is another winner: entrees, $4.25 to $6.95, are served with fresh fruit and homemade blueberry muffin. Try the eggs Blackstone or the french toast with Canadian bacon. Yes, they have Mud Pie here too. Service is professional and not cloying, as it can often be in the islands.

There's an informal, relaxed feeling about dining at **Quinn's,** 75-5655A Palani Rd. (tel. 329-3822), next door to the King Kamehameha Hotel. A lively young crowd hangs out in the garden dining lanai, whose two open walls and one of lava rock give an outdoor feeling. Blue canvas director's chairs and glass-topped wooden tables continue the same mood. Dinner entrees average $8.95 to $13.95, and best bets are such seafood dishes as shrimp continental (sautéed in wine, herbs, mushrooms, and tomatoes). Entrees include salad, vegetable, and potato or rice. French dip, burger, and roast beef sandwiches are fine at lunch, from about $4.50 to $6.95. Lots of cheer inside at the bar. Local residents consider this place a favorite. Lunch from 11 a.m. to 5:30 p.m., dinner from 5:30 p.m. to 1 a.m.

For seafood in a sunset setting the **Kona Galley,** right on the bay on Alii Drive (tel. 329-3777), will do nicely, thanks. The sides of this one-flight-up restaurant, nautically decorated with wooden tables, leather and wicker chairs, are all open to catch the ocean breezes, very welcome on a tropical night. The menu leans heavily to seafood, with such specialties as coquilles St-Jacques, shrimp Bombay, and crab Newburg en casserole, from about $11.75 to $14.75. Mahimahi, the most popular native fish, is always available, as are other native fish when the Galley can get them. Steak entrees, too. The generous portions are served along with salad, bread, rice or french fries, and beverage. Potent, exotic drinks are at the ready, and there is a good wine list. Lunch consists mostly of hot sandwiches and some very good seafood salads, with a daily special and fish 'n' chips at $5.25.

Very good, moderately priced food in two charming settings is offered by the Hawaiian family who run Uncle Billy's Kona Bay Hotel, at two central Kona locations. **Cousin Kimo's Steak 'n' Seafood Restaurant** (tel. 329-1393) is right out in the garden of the hotel on Alii Drive. Prices start at around $5.95 for salad bar, but you can also have shrimp, scampi, chicken, steaks, and fish of the day—all from about $8.95 to $10.95, including fried rice and all you want of soup and salad bar. While you're feasting, enjoy a free Hawaiian show at 6:30 and 7:30 every night. Right across the street is **Hurricane Annie's** (tel. 329-4345), at the Kona Inn Shopping Village, a nautical charmer. You dine on a variety of pastas and Italian dishes, roast beef, spare ribs, steak, fish of the day, and more, from about $6.95 to $11.75. All entrees come with salad bar. Lunch and dinner are served at both restaurants; breakfast too at Cousin Kimo's.

Uncle Billy's crowning achievement in the restaurant field, **Fisherman's Landing,** on the oceanfront of the Kona Inn Shopping Village, was being called a "landmark restaurant of the islands" almost as soon as it opened its doors in 1986. And well it might: Uncle Billy spent years studying restaurants around the world before he came back home with his concept for the first fully computerized restaurant in Hawaii. The efficiency in the kitchen explains how they are able to serve almost 200 guests at a time, so expertly and with no feeling of rush. You enter the restaurant via a cobblestone walkway shaded by ancient banyan trees and move on into a series of indoor-outdoor dining areas, skillfully arranged to create a feeling of privacy as you enjoy the fountains, the pool, the ocean waves rolling up on the beach in front of you. An ice sculpture near the entrance displays the fish caught that day in Kona waters: kiawe-broiled, priced from $15.95 to $17.95, they are the restaurant's star attraction. But there are also other seafood specialties, Oriental and wok dishes, Chateaubriand, saltimbocca, filet mignon, and New York steak, all from about $12.95 to $16.95. Entrees include soup or salad and home-baked bread. Appetizers like shrimp scampi or fresh oysters on the half shell, desserts like the sensational lava pie, Irish mousse cake, or fresh lychee sherbet round out a perfect dining experience. Lunch, priced from about $5 to $7, offers a deli for made-to-order sandwiches, broiler items and salads. And you can always stop at the attractive patio bar for drinks and pupus.

Fisherman's Landing is open every day, from 11 a.m. to 2 p.m. and from 6 to 11 p.m. Reservations are essential, as this one is a sellout (tel. 326-2555).

There's something really likable about the **Old Kailua Cantina,** a Mexican restaurant and bar at 75-5669 Alii Drive, mauka side (tel. 329-TACO). Perhaps it's the casual atmosphere in the lounge and dining room, the lively crowd, the terrific margaritas, the special keiki menus, and the number of Happy Hour and Early Bird specials they offer (six dinners from $4.50 to $6.95 served between 4 and 6 p.m.). At any rate, the food is typical Tex-Mex, very tasty, and it will not overly deplete your supply of pesos: combination plates are $6.50 to $7.50; most specialties run around $7.95 to $8.95. Open every day from 11:30 a.m. to 10:30 p.m.

The **Pottery Terrace Restaurant,** on Kuakini Hwy., just up Wailua Road from the Kona Hilton (tel. 329-2277), no longer has its working gallery, but the pottery decor is still here, and the food is still excellent. Entrees come served with soup or salad, rice or baked potato, vegetable and garlic bread. You can have a variety of steaks from $12 to $18; other good choices are mahimahi or fresh catch of the day, and boned Cornish game hen stuffed with wild rice. And for that after-dinner treat, finish up with the very special Potter's coffee. Dinner only is served, from 6 to 10 p.m.

Also on Kuakini Hwy., in Kuakini Plaza South, is a change-of-pace restaurant for Kona: instead of open lanais and a view of the harbor, **La Bourgogne** offers a quaint, cozy, European country atmosphere. Guy Chatelard, one-time chef at the prestigious Mauna Kea Beach Hotel, began his apprenticeship in his native

France at the age of 15. Now he and his wife, Jutta, run their own charming little place and serve up traditional French interpretations of seafood, steak, lamb, and veal dishes. The à la carte menu ranges in price from $12 to $20. Entrees are served with fresh vegetables of the day and freshly prepared potatoes. Everything is homemade, from the onion soup and lobster bisque, to the crème au caramel, and very nicely done. There is a good wine list, and cocktails are available. Dinner only, Monday through Saturday, from 6 to 10 p.m. Closed Sunday. Reservations: 329-6711.

There are three areas to hit when the travelers checks are running low. The first are the arcades on Alii Drive, which house a number of tasty fast-food operations: **Sibu Café,** in Banyan Court, is one of our favorites for its exotic Indonesian food. Delicious satés of marinated meats and vegetables are reasonably priced, around $5 to $6. Fast foods with a gourmet touch are created at the **Little Sandwich Shack** on Alii Drive, just across from Hulihee Palace. Sample the homemade soups and salads, the macadamia nutburgers, roast beef tacos, and lots more. Prices go from about $2 to $5. If you have a car, drive over to the industrial area and have a moderately-priced Thai meal at **Lanai's Siamese Kitchen,** 74-5588A Pawai Place ($5 lunch specials, dinner under $10), or enjoy a natural-food, organic meal at **Amy's Café,** 75-5629 Kuakini Hwy., at Palani Rd. (lunch $4 to $5, dinner under $10). The third area to remember is the **Kona Coast Shopping Center,** near the intersection of Hwys. 11 and 19, which boasts **Betty's Chinese Kitchen** for some of the freshest and best manapua (dim sum) in these parts; **Paniolo Pizza** for good Mexican food, salads, and subs as well as pies; and the amazingly low-priced **Sizzler Steak House,** a steak cafeteria, where you can get, among many other offerings, a teriyaki steak platter for $6.29. And don't forget **Tom Bombadil's** on Alii Drive, across from the Kona Hilton, for terrific broasted chicken, pizzas, pastas, fish 'n' chips, and the like, at very low prices.

KONA AFTER DARK: There's plenty of excitement in the Kona night, and much of the action is centered around the big hotels. At the **Kona Surf,** at this writing, there's a terrific free show, "A Night in Hawaii." It's on every night at 7:45 at the Nalu Terrace, overlooking Keauhou Bay. . . . There's a terrific $30 luau at the **Keauhou Beach Hotel** on Sunday, Wednesday, and Friday at 6:30 p.m. Reservations: 322-3411. The same hotel features live music for dancing on Thursday, Friday, and Saturday from 7 p.m. on.

. . . They pop the pig into the imu every Sunday, Tuesday, and Thursday at the **Hotel King Kamehameha.** The tab for this in-town luau is $34, all inclusive. . . . It's worth a 15- to 20-minute drive out to Kaupulehua for the festive $39 luau given every Friday night at the **Kona Village Resort.** For reservations, phone 325-5555. . . . Dancing to the "West Hawaii Revue" in the Windjammer Lounge of the **Kona Hilton** is always fun. . . . For a change of pace, take to the ocean on **Captain Beans' Royal Canoe** for a sunset or moonlight cruise. It's open bar, plus all you can eat, music, and entertainment, for $34 per person. Adults only. The Canoe usually sails at 5:15 and 8:15 p.m. from Kailua Pier; phone 329-2955 for reservations. . . . For all entertainments, check the papers when you arrive, since times and schedules may change. Children are usually admitted to luaus at half the adult price.

BETWEEN KONA AND HILO—ROOM AND BOARD: If you're driving the southern route (11) between Hilo and Kona, or vice versa, you'll certainly stop off at Volcanoes National Park, and you may become so enchanted with the area that you'll want to stay there for a few days. Great idea! The place to stay is **Volcano House,** Hawaii Volcanoes National Park, HI 96718 (tel. 967-7321), which is situated in an incredibly exciting spot on top of Kilauea Crater. If Pele happens to be acting up, you'll have a ringside seat for the fireworks, and even if not, you'll have an attractive room ($44 single, $47 double, garden view; $48 single, $51 double, crater view), plus a chance to take a sauna bath in live volcanic steam, and a tingling-fresh mountain atmosphere to enjoy. For toll-free reservations, call Sheraton at 800/325-3535.

If you're ready for lunch now, you have several choices. The famous buffet lunch at Volcano House is good, but it attracts crowds of hungry tourists. Local people like the restaurant at the **Volcano Golf and Country Club** for good burgers and daily Oriental, Hawaiian, and American specials in a stylish atmosphere; and in the town of Volcano itself, there's **Volcano Country Kitchen,** a simple and cozy café for snacks and light meals. In a glorious beachfront setting, the **Punalu'u Black Sands Restaurant** at Punalu'u serves a fabulous luncheon buffet, with over 18 dishes displayed in a native canoe, plus elaborate desserts. And the **Naalehu Coffeeshop,** in the little town of Naalehu, the southernmost community in the U.S.A., serves delicious food at very modest prices. But don't just eat and run; take a look at owner Roy Toguchi's garden in back, his collection of bonsais, and the informal "gift shop," filled with paintings and handcrafts. A delightful interlude.

The Sights and Sounds of the Big Island

If you really want to see the Big Island, you should plan on at least four days. The ideal way would be to spend the first day in the city of Hilo; the second, driving to Volcanoes National Park; the third, taking the Hamakua coast trip across the island, driving through the cowboy country of the Parker Ranch; and the fourth, exploring the Kona coast and luxuriating in the sun and water. You could also start your trip at Kona and work backward. We'll suppose, though, for the purposes of this discussion, that you're starting out—in your own rented car—from General Lyman Field, the Hilo airport.

THE FIRST DAY—SEEING HILO: We hope you'll start your trip early, since the first sight to see is at its most beautiful when the sun is new and the world is not yet too warm. From the airport, take H-12 (Kamehameha Avenue) all the way around the curve in the bay until you reach Waianuenue Avenue, which you'll follow until you get to Rainbow Drive. Here you'll find the glorious **Rainbow Falls,** so named for the transparent rainbows that appear in the mist from the falls when the morning sun glances through it. Drive on a little farther, up to Peepee Street, and you'll see the **Boiling Pots,** another scenic vista. Such beauty so close to the city is no surprise, since the city itself is a spot blessed by nature. It curves around a crescent-shaped bay, and always in sight are the two homes of Pele: the larger, extinct volcano, **Mauna Kea,** and the sporadically active, only slightly smaller one, **Mauna Loa.**

Turn around now, and make a right on Puu Hina and another right on Kaumana. Follow this a few miles to the site of the **Kaumana Cave,** a lava tube similar to those you will be seeing later along the circular drive in Volcanoes National Park. This one was formed in 1881, when Pele came close to destroying the city of Hilo. The cave extends about a mile in the direction of the city, and a hardy spelunker could traverse the entire length with the help of a flashlight. The less adventurous can admire the lovely fern grotto at the entrance to the tube on the right (the one on the left is dangerous), and continue on.

Swing back the way you came, but make a right at Laimana Street, then left onto Haili Street. Follow it almost until Kapiolani Street, and in the middle of the block you'll find an impressive New England–type white building with green shutters. This old missionary home, built in 1839, is part of the **Lyman House Museum** and has been restored to look as it did in the mid-19th century. The ground floor contains a parlor and dining room plus others, furnished with authentic antiques. Upstairs are four quaint bedrooms, complete with four-posters, marble-topped dressers, and washstands. Adjoining is the modern museum building built to house the many artifacts of the seven ethnic groups living in Hawaii: you'll see a full-size grass hut of the early Hawaiians, artifacts from the missionary era, a 300-year-old Taoist shrine of gold leaf on intricate woodcarvings, plus exhibits reflecting the culture of the Japanese, Portuguese, Korean, and Filipino settlers. The top-floor galleries contain, among other exhibits, one of the largest mineral collections anywhere, and a world-class seashell exhibition. Admission to both buildings is $2.50 for adults, $1.25 for children. Hours are from 9 a.m. to 4 p.m., Monday through Saturday.

After you've finished here, turn left on Kapiolani and make a right back to Waianuenue Street. On your left you'll notice the Hilo Branch of the Library of Hawaii. Right out in front is the legendary **Naha Stone,** believed to be a gift of the gods to mortals. It was believed that any man strong enough to lift the stone would be able to unite the islands of the Hawaiian chain. Kamehameha, the island's favorite son, was able to do so, or thus goes the legend. At any rate, he went on to become first a chief, then king, and the rest is history.

Make a right now when you get to the corner of Kinoole and Waianuenue. Before you turn, though, notice the shaded, somber building in front of you. This is one of the buildings of the Hilo campus of the **University of Hawaii,** the second-biggest center of higher education in the islands. You can complete that turn now, take the next available left, get back onto Kamehameha Avenue, and swing out around Hilo Bay.

Continue on past Pauhi Street until you can make a left onto Lihiwai. Just before you reach the intersection of Lihiwai and Banyan Drive, you'll see an HVB marker on the right side of the road pointing to the fish-auction area. If you can manage to get up with the birds tomorrow morning, you can join the local dealers in a colorful 8 a.m. auction. Now, however, continue on Lihiwai as you swing in a circle around beautiful **Liliuokalani Park,** where a Japanese Yedo garden has been completely reconstructed. Stone lanterns and bridges accent the lovely setting here on the shore of Hilo Bay. The **Japanese Cultural Center,** a restaurant, art gallery, tea room, and exhibition space, comes up soon. Off to your left is **Coconut Island,** which used to be a popular recreation spot for the people of Hilo until the 1960 tidal wave carried a good portion of the island soil into the ocean.

Now you can continue around the lip of Lihiwai and turn left onto **Banyan Drive,** so named for the small banyan trees (as banyans go) planted along the middle of the highway by famous people in the past half century. Most of the hotels in the city are ranged along here, and the setting is cool and easy. Follow Banyan Drive to its intersection with Kamehameha Avenue and drive left out of town, taking a left fork shortly to get onto Kalanianaole Avenue.

Now you're approaching one of the best spots for swimming and picnicking in the Hilo area (Hilo is not known for good beaches), an easy drive along Kalanianaole Avenue; it's **Onekahakaha Beach Park.** Here you either swim in the bay or wade in several wading pools—natural, of course—that the ocean constantly refills. Fishing is permitted from the rocks on shore. There are several pavilion areas, rest room accommodations, firepits for barbecuing, and a tiny but growing children's zoo that exhibits small samples of wildlife. All in all, there's quite a lot to do here. After you've done it, drive back out onto Kalanianaole and turn right to return to the center of Hilo.

Shopping in Hilo

Since many artists, craftspeople, and people of originality and good taste live on the Big Island, shopping in Hilo can be quite interesting. Head downtown, along Kilauea, Kinoole, and Keawe Streets, and Kamehameha Avenue, where you'll find many appealing local shops. **The Most Irresistible Shop in Hilo,** at 98 Keawe St., is laden with tasteful cards, T-shirts, kitchenware, as well as beautiful hand-turned pottery, featherwork, patchwork, stained glass, etc. Kids will be enchanted by the toys and dollhouse furniture, and everyone will want to have a drink and a pastry or a light meal at the adorable **Bears Café** adjacent. In the same Pacific Building which houses this shop are several other places you will want to browse through: the **Futon Connection,** with such wonderful decorator items as futons, wall fans, handcarved banana trees from Bali, porcelain, silks, and much more; the **Chocolate Bar,** for homemade candies that include chocolate greeting cards and coconut/chocolate sushi; the **Picture Frame Shop,** which frames and sells prints and paintings by island artists, specializing in local koa-wood frames.

The Gardens of Hilo

You'll want to take time to soak up the beauty of the many gardens of Hilo, and a good place to start is at its most unique: the **Hawaii Tropical Botanical Garden,** a 17-acre nature preserve and sanctuary developed to protect the natural beauty of a tropical rain forest. Bordered by the ocean, the valley is dotted with waterfalls, streams, and an amazing variety of tropical plants, birds, and marine life; shore birds, forest birds, and giant sea turtles inhabit the nature preserve. Trails take visitors from coconut groves to palm jungles to fern forests, to spend as long as they like enjoying, exploring, and—of course—photographing the wonders therein.

Admission to the Garden, a nonprofit foundation, is a tax-deductible $6. No picnic areas, no food sold. Open Monday to Saturday, 9 a.m. to 5 p.m.; Sunday, 11 a.m. to 5 p.m. For information and driving directions (it is five miles from Hilo), phone 964-5233.

Another eminently worthwhile stop is **Nani Mau Gardens,** 20 acres of the fruits and flowers of many lands, with a special emphasis on those that have figured in the life of the islands. Orchids, of course, but also macadamia-nut trees, rare Hawaiian medicinal herbs, and acres and acres of fragrant hibiscus, torch ginger, and bird of paradise. After your one-hour tour, you can stop for a picnic lunch; and you'll be given free "samples" of ripe fruit from the fruit garden. Open daily from 8 a.m. to 5 p.m. Admission is $3 for adults, $1.50 for children. To reach the gardens, drive about 3½ miles south on Hwy. 11 (the road to the volcano) from Hilo Airport. Take the left fork where Hwy. 11 divides onto Makalika Street, and the gardens are right ahead.

More treats for lovers of gardens and flowers include visits to the charming **Hilo Tropical Gardens,** 1477 Kalanianaole Ave. (free admission, 10:30 a.m. hula show on Saturday); **Orchids of Hawaii,** 2801 Kilauea Ave.; and **Kulani Flowers Anthurium Farm,** about a mile further on the same road (take Hwy. 11 toward the volcano to Mamaki Street).

The local natural-living set hangs out at two places: **Abundant Life Natural Foods** at 90 Kamehameha Ave., corner of Waianuenue Avenue, whose selection of locally produced fruits, vegetables, honey, herbs and foods to go is outstanding; and at **Hilo**

Natural Foods, 308 Kilauea St., also plentifully stocked, which has a small natural-foods counter restaurant. **Basically Books,** 169 Keawe St., offers an excellent selection of books on Hawaii, including those published by their own Petroglyph Press.

Hilo has a brand-new, multimillion dollar shopping center out on Hwy. 11, **Prince Kuhio Shopping Plaza.** Stop in at **Liberty House** or **Sears,** wander through some upscale boutiques like **Imagination Toys,** for educational and creative playthings; **Limited Editions,** for children's wear and patchwork quilts; **Once Upon a Time** for stuffed animals, teddy bears, Victorian dolls; **Chef's Heaven** for gourmet cookware and accessories. Sister shops to The Most Irresistible Shop in Hilo and The Chocolate Bar can also be found here.

A popular older shopping center is **Kaiko'o Mall,** just behind the County and State Buildings, a big, handsome place where the locals buy everything from clothes to crafts to papayas and soapsuds. **J.C. Penney, McInerny, Book Gallery,** and **Hilo Hattie's Resort Shop** are some good places to know about.

THE SECOND DAY—IN THE WAKE OF PELE: Although volcanology is now an exact physical science, you could never prove it to some of the residents of the Big Island. As far as they are concerned, Pele, the flaming goddess of the volcanoes, is still alive and well, and she lives in Halemaumau Crater on Kilauea. You'll have to see Pele before you leave the Big Island; you may observe her in action, or you may just see what she's been up to. Either way, the sights are unforgettable. You can follow in her trail all along the road up to **Volcanoes National Park** and even right up to the shoreline—an exciting territory that's well worth exploring.

To begin your drive to the Puna region, take the southern route, H-11, out of Hilo. Six miles out of town, and across the divided highway, you'll see the **Mauna Loa Macadamia Nut Corporation,** where, if you can get Pele out of your mind for a few minutes, you can take yourself on a quick tour of the grounds, between 9 a.m. and 5 p.m. daily. Macadamia-nut raising is one of the fastest growing industries in the state, and once you taste them—free tastings are offered—you'll understand why.

But back to volcanoland. Continuing on your journey, you take H-12 on its rain-forested drive along the sea. At the fork in the road coming up later, take H-132 and head makai. You'll pass **Lava Tree Park,** where you could have a hike or a picnic while you observe the work of the molten lava all around. The casts of tree trunks in solidified lava still stand here; the lava burned out the trees inside and went hurtling on. There are also a few tremendous earth faults, which are fenced off. You can look into mini-canyons for a glimpse of the rock layers under the surface. Continue on, passing fertile papaya fields and orchid farms. Just before the intersection with H-137, you'll pass the village of **Kapoho,** buried under tons of lava in a 1960 eruption that added several square miles to the island's geography. You might even notice the lighthouse, standing isolated and strangely inland. A few signs of village life remain, sticking out from under the smothering lava rock.

Now you turn right onto an unearthly stretch of highway that careens wildly along the seashore, giving you an unforgettable picture of what volcanic fury does to the land. Mound upon mound of rolling lava rock spills down to the ocean on your left, and on the right a few cinder cones, some wisping meaningless smoke, play hide and seek with the foliage that has managed to take root in the rich volcanic soil. The plant life reworks the volcanic earth, producing red dirt, which blows across and colors the highway on which you are riding. The road will dip into shady grottoes and emerge into the brilliant sunlight where nothing but black, frozen rock stares back at you from every side.

Note the intersection of the road now with the H-13, but continue on just past it to see a beach unique unto the islands: **Kaimu Beach,** known popularly as the **Black Sand Beach,** at Kalapana. Here volcanic rock has been beaten into fine sand, as brilliant in its ebony texture as other beaches are in their golden hues. With swaying palm trees in the background, it's picture-postcard Hawaii, but the tides are too tricky for safe swimming. Instead, continue down the road a bit for a picnic at **Harry K. Brown Beach Park,** where lava rock has been used in the creation of the picturesque picnic tables and stools. Across the street is a man-made pool constructed completely of lava stones and fed with ocean water. A bit down the road, you'll pass the **Star of the Sea Painted Church,** one of two "painted churches" on the island. Since the ancient Hawaiians were accustomed to outdoor worship of their pagan gods, the murals on the walls of these little churches are designed to create an outdoorsy feeling. (This little church, however, is rather recent; you'll see a much older one just off the road to Hoonaunau, when you explore the Kona coast on the other side of the island.) About five miles from this spot is the **Queen's Bath,** a pond where those enormous and matronly monarchs of

THE ISLAND OF HAWAII

old Hawaii allegedly came to bathe. According to the old legend, any citizen found watching was immediately put to death—no questions asked. Don't worry, democracy reigns, and anybody can swim here, especially the local kids who have turned it into a favorite swimming hole.

On to the Volcano

Every visitor to the Big Island has one important question: "Will I see the volcano erupt?" Since Kilauea erupts only sporadically, the answer will have to be "maybe." But if Pele answers your prayers—as she once did ours—you're in for a fantastic experience. Several years ago, one of the fire pits along the Chain of Craters Road went into sudden action for only one night. We, along with several hundred others, queued up in park headquarters to see the raging fountains several miles away. The sky was painted red with the glow of lava, and sometimes the fiery geysers shot up over 1,000 feet in the air. It was quite a show. We hope you'll catch a similar performance somewhere in the volcano area, and there's a good chance that you will, as there has been a great deal of activity in some of the craters in recent years. You can call the park before you start out (tel. 967-7311) for news of latest eruptions and viewing conditions, and check with the rangers as soon as you arrive for directions to the site. For recorded information on eruptions, you can phone 967-7977 at any hour.

But even if there are no eruptions at the moment, you will, of course, visit the home of Pele, which the United States government has thoughtfully and handsomely turned into a national park. To reach **Hawaii Volcanoes National Park,** your best route is to continue a few miles to the Wahaula Visitor Center, which takes you to the Chain of Craters Road, which leads right into the park. If time is short and you decide to skip the shoreline trip completely, simply take Hwy. 11 out of Hilo and stay on the road all the way to Kilauea. Park headquarters should be your first stop. The rangers on duty there will give you driving maps and information on nature walks, and tell you when the next movie on volcanology will be shown. It is well worth seeing.

To really see and experience the volcano, you should take one of the hikes that start out from behind Volcano House, across the street; the air is deliciously crisp (we hope you've brought a jacket with you), the views eye-filling, and the mountain flowers and trees different from what you've seen on the tropical beaches below. But if time and energy are lacking, you can get the impact of the place simply by taking the circular drive that surrounds the park and leads you alongside every major point of interest. First you'll come to the **Sulfur Banks,** just out of park headquarters territory, and farther on are the steam vents where clouds of evaporating rainwater hiss off hot stones underground.

Farther ahead, you can swing to the right on Mauna Loa Road and come upon the **Tree Molds,** similar to the ones you saw earlier at Puna, and **Kipuka Puala Bird Park,** perfect for a nature walk or a picnic. Head back to Crater Rim Drive now, and continue on around the rim of **Halemaumau Crater,** which stretches below you for half a mile. You can completely circle it by car and then walk to the observation platform and inspect the 300-foot-deep crater, spilling forth sulfur fumes at what is sometimes a pretty impressive rate. Continue on to the **Devastation Trail,** a man-made walkway stretching with spooky certainty through a forest of dead trees and winding around inert cinder cones. This walk takes about 15 minutes, so, to conserve energy, you might send one member of your party back to the parking lot to bring the car around to the lookout area at the end of the walk.

Back to the beauty of the forest you go now, and in the midst of an indescribably lush tropical setting you'll find the **Thurston Lava Tube.** Like the Kaumana Cave in Hilo, the tube was formed by cooled lava forming around a molten core that kept moving and eventually emptied the circular shell. The short path through the tube is clear enough, and you'll emerge into more forest at its end. Kilauea Iki and Waldron Ledge Overlooks comprise the last two stops on the loop.

Since this is a circular drive, you're now back where you started from, and you've seen the major sights of the volcano. Before you leave the area, stop in to see the tasteful collection of arts and crafts, most of it by Big Island artists, at the **Volcano Art Center,** a rustic gallery occupying the original (1877) Volcano House Hotel. Many items here would make excellent gifts.

Where you go from here depends on you. If you haven't seen the Puna shore area on the way up, you can take the Chain of Craters Road to the Wahaula Visitor Center, then head back to Pahoa, Keaau, and ultimately Hilo. Or you can return directly to Hilo via Hwy. 11. A third alternative is to continue from the volcano for another 96 miles to the Kona coast. The highway is good, but not especially interesting. You can stop at another black-sand beach—at **Punaluu**—and in **Kau** you can still see in the cooled lava the footprints of Hawaiian warriors routed from a battle by a sudden outburst of Pele. Our personal preference is to go back to Hilo for the night, starting out the next morning for Kona by way of the varied and beautiful Hamakua coast.

THE THIRD DAY—FROM HILO TO KONA: The intriguing thing about driving the **Hamakua Coast** is that, in a mere 96 miles, you pass scenery so unusual and so varied that it's difficult to believe it's all part of the same island—from lush sugar plantation fields curving around the base of Mauna Kea on the Hilo coast, through the grassy pastures of the Parker Ranch, into remote mountain regions, posh seaside watering holes, and across barren lava landscapes until you reach the green and gold of the Kona coast. Plan on a full day and savor it all.

Begin your travels on H-19 in Hilo, which continues straight out of the city. After about five miles, you will see a blue sign on the right which reads: "Scenic Route, 4 miles long." Take this and you will be driving around picturesque Onomea Bay. If you've not yet seen it, this is a good time to visit **Hawaii Tropical Botanical Garden** (see above), which you reach after one mile on the drive. Continuing on, you'll hug the northern shore of the island now, with Mauna Kea on one side, the surging sea on the other. The rich earth yields a bumper crop of sugarcane here. Your next stop should be in the little village of **Honomu,** ten miles out, where an HVB marker will point the way up a country road to **Akaka Falls,** a glorious waterfall surrounded by an incredibly rich bit of jungle, tamed enough to turn it into an idyllic little park where you might want to spend all day. But get back to the highway and continue on; there's another pretty park at **Laupahoe-hoe,** down on the shore. Back in 1946 this village bore the brunt of a tidal wave that swept a school and its occupants into the sea. Swimming, as you will notice, is terribly dangerous in the pounding surf near the jutting rocks. A picnic or a look is enough.

In **Honokaa,** 20 miles ahead, you'll find Waipio Valley Lookout, the takeoff point for a 1½-hour Jeep trip into dreamy **Waipio Valley.** (It's best to have made advance reservations by phoning 775-7121. The cost is $15 for adults, $5 for children 2 to 12.) If you don't have time for that 1½-hour excursion, you might stop in at the venerable **Hotel Honokaa Club** for lunch, or visit **Hawaiian Holiday's** macadamia-nut-processing plant (open daily 9 a.m. to 6 p.m.; macadamia-nut gifts mailed anywhere; free sample), relax, and continue on your way.

A Stop at Parker Ranch

Now Hwy. 19 heads inland, and soon you're in cowboy country (they call them *paniolos* here), careening along the highway that borders grasslands reminiscent of Texas. This is **Kamuela** (also called **Waimea**), home of the enormous **Parker Ranch,** one of the largest cattle ranches in the United States under single ownership. Although most of us don't associate Hawaii with ranching, it is a major industry on the Big Island. Parker Ranch was begun in 1847 when King Kamehameha III deeded a two-acre parcel of land to John Palmer Parker, a sailor from Newton, Massachusetts, who had managed to tame some wild cattle for the king. Today, the ranch covers approximately 225,000 acres, and Parker's great-great-great-grandson, Richard Smart, is its owner. It's here in Kamuela that you may want to stop to see the **Parker Ranch Visitor Center Theater/Museum.**

Plan on about 45 minutes to see the complex. First, browse through the John Palmer Parker Museum with its Hawaiiana and Parker Ranch artifacts (there's a tapa bedcover from the old Parker homestead and a gown worn by Thelma Parker), and stop also to see a special section filled with mementos and trophies of Duke Kahanamoku, Hawaii's greatest swimming star and Olympic champion. Then, in the Thelma Parker Theater, you'll see a 15-minute narrated color-slide presentation depicting the history and workings of the Parker Ranch; it's very well done. Located in the Parker Ranch Shopping Center, the Visitor Center is open Monday to Saturday from 9:30 a.m. to 3:30 p.m. Admission is $2.25 for adults, $1.25 for those 12 to 18, 75¢ for children 7 to 11; under 6, free.

Of course, you'll want to stop next door and visit **The Paddock,** whose tiny shops display arts and crafts that reflect Hawaii's ranching tradition. We found many unusual things here, many of them made right in the community, like the strawflower leis that paniolos wear at rodeos, owl-feather pins, and Parker Ranch print shirts, belt buckles, and T-shirts. Then finish your visit with a meal at the superb **Edelweiss Restaurant,** on Kawaihae Road, where chef Hans Peter Hager turns out extraordinary continental cuisine in a country atmosphere (no reservations, and about an hour's wait at dinner); or at the plushly decorated **Parker Ranch Broiler,** which specializes in steaks and oven-roasted prime rib at dinner. (At both, expect to pay $5 to $7 for lunch, $10 to $20 or more for dinner.) If you like this area well enough to stay a bit, try the **Parker Ranch Lodge,** a modern motor-hotel offering spacious rooms, kitchenettes, and rates of $36 single, $42 double, $48 for two queen-size beds.

More About Waimea

Waimea is such a pleasant little mountain town that you may want to spend an hour or so wandering about, perhaps doing a little shopping. The shops in the **Parker Ranch Shopping Center** are a good place to start: especially interesting is **Setay,** originally of Beverly Hills, with a great deal of original jewelry, like gold and silver charms in the shapes of Hawaii potato chips, Maui onions, paniolo hats, or lei sellers. Drive up the road a bit to the **Waimea General Store,** which is just what its name implies, but with many sophisticated craft and gift items. **Kamuela Country Living** on Hwy. 19 shows lots of gourmet kitchenware and gifts, bath accessories and soaps, plus a large book selection—for children, cooks, equestrians, and collectors of Hawaiiana.

There's one more stop you might want to make in Waimea, and that's at the **Kamuela Museum.** John Parker's great-great-granddaughter and her husband, Harriet and Albert K. Solomon, Sr., are the founders, owners, and curators of this largest private museum in Hawaii. It's located at the junction of Rtes. 19 and 250, open daily including all holidays from 8 a.m. to 5 p.m., and boasts a collection of ancient and royal Hawaiian artifacts (many of which were originally at 'Iolani Palace in Honolulu), as well as European and Oriental objets d'art. Among the treasures: an ancient Hawaiian 61-pound, hammer-type stone canoe-buster, the only one in existence, used by warriors to smash enemy canoes; many ancient temple idols; a royal Hawaiian marble-top teak table once owned by Kamehameha III; and a traveling clock given to Queen Liliuokalani by Queen Victoria of England. Admission is $2; children under 12, $1; phone: 885-4724.

Now some of you might want to take a little side trip up into the **Kohala** region of the Big Island. It's an uphill drive along Rte. 25, and it's 22 miles in each direction before you can get back to Kamuela or Kawaihae and continue your cross-island jaunt to Kona. But the scenery is among the most spectacular we've found in the island. The Pacific drops off into a far-away, misty horizon, and the snow-topped cliffs of Mauna Loa and Mauna Kea provide an alpine-like background to the drive up the slopes of the Kohala Mountains. At the end of the road, and the end of the island, is the little village of **Kapaau,** the birthplace of Kamehameha and the site of the original statue of the warrior chief (you've probably seen its copy in front of 'Iolani Palace).

Still game for a side trip? This one is a simple 12-mile jaunt to the deepwater port of **Kawaihae,** where you can either have a swim with the local people at **Samuel Spencer Park** or **Hapuna Beach,** considered the best beaches on the island, or watch the jet set at play at **The Westin Mauna Kea.** Their $16.50 buffet lunch is sumptuous, and you couldn't ask for a more perfect spot for a swim or a stroll. To reach the hotel, take Rte. H-26 from Kamuela, which will go past the Puukohala Heiau, and then, on the road to Samuel Spencer Park, to the hotel.

As an alternative to the Mauna Kea trip, you might want to drive farther south along Hwy. 19 until you reach the splendid new **Sheraton Royal Waikoloa** at Aneehoomalu Bay; this hotel too welcomes you to use its superb beach. After your swim, you can visit the archeological sites and explore some of the oldest petroglyphs in Hawaii. The Sheraton's near neighbor, the **Mauna Lani Resort,** is well worth another stop, just to soak up the beauty of its gardens and grounds and seaside vistas everywhere. Have a look at the splendid offerings at the Connoisseur's Gallery here, and perhaps partake of their excellent buffet lunch on Saturday and Sunday from noon to 2 p.m.

Now, whether or not you've made any of these side trips, get back on (or continue along) Hwy. 19 or 190 (the latter trip is a bit shorter) and follow the road south to Kona. Along the side of the road you will see stone walls all the way. These are the remains of border fences, constructed when Hawaii was not yet united and various chieftains would lay claims to territories stretching from the slopes of Mauna Kea (the austere mountain peak on your left) down to the ocean in almost pie-shaped wedges. The fences were such a tremendous engineering achievement, however, that they were never torn down, even after the coming of the white man. The landscape turns into a volcanic wasteland now, with HVB markers dating the lava flows before you, and finally you escape the path of Pele into the golden, glowing welcome of the Kona coast.

THE FOURTH DAY—EXPLORING KONA: Let's face it. Getting up enough energy to go sightseeing in Kona is difficult. The sea is so beautiful, the colors of the tropical blossoms so brilliant, and the mood so deliciously lazy, that you may want to spend all your time fishing or golfing or swimming or just plain doing nothing. But we think you'll find it more than worth the effort to spend a few hours sightseeing, since the culmination of your efforts—a visit to the Pu'uhonua o'Honaunao National Historical Park—is certainly one of the highlights of a trip to the Big Island.

Preliminary sightseeing in Kailua-Kona is simple. The main street, Alii Drive, covers the entire length of the village in less than a mile. Situated in the middle of town is the **Mokuaikaua Church,** dating from 1823, and built by the Hawaiians at the request of the missionaries from lava stones and koa wood from the uplands. It is one of the oldest churches in the islands. Across the street is **Hulihee Palace,** the summer home of Hawaiian royalty, now converted into a museum showing furniture and accessories of Hawaiian royalty plus ancient artifacts. It's open daily from 9 a.m. to 4 p.m. Admission is $4 for adults and $1 for children. Just down the street, in the Kona Plaza Shopping Arcade, Ami Gay dispenses tourist information for the **Hawaii Visitors Bureau.** She is truly one of Kona's wonders and deserves a place on any map. Walk around Kona to get the feel of the place and relax in its atmosphere. There's a public beach area in front of the Hotel King Kamehameha, boats and guides for rent at every turn, and you can even take skin-diving lessons if you fell like it. For a great adventure, try **Pacific Sail & Snorkel's** snorkeling cruise that includes everything from transportation, equipment, and the inner tube in which you enter the water to a glass of passion-fruit juice for your $25. Phone: 329-2021. The lazier ones can see the wonders of the underwater world via **Captain Beans' Glass Bottom Boat Cruise:** around $6 for adults, $3 for children (tel. 329-2955).

Now, to start your serious sightseeing, get into your car and follow Alii Drive until it becomes a two-way street; take the mountain road and get onto Kuakini Hwy., H-11. Now you're in Kona "up mauka," an area of small coffee plantations (this is where they grow that rich, wonderful Kona coffee), and if it's fall harvest time you'll see little red beans glistening against the green leaves of the coffee bushes lining the road. There are also small cattle ranches here. Follow the road past the Hongwanji Mission down the slopes of the mountains until you reach the sea at **Kealakekua Bay.** Across the bay, you can see a white monument that was erected to mark the spot where Capt. James Cook was killed by Hawaiian natives in a scuffle in 1799. At the very spot where you park your car, however, you'll see two shrines: one that commemorates the first Christian funeral in the islands (performed by Captain Cook for one of his sailors) and another in honor of Opukahaia, a sailor who became the first Christian convert in the islands (he was instrumental in bringing those New England missionaries here in the first place).

Continue along the shore road now for your major destination —**Pu'uhonua o'Honaunau National Historical Park,** formerly known as the place of refuge. This ancient, partially restored *pu'uhonua* still has about it the air of sanctuary for which it was built over 400 years ago. In the days when many chiefs ruled in the islands, each district had a spot designed as a refuge to which kapu-breakers, war refugees, and defeated warriors could escape; here kapu-breakers could be cleansed of their offenses and returned, purified, to their tribes. (There is another such place of refuge on the island of Kauai, near Lydgate Park, but this one is far better preserved.) The *heiau* has been reconstructed, and all-wooden images (known as *Ki'i* in Hawaiian) guard its entrance. A great wall surrounds the purification site, and next to it is a little cove, shaded by coconut palms, where the chief could land his canoe. Although you can wander about this place on your own, swimming (but *not* sunbathing) and picnicking and enjoying the peace, you should attend one of the orientation talks given at 10, 10:30, and 11 a.m., and 2:30, 3, and 3:30 p.m. in the amphitheater by the National Park Service. Several "cultural demonstrators" are also on hand; they carve wood and demonstrate poi-pounding and ancient Hawaiian crafts.

On your return to Kealakekua and on up the hill to H-11, take the turnoff to the **Painted Church,** about one mile in, on a bumpy side road. This tiny church was the first of all the similar churches on the island.

For one more possible stop on your way home, turn left on Kuakini Hwy. in the Keauhou area and descend to sea level; opposite the Keauhou Beach Hotel you'll find **Kona Gardens,** a multimillion-dollar botanical and cultural park. Flowering plants from all of Polynesia are beginning to grow amid the lava flows, highlighting historical sites: *heiaus,* the ruins of a temple, petroglyphs. The 12-acre park offers botanical tours from 9 a.m. to 5 p.m. Monday through Friday, plus an audio-visual show about Hawaii and arts and crafts demonstrations. Admission is $5 for adults, free for children. Closed Sunday and Monday. On Saturday between 8 a.m. and 2:30 p.m. this is the site of a flea market that the locals rave about: locally grown fruit, Hawaiian books, crafts, junk, and treasures are all here at bargain-hunter prices. No admission fee to buyers.

Shopping in Kailua Village

Return now to the sun and fun of Kailua-Kona. It's a great place to shop, so poke in and out of the arcades along Alii Drive. The **Kona Shopping Village,** oceanside, has a huge collection of tasteful shops: **The Shellery,** for one, with its outstanding collections of pearls, coral, jade, lapis, and specimen shells, is a favorite of ours, as is **Noa Noa,** which offers hand-printed cotton batiks and other exotic clothes and jewelry from Bali and Indonesia. . . . Across Alii Drive, the **Kona Arts & Crafts Gallery** is a must stop for those interested in native Hawaiian crafts, everything from koa carvings to seaweed art to genuine hula instruments. . . . **Gifts for All Seasons** at the Hotel King Kamehameha shopping mall is known for wonderful soft-sculpture dolls, crocheted

pillowcovers from the Philippines, and many Christmas ornaments with a Hawaiian touch. . . . There are dozens of shops for
clothing that come and go, but you can always count on **Marlin
Casuals** in the **Kona Plaza Shopping Arcade** for lovely resort wear
at good prices. . . . And, in **World Square, Smuggler's Loft** is
crammed full of nautical brass, plus scrimshaw, jewelry, unusual
art works, and lots more.

Chapter X

THE VALLEY ISLAND: MAUI

THERE IS A LEGEND in the Valley Island that the great god Maui was powerful enough to stop the sun in its tracks. He lassoed the sun as it was making its way across Haleakala Crater one morning, and held it captive until it promised to slow up its route across the heavens, making the days longer and the skies brighter. The primitive Hawaiians never doubted the truth of this legend, and we are beginning to half-believe it too. For any force that could have created the island of Maui must have been doing something right. Oahu is 20th-century brilliant; Kauai is green and lush; Hawaii is immense and exciting—but Maui is pure gold. By all means, make a point of seeing it.

Fortunately, the treasures of Maui—its glorious beaches, its swinging little boating-shopping town of Lahaina, its remote jungle valleys, and its mighty giant of a sleeping volcano—are all just 88 miles from Honolulu. It's a short hop by jet to either Kahului Airport or the landing strip at Kaanapali, site of a resort-hotel building boom that, some claim, will make it another Waikiki in ten years. Don't wait. Get there now.

Plan to spend a minimum of three days, four or five if you have them, to sample the island's various charms. The Kahului area (on the bay, but no beach) is centrally located for sightseeing, but hotels here now cater mostly to large tour groups and local business people; the Kihei-Wailea area, about a 15-minute drive from Wailuku and on the beach, is the major destination in eastern Maui. Our personal favorite is the Lahaina-Kaanapali-Napili-Kapalua area in western Maui; although it is a 45-minute drive from Kahului, you'll be living at an exciting beach area, and the coastline is so gorgeous that coming home in the afternoon becomes just as much fun as starting out in the morning for a day of sightseeing.

WELCOME TO MAUI: The natives say that *Maui no ka oi* (there's no place better than Maui), and you'll begin to see why as soon as you arrive at Kahului Airport. The large reception lounge, with its contemporary architecture, is open at one end, so the outdoors beckons immediately. A car is a must, since there is very little public transportation. At the airport, **Holiday Hawaii Car Rentals** and **Budget,** among others, offer bargain rates. A phone call brings **Tropical Rent-A-Car** (tel. 877-0002) or **Atlas U-Drive** (tel. 244-7408) with other attractive deals. Best to reserve in advance.

Note: The local airlines and car-rental companies often offer special package deals with hotels on Maui; you might get a room and a car for $40 to $50 a day. Many of these offers can be booked only in Hawaii.

The telephone area code for all phones in the state of Hawaii is 808.

Hotels of Maui

HOTELS IN KAHULUI: The **Maui Hukilau,** Kahuli, HI 96732 (tel. 877-3311), is a cute little place right on Kahului Bay. The sandy beach that it fronts was once the site of an old *hukilau* fishing beach, and it's okay for swimming even though the currents are strong; but most of the hotel guests prefer to use the pool. The rooms are all attractively furnished and the rates are good: $40 standard, $44 superior, $48 deluxe, single or double; extra person, $5. Hotel, car, and breakfast plans are often available at good rates. The hotel has a pleasant dining room and bar, and many nights you'll get a good Hawaiian show along with your meal. See below for reservations information.

Also on the white-sand beach at Kahului is the pleasant **Maui Seaside Hotel,** Kahuli, HI 96732 (tel. 877-3311), all of whose rooms are air-conditioned, and have color TV, double beds, and a refrigerator. It's next door to the Maui Hukilau and uses the same swimming pool and dining facilities. Rates are $44, $50, and $55, single or double; extra person, $5. Hotel, car, and breakfast plans are available here, too. For reservations for both hotels, write to Hukilau Resorts, 2222 Kalakaua Ave., Suite 714, Honolulu, HI 96815, or phone toll free 800/367-7000.

HOTELS IN KIHEI AND WAILEA: For centuries, the calm beaches and

windswept sands of the Kihei area of Maui were left relatively
untouched. Even as tourist development boomed in the rest of
Maui, this dry, sunny area just a 15- to 20-minute drive from Kahului was practically undiscovered—one hotel, a few cottages,
that was it. But in the last ten years or so, Kihei has been discovered in a big way, and now, as the islanders say, it's wall-to-wall
condominiums. In the neighboring Wailea area, more condominiums as well as two luxury resorts, Hotel Inter-Continental Maui
and Stouffer's Wailea Beach Resort, have sprung up. And further along this coast, the super-luxurious Maui Prince Hotel has
opened at Makena. While Kihei lacks the heady excitement of
the Lahaina-Kaanapali-Napili area (less in the way of restaurants, nightlife, and shops), it is growing more interesting all the
time. And it does offer excellent, safe swimming beaches, acres
of peace and quiet, and plenty of apartment hotels that offer
space and comfort enough for a long stay. Many guests do, in
fact, winter in Kihei. The tourist who wishes to stay in Kihei has
literally dozens and dozens of choices that would require a book
in themselves to detail. The few mentioned below are among the
most attractive, and are typical of the many in the area. Note that
daily maid service is not the rule in the Kihei condominiums (although it is usually available at an extra price), so be sure to check
if this factor is important to you.

Each of the two-bedroom apartments at **Kihei Sands,** 115
North Kihei Rd., Kihei, HI 96753 (tel. 879-2624), is actually a
tiny little house; one of the bedrooms is on a balcony right above
the living room, the other is to the side. These cute, compact little
units also have two baths, a fully equipped kitchen, and a private
lanai, and they rent for $60 and up for four, with each extra per-
son charged $6, from April 16 to November 30. They can com-
fortably sleep up to six people. There are also pretty
one-bedroom apartments (without the upstairs) and these, capable of housing up to four, go for $45 and up double, with each
extra person charged $6. From December 1 to April 15, prices go
up $15 a day. Although the white-sand beach with its oh-so-calm
waters is perfect for swimming, Kihei Sands also boasts a freshwater pool. The shake roofs give this place a modern Polynesian
feeling that is quite charming. Three-day minimum stay.

High-rise rather than low-slung, **Kihei Beach Resort,** 36 South
Kihei Rd., Kihei, HI 96753 (tel. 879-2744, or toll free 800/367-
6034), is a handsomely modern place each of whose apartments
faces directly on the white-sand beach. The apartments are spacious and comfortable, the living-dining area is carpeted wall to
wall, and the electric kitchen is complete with every convenience.

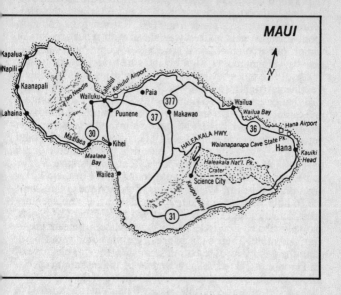

From April 16 to December 15, the one-bedroom apartments, big enough to sleep four (sofa bed in the living room, queen or twin beds in the bedroom), go for $58 for a double; $8 per extra person. The two-bedroom units, big enough for six, are $86 for four, $8 per extra person. Maid service is included in these rates. The rest of the year, prices are $16 to $22 higher. More pluses for the Kihei Beach: free coffee in the morning; a freshwater pool for swimming; the fact that you're within walking distance of Robaire's, a fine French restaurant and one of the better eating places in the area. Three-day minimum stay.

If you choose to stay at the **Punahoa Beach Apartments,** 2142 Iliili Rd., Kihei, HI 96753 (tel. 879-2720), you know that you'll be in good hands. Punahoa is a small place with just 15 units, all of which have a private lanai, ocean views, a fully equipped kitchen, telephone, and smart, modern furnishings. It's surrounded by gardens, and it's right on the ocean; sandy beaches, with good swimming and surfing, are adjacent; children love it around the rocks because of the fish. The studio apartments rent for $52 daily in winter (December 15 to April 14) and $39 in summer

(April 15 to December 14); one-bedroom units are $68 and $50; the one-bedroom penthouse is $70 and $52; and the two-bedroom apartments are $75 and $60. Rates may be going up soon. Punahoa gets booked way ahead with repeat visitors in winter, but accommodations are easier to come by in summer. Five-day minimum stay. Monthly rates are available year round.

About five miles beyond Kihei, in Wailea, is the **Maui Inter-Continental Wailea** (tel. 879-1922), a 600-room, 18-acre luxury villa that has managed to translate the island feeling of comfort and casual living into a setting of relaxed elegance. Grounds are spacious, vistas are large, and there seems to be no separation between indoors and outdoors. Just about everything one could want from resort life is here, including two beautiful ocean beaches and three freshwater pools. Tennis buffs have 3 grass courts and 11 all-weather Laykold courts (three of them lit for night play) at nearby Wailea Tennis Club; and the golfers have the 36-hole Wailea Golf Course very close by. Complimentary guest activities range from windsurfing and Hobie Cat clinics, snorkel/scuba classes, to lei making, hula classes, pineapple cutting, and more. There's no chance of getting bored eating here, since there is a slew of restaurants, ranging from the elegance of La Perouse, a *Travel/Holiday* award-winning restaurant specializing in seafood, to the relaxed island charm of the inexpensive Makani Restaurant. The hotel is *the* evening entertainment spot on this part of the island, with Hawaiian entertainment, dancing, and disco every night.

Newly renovated guest rooms and suites utilize beautiful island woods, rattan headboards, and color schemes of peach and turquoise. They are large and comfortable, with king-size or twin beds, private lanai, air conditioning, radio, color TV. Rates for a single or double twin room from December 20 through April 30 are $133 mountain view, $155 ocean view, $175 oceanfront; the rest of the year, they go down to $110, 130, and $150; a third person is charged $15 more. Inquire about special room-and-car and family-plan packages.

For toll-free reservations, phone 800/367-2960. In Honolulu, phone 537-5589.

It's luxury all the way at the **Stouffer Wailea Beach Resort,** 3550 Wailea Alanui Dr., HI 96753 (tel. 879-4900), one of Maui's premier resorts, a playground for sybarites set in lush tropical gardens sloping to the sea on 15 beachfront acres. From the stunning weavings and murals in the lobby to the outdoor sculptures in the seaside gardens to the glamorous dining spots and beautifully furnished accommodations, there's a high standard of taste and elegance here that makes it easy to see why the Wailea Beach is the only Hawaii resort to receive the A A A Five Diamond Award for five consecutive years—not to mention the *Travel/Holiday* award for Raffles, its fine dining restaurant, for six years. The hotel has just about everything for an active or blissfully lazy vacation, including shuttle service to two 18-hole championship golf courses and the Wailea Tennis Club (dubbed "Wimbledon West" with its three grass and 11 Laykold courts, three lit for night play); swimming at five sandy beaches or a superb pool; snorkeling off a coral reef; classes in lei making or hula or aerobics. In addition to the prize-winning Raffles (patterned after the famous Raffles' Hotel in Singapore, and known for continental cuisine and the most elaborate Sunday champagne brunch in Maui), there's the delightfully casual Palm Court, which features a different international buffet nightly; the cute little Maui Onion, a gazebo restaurant poolside; the Sunset Terrace for cocktails with a view; and Lost Horizon, a contemporary nightclub for dancing. Tuesday night's luau is considered one of the best on Maui.

The 350 rooms are lovely in an elegantly understated way—quite large, done in a contemporary Hawaiian motif, with bamboo, wicker, or rattan furnishings. All have a private lanai with an ocean, garden, or mountain view; a refrigerator with stocked bar; color TV with in-room movies; individual air conditioning controls; and a direct-dial telephone. The morning wakeup call brings complimentary coffee and the daily paper.

Room rates (subject to change) are $185 double for deluxe on the mountain side, $215 for deluxe oceanside; rooms at the Mokapu Beach Club and suites go much higher. A third and fourth person in a room is $25 each; children 18 or under stay in their parents' room free; an extra room required for a family is 50% less, complimentary during the summer. Families will also do well to take advantage of the Stouffer Family Summer program, which offers a special rate—it could be as low as $125—for vacations between mid-May and mid-September. And that includes complimentary breakfast or dinner for children, too. In addition, there's an excellent activities program for kids 5 to 12, available at a nominal fee.

For information and reservations (inquire also about special packages), phone toll free 800/HOTELS-1 from U.S. and Canada.

HOTELS IN LAHAINA: Although the major resort areas of Kaanapali and Kapalua are not far away, there's a certain ramshackle charm about staying right in Lahaina. Once the capital of the islands, a town with a history as a whaling port and a current free-wheeling ambience that matches those lusty days, Lahaina is a fun-and-games town from morning through night.

If you'd like to settle into your own little apartment right in Lahaina, then **Lahaina Roads,** 1403 Front St., Lahaina, HI 96761 (tel. 661-3166, or toll free 800/624-8203), could be your place. The five-story elevator building at the Kaanapali end of Front Street sits in a cool and breezy spot right on a good snorkeling beach; you can look down at the ocean—and watch some spectacular sunsets—from your own lanai. A swimming beach is half a mile up the road, but there's a freshwater pool right at home. These are condominium apartments, many of them exquisitely furnished by their absentee owners. They are soundproof, with wall-to-wall carpeting, fully equipped kitchens with washer and dryer, large living rooms with convertible couches, and there are phones for free local calls in your room. One-bedroom apartments go for $60 a day double in summer, $65 in winter (they can accommodate up to four people); two-bedrooms for $68 and $73 double (capable of accommodating up to six); and there are two delightful penthouses (that can house up to six of you) for $120 and $130 for four. Additional persons are $6. Three-day minimum stay. Write them in advance.

Situated right in the heart of Lahaina town, the **Maui Islander,** 660 Wainee St., Lahaina, HI 96761 (tel. 667-9766, or toll free 800/367-5226), is great for anyone who doesn't want to be bothered driving everywhere; it's within a short walking distance of a good swimming beach, the activities of Lahaina Harbor, and all the shops and restaurants and nightlife of Front Street. Set amid nine acres of tropical grounds, the Maui Islander consists of nine two-story buildings containing 374 units, a combination of hotel rooms, studios, and apartments, all of which offer daily maid service, telephone, and color TV. All except the hotel units also have a fully equipped kitchen for cooking at home. There's an attractive pool and sunning area, a tennis court lit at night, a recreation room, a hospitable staff and plenty of activities. The price is excellent: $65 for two people in a hotel room, $75 for three in a studio, $85 for four in a one-bedroom. From December 20 to March 31, add $8 per unit.

HOTELS AT KAANAPALI BEACH: Just three miles north of Lahaina is what surely must be one of the great resort areas anywhere in the world—Kaanapali Beach. Stretched out along this fabled strip of white sand, crystal waters, and gentle, rolling surf, with a championship golf course sloping down to the sea and the West Maui mountains offering spectacular vistas in the background, is a small cluster of luxury hotels. We doubt if you could go wrong at any of them, but each offers something a little bit special.

Perhaps the grandest of these resorts is the $80-million **Hyatt Regency Maui** (tel. 677-7474, or toll free 800/228-9000), which opened in 1980. Breathtaking is the word for this 815-room seaside caravanserai, which covers 18 acres of prime beachfront and is spangled with eight major waterfalls, Japanese gardens and lagoons, underground grottoes, meandering streams along which swans glide, and an exceptional pool—half an acre of fresh water that roams under waterfalls and bridges, along gardens and lava rocks, and offers swimmers a sensational 130-foot slide. A 70-foot-tall banyan tree dominates the atrium lobby, which is dotted with plantings, gardens, and tropical birds—flamingos, parrots, peacocks, even penguins. And throughout the lobby and the adjoining luxury shopping arcade (a kind of Rodeo Drive of the islands) is $2-million worth of original artworks, mostly from the Far East and the South Pacific. Such a setup is, of course, a sightseeing attraction; tours for the public are held daily at varying times.

But if you are a guest at this hotel, you have a wealth of activities to choose from—Robert Trent Jones's 36-hole golf course right at hand, five all-weather-surface tennis courts, an underground health spa. Classes and clinics go on all day, in sailing, aquatrimatics (water exercises), hula, and coconut weaving, to name just a few. And dining facilities are as splendid as you would imagine. There are the Swan Court (with real swans) for continental and seafood specialties; Lahaina Provision Company, a garden-like, casual setting for grilled-to-order meats and huge salads; Spats, an Italian café where the pasta is fine, the decor is early 1920s, and disco rules the night; the Pavillion, for poolside cafeteria dining; and several bars and lounges, including the "sunken" Grotto pool bar. The Sunset Terrace is the scene of Hyatt's Polynesian Revue, *Drums of the Pacific*.

As for the rooms, they are spacious, artfully decorated in quiet earth tones, and provide every comfort: air conditioning, color TV, private phones, full bathrooms, sitting areas, tasteful artworks on the walls. Prices vary according to the view, from garden to golf/mountain to oceanfront. Single or twin, they are $155, $185, $215, and $255 to $285 for Regency Club. Suites range all the way from $400 for a Golf Suite to $1,400 for the Presidential digs. Each additional person is charged $25; children under 12 stay free with parents; maximum of three in a room.

A longtime favorite at Kaanapali is the **Royal Lahaina Resort,**

2780 Kekaa Dr., Lahaina, HI 96761 (tel. 661-3611, or toll free 800/227-4700), with 514 rooms, cottages, and suites spread out on 26 acres of beautiful tropical gardens fronting the beach. Recreational facilities are magnificent: you can play at 11 tennis courts (including one stadium court), six of them lighted at night; golf at the magnificent Robert Trent Jones courses adjacent to the hotel; swim at any of three pools or in the glorious ocean; or indulge in a multitude of water-sports activities. You can shop at some of the best stores in Maui in two separate shopping arcades, and dine at a bevy of splendid restaurants including **Moby Dick's** for seafood as good as it is in New England, **Don the Beachcomber** for Polynesian and Cantonese specialties, and the **Royal Ocean Terrace** for all three meals, plus a great Sunday champagne brunch. There's an old-fashioned ice-cream parlor, three cocktail lounges, even a nightly luau. Once you've settled in here, there's little reason to go anywhere else.

Now for the rooms. Even those at the lowest rate—$95, single or double—are spacious and equipped with color television, air conditioning, phone, refrigerator, and a combination bath and dressing room. Rooms go up to $200, single or double, while the one-, two-, and three-bedroom suites are in the $350 to $500 range; a third person in the room is $15, which includes a rollaway; no charge for cribs. Request king- or queen-size beds in advance. Full American Plan is available at $51, MAP at $40.

Surrounding the Royal Lahaina are the spectacular Maui mountains, incredible views of Lanai and Molokai, and of course the sparkling Pacific. For reservations, write AmFac Hotels, P.O. Box 8519, Honolulu, HI 96830; or write directly to the Royal Lahaina.

Maui's newest showplace is the **Westin Maui,** a $125-million remake of the venerable Maui Surf Hotel. And investor Christopher Hemmeter (the force behind the new Westin Kauai and Hyatt Regency Maui, among others) has seen to it that this will be one of the ultimate luxury playgrounds of the islands. Situated on 12 acres of glorious sandy beach, great for swimming, snorkeling, windsurfing, the Westin Maui (still under construction at the time of this writing) will also feature a spectacular, multilevel swimming pool complex: five pools, fed by four waterfalls, connected by a network of super-slides and bridges, with the Island Bar in the center, so guests can swim right up for a drink. At 25,000 square feet, it's over twice the size of the gigantic pool at the Hyatt Regency Maui. Sports and recreational facilities will also include a European-style health club, access to Kaanapali's two famed 18-hole, par 72 golf courses, and tennis nearby.

Guests enter the hotel through a spectacular lobby cooled by waterfalls and exotic plantings, with swans gliding just a few feet away from the registration desk. Two millions dollars' worth of art work will grace the public areas and gardens. Restaurants and lounges include everything from a 250-seat coffeeshop to the luxurious Villa Restaurant, where guests will dine on continental cuisine with a view of ocean, pools, slides, and waterfalls. The 762 guest units, including 28 suites and 43 rooms at the Royal Beach Club, will be handsomely decorated, each with a mini-bar and refrigerator. Rates will definitely be in the luxury category.

For reservations and information, call toll free 800/228-3000, or write the Westin Maui, 1775 Ala Moana Blvd., Suite 221, Honolulu, HI 96815.

One of the first hotels to be built on the Kaanapali strip, the **Sheraton-Maui** (tel. 661-0031; reservations, toll free 800/325-3535) has been blessed with a spectacular location. It is wrapped around a crater called Black Rock (the ancient cliff from which souls of Hawaiians were said to leap to the spirit world beyond), and its main building winds around the rock in a series of descending, curving parapets that are really the balconies of individual rooms. There's also another wing that is more conventionally high-rise. In both buildings, each room is of good size, has its own private balcony or garden, and tub-shower combination, plus an optional refrigerator on wheels for a modest rental fee. Depending on the view, doubles run from $105 to $165 for rooms in various buildings, the top price being for oceanfront cabañas or "cottages." Ocean-view suites are $250 to $650; a third person in the room costs $15 more; no charge for children under 18. From December 21 through March 31, there's a $10 to $25 increment.

There's a great deal to look at in this hotel. The old lobby with the sky for a roof from which you take the elevators *down* to everything is beautiful, with its pool, fountains, and sculpture; off it is the stylish Discovery Room, for continental dining and nightly entertainment. The Black Rock Terrace at poolside serves breakfast, lunch, and casual evening meals. The beach here is one of the favorites at Kaanapali. Snorkeling buffs love the long reef that goes out from Black Rock, and golfers have the Robert Trent Jones Royal Kaanapali Golf Club next door—so everybody's happy.

Indoors and outdoors merge gracefully at the **Maui Marriott Resort,** 100 Nohea Kai Dr., Lahaina, HI 96761 (tel. 228-9290, or toll free 800/228-9290), which opened in 1981. Since the hotel is built around a courtyard, there's an outdoorsy feeling to the lobby and shopping arcades. The resort, very popular with families, has a pool with whirlpool spa, its own catamarans to use sailing at the beautiful beach, a game room, an exercise room, tennis courts, golf nearby, and four restaurants, including the airy Moana Terrace, where you can have your meals overlooking the water; and Nikko, a Japanese steakhouse (the only teppanyaki restaurant in the Lahaina-Kaanapali area). The rooms, done in subtle earth tones of browns and muted golds, are furnished very tastefully; much use is made of rattan and dark woods. All have lanais and the usual luxury hotel amenities. Rates are for single or double occupancy; except for "parlors" and suites, all rooms are basically the same (the view and location account for the wide disparity in price). Rooms facing the mountains or golf course are $135; those with partial ocean view are $165; ocean view is $190 and oceanfront—nothing between you and the deep blue sea—is $205. Large suites go from $375 to $1,000, depending on location. An extra person in the room is charged $25 a day! With rates like these, your best bet here is to take the "Aloha Plan"; based on double occupancy only, it is $87.50 per person. For that price, you get a mountain/ocean-view room, a breakfast buffet for two, a National rental car, and a free hour's use of the tennis court or beach services.

A budget hotel on Kaanapali Beach? There's really no such animal, but rates are a bit lower at the **Kaanapali Beach Hotel**, 2525 Kaanapali Parkway, Lahaina, HI 96761 (tel. 661-0011), and it's also a lovely place, right out on the ocean, with an intriguing swimming pool shaped like a whale, acres of trees and flowers, and a full complement of restaurants and drinking spots. Each room has its own private lanai, and is large, air-conditioned, attractively decorated, with the convenience of a refrigerator and color television set. The price for minimum rooms is $100. Medium, deluxe, and waterfront rooms and suites go up the scale to $150, single or double. And for those budget meals, it's nice to know that the coffeehouse offers dinners from about $7 to $9.

HOTELS BETWEEN KAANAPALI AND KAPALUA: Once you pass the big hotels of the Kaanapali area, you're smack into condominium country. Between Kaanapali and Kapalua, miles and miles of curving coastline are being given over to small apartment hotels that provide every home-away-from-home comfort in an idyllic setting that's nothing like home. Most of these operate exactly like a hotel. Apartments can be rented on a daily, weekly, or monthly basis; frequent maid and linen service are provided, and the management takes care of all repairs and services. Most do not have restaurants on the premises, but they all have kitchen facilities, and restaurants abound all over the area. *Note:* Since some condominiums do expect you to do your own housework, be sure to inquire about all such details before you send your deposit.

Just about our favorite place here, the **Maui Sands Hotel,** 3559 Lower Honoapiilani Rd., Lahaina, HI 96761 (tel. 669-6391, or toll free 800/367-5037), is only a mile from the Kaanapali hotels, and has accommodations as comfortable as any luxury suite at about one-third the price. The 76 one- and two-bedroom suites are set in either a beautiful tropic garden or on the oceanfront. These have enormous living rooms with private lanais (great for star-gazing at night), comfortable-size bedrooms, full electric kitchens, tropical ceiling fans, air conditioning, and color television; a family has plenty of room to really stretch out and relax here. Since each apartment is individually owned, the furnishings are slightly different in each, but all are well appointed and comfortable. Everything has been newly refurbished. The top accommodation, a two-bedroom apartment overlooking the beach, goes for $108 for four persons. In the garden, it's $89; and near the road, $77. One-bedroom apartments for two people are $83 for oceanfront, $68 for the garden, and $55 for standard. Extra persons are charged $6. Kids love the swimming pool and sunning area, mom appreciates the convenience of the laundry, and everybody loves the beach. You'll get free Hawaiian entertainment once a week in season, cocktail parties every other week, and a cordial reception up at the front desk. Inquire about their luxury units on the beach at Papakea, next door.

Just a bit farther north in Honokowai, **Hale Ono Loa** (the "House of Good Living"), 3823 Honoapiilani Rd., Honokowai, Lahaina, HI 96761 (tel. 669-6362, or toll free 800/367-2927), offers just that. Some 67 condominium apartments in a four-story building are set in a very beautiful garden, with a large pool area in the central courtyard ringed by palm trees. The pool and sundeck—big enough so that guests can play coconut checkers, shuffleboard, or Ping-Pong—is the center of social life here. You can wade out between the coral reefs for swimming and snorkeling, or walk 2½ blocks to a sandy beach. Apartments are individually furnished and decorated, and have very well-equipped kitchens and either one or two bedrooms. Rates for a one-bedroom suite with a garden view are $75, single or double; with partial ocean view, $80; with full ocean view, $85. For a two-bedroom suite, the rates are $100, $110, and $120. These rates apply to stays of one or two days; on stays of three days or more, they go down $10 in each category. During the winter season, December 15 to April 15, rates go up $10 to $20 in each category. All apartments are oriented to the trade winds, and have a large lanai, which makes sunset watching, whale watching and just plain relaxing very popular activities here.

Surprisingly enough, really good beaches are not so easy to find along the coastline. Many of the apartment hotels are built on rocky beachfronts or storms have blown away sandy beaches, so guests do most of their swimming in pools. One place that is, however, blessed with a beautiful, reef-protected crescent beach is **Kahana Sunset** on Kahana Bay, about midway between Kaanapali and Napili (P.O. Box 10219, Lahaina, HI 96761; tel. 669-8011). There are other things to commend this place too, notably the 79 units that meander down a gentle hillside and are adequately spaced for privacy, comfort, and good ocean views. We especially like the two-bedroom units, which are like little two-story town houses with twin stairways leading to the bedrooms and two baths; from April 15 through December 15, they run from $105 for two, up to $129 for six. There's a $20 surcharge during high season. Slightly larger two-bedroom, 2½-bathroom units—called executive town houses—go from $145 to $169, and one-bedroom apartments run from $80 to $92 in season, with surcharges of $10 to $20 during high season. It's $6 for each additional person (maximum of four in the one-bedrooms, six in the two-bedrooms). All the units are handsomely furnished and have a full electric kitchen with all the comforts a suburban matron might want: dishwasher, garbage disposal, self-cleaning oven, refrigerator and freezer with an automatic ice-maker, even one's own washer-dryer. Besides the good beach, there's a freshwater swimming pool, croquet, and barbecue pits down on the beach. The Quigley family are in charge here, and every Friday night they offer a fish fry for their guests.

You can also be assured of an excellent swimming beach at a clutch of small hotels coming up now on Napili Bay. Here's where the **Mauian Hotel,** 5441 Honoapiilani Rd., Lahaina, HI 96761 (tel. 669-6205, or toll free 800/367-5034), one of the first in this area, is still going strong. Its 44 Polynesian-style units are fitted out with a queen-size bed and two twins to accommodate four persons. They boast fully equipped electric kitchens, private lanais, and plenty of ocean breezes whooshing through. There's a pool for those who can forgo the superb beach, a laundry area, even an island-style mini-supermarket that makes cooking a breeze. There are golf courses and many good restaurants nearby. Rates are $70, $75, and $90 daily, single or double. Maid service every three days; 10% more for daily service.

Napili Village, 5425 Honoapiilani Rd., Lahaina, HI 96761 (tel. 669-6228, or toll free 800/336-2185; from Canada, call collect), a stone's throw away from the Mauian, is another popular and well-established place in the lovely Napili area. Each of the 28 units is capable of housing four, with a folding door creating two separate sleeping areas, one with a king-size bed and the other with twins or a queen-size sofa sleeper. An all-electric kitchen, a large lanai, wall-to-wall carpeting, cable TV, radio, and daily maid service make for comfortable living. You have a lovely pool and the beach is just a few steps away, but there are no beach-front accommodations. The mini-supermarket, mentioned above, is just behind the pool, and there are also barbecues. Rates begin at $55 in summer, $65 in winter, double or single; $5 for each extra person.

A true luxury setup on Napili Bay is **Napili Surf Beach Resort,** Napili Bay, HI 96761 (tel. 669-8002 or 669-8003), which offers plenty of aloha along with beautiful beachfront accommodations. Spaciousness and comfort are the big things here: the studio apartments each contain 500 square feet; the one-bedroom units contain 670 square feet. Each apartment has an all-electric kitchen. All units are soundproof, carpeted, and handsomely furnished. The choice of either the freshwater swimming pool or that blue Pacific is yours. Rates are $59 single and $64 double in the smaller but cozy Puamala garden studios; $69 and $74 in the ocean-view studios; and $97 in the one-bedroom apartments on the beachfronting property. It's $10 for an extra person. Summer specials usually offer lower rates. The managers can usually arrange car rentals and trips at 15% to 20% discounts.

Perched on a hill overlooking Napili Bay, **Napili Point Resort,** P.O. Box 5183, Lahaina, HI 96761 (tel. 669-9222), is a beautiful hotel in a dramatic setting. Gently sloping lawns, along which the 100 all-suite units are set, lead down to a sandy beach fine for snorkeling; a better swimming beach is just a few steps away. There are two freshwater pools (one out on a cliff overlooking the bay) and a picnic area for barbecuing; guests enjoy complimentary tennis privileges at a nearby condo. Each of the units is a charming little home, tastefully decorated, with a dropped living room, white furniture, good art on the walls. Spacious lanais afford ocean views. Each includes an all-electric kitchen with washer-dryer and dishwasher, and each has direct-dial telephone and color cable TV. Napili Point is a condo, but it offers hotel services: a resident manager on duty around the clock to provide assistance, and daily maid service. From April 1 to December 19, the rate for a superior one-bedroom suite with ocean view, is $100 for up to four persons; deluxe oceanfront is $110. A two-bedroom, two-bath suite with ocean view is $130 for up to six persons; deluxe oceanfront is $145. During the peak winter season, rates go up $20 per unit. Reservations: Write Aston, 22255 Kuhio Ave., Honolulu, HI 96815, or call toll free 800/367-5124.

The **Napili Kai Beach Club,** 5900 Honoapiilani Rd., Lahaina, HI 96761 (tel. 669-6025, or toll free 800/367-5030), offers luxury-plus accommodations on gorgeous Napili Bay, as well as tennis courts, four swimming pools and a 20-foot whirlpool, two putting greens, and a very good dining spot: the Sea House Restaurant. Guests here say they never want to leave. You can get a standard room for $105 single, $110 double. Deluxe ocean-view and oceanfront rooms are $130 and $150 respectively. Suites for two are $140 to $170; for three to four, $115 to $275. (Rates subject to change.) The rooms all have kitchenette, lanai, color TV, and telephone. The ocean swimming is great.

Should you happen to have a generous fairy godmother (or godperson, as the case may be) who will grant you a special wish, ask for a stay at **Kapalua Bay Hotel,** 1 Bay Dr., Kapalua, HI 96761 (tel. toll free 800/367-8000), near the northern tip of the island. Picture a 750-acre resort complex, surrounded by ocean and bay, by coconut palms and tall pines, by flowering gardens and gentle landscapes at every turn, combining the ultimate in continental hotel service and elegance with the graceful aloha of island living, and you'll get some idea of what Kapalua Bay is all about. "No compromise" is the watchword here. Kapalua Bay provides three sandy ocean beaches for swimming; a freshwater pool; two 18-hole championship golf courses designed by Arnold Palmer; a "tennis garden" (ten courts surrounded by lush greenery); many dining facilities, including the intimate Plantation Veranda, which has won awards from *Travel/Holiday* magazine for gourmet cuisine, the Grill & Bar for informal food and panoramic views, and the Bay Club, just above the beach, for drinks and dining overlooking a spectacular setting—for starters. Buffet lunches served daily in the Mayfair Buffet are among the special treats of the islands (see ahead).

The guest rooms are gracious beauties, tastefully decorated in subdued South Seas style, all in tones of rust or blue. They have twin or king-size beds, his-and-hers baths, small refrigerators in the dividers between bed and sitting areas, floor-to-ceiling shutters leading out to large lanais, and high ceilings (they are reminiscent, in fact, of rooms at the Kahala Hilton in Honolulu and were designed by the same person). Rooms are all the same; only their location makes for a price differential. From December 20 to April 15, standard garden-view rooms are $150, single or double; prime garden-view rooms are $175; standard ocean-view rooms are $225; prime ocean-view rooms are $250; and ocean-front rooms are $300. Between April 16 and December 19, rates descend a bit to $120, $150, $175, $225, and $275, respectively. An extra person is charged $35 more per day. Prices are subject to change. Family Plan is sometimes available. Modified American Plan is available for an extra fee. Discounts are offered on greens fees, golf carts, and tennis.

Kapalua Bay also boasts one of the most tasteful shopping arcades in the islands. The Shops at Kapalua, which contains its own little European-style Market Café.

Should you prefer your own apartment at Kapalua, the **Bay Villas,** 1 Bay Dr., Kapalua, HI 96761 (tel. toll free 800/367-8000), are for you. There are 141 of these condominium apartments on the grounds, and it's luxury all the way—beautiful furnishings, spectacular views, sunken tile baths, wall-to-wall carpeting, washer-dryers, complete kitchens, plus daily maid service. From December 19 to April 16, one-bedroom apartments are $175 fairway view, $225 ocean view, $300 oceanfront. From April 17 to December 18 they go for $125, $150, and $200, respectively. Two-bedroom apartments, in season, are $275 for fairway view, $325 for ocean view, and $400 for oceanfront; off-season, rates are $180, $225, and $290. These rates are all subject to change.

HIDEOUTS IN HANA: Because of its remoteness, separated as it is from the rest of Maui by the mighty bulk of Haleakala, Hana has remained one of the few places to maintain the spirit of Old Hawaii. And nowhere is this spirit more evident than at **Hotel Hana-Maui** (reservations, toll free 800/321-4262), a favorite retreat for the privileged few since it opened its doors in 1946. Now that a new management has taken over, changes are evident—in the new porte-cochere and series of open-air courtyards leading to the main lobby; in the dramatically redesigned dining room with an ocean-view terrace; in the guestrooms redone with French windows, new furnishings, and large expanses of French doors opening onto trellised verandas. New cottages take advantage of sweeping ocean views. But the gracious, garden setting, with one-storied bungalows (there are only 82 rooms and suites on the 23-acre property) spread out on lush tropical grounds, and the central building with its open courtyard housing the lobby, restaurant, bar, library, and gift shop, is still the same. The Hana-Maui's staff, most of them Hawaiian, are family members who have been welcoming guests here for generations. Days are given to horseback riding on the gorgeous trails, swimming at beautiful Hamoa Beach or in the heated swimming pool, playing tennis on two courts, trying the par 3, 18-hole pitch 'n' putt golf course, participating in such events as ukulele or hula lessons, lei making, rock painting, or just gathering around the lava-rock fireplace in the library for games or conversation. Luncheon barbecues, cookouts at a secluded beach, as well as a cocktail party at the former plantation manager's home, are all weekly events.

All rates at Hana-Maui include meals, a skillful blending of international, American, and Hawaiian cuisines. For one person, Full American Plan is $241, $321, $331, and $341 per day; for two persons, it is $380, $390, and $400; a child up to seven is charged $43 in his parents' room; an extra adult, $85.

For budget accommodations in Hana, try the comfy little **Aloha Cottages,** (P.O. Box 205, Hana, HI 96713; tel. 248-8420), where Mr. and Mrs. Nakamura will make you feel right at home. A mere $45 to $48 per night gives you a two-bedroom redwood cottage with living room, complete kitchen, and bathroom, very clean and tidy, and with a view of Hana Bay. Write to them at the address above, or write to Stan and Suzanne Collins, the managers at **Hana Bay Vacation Rentals,** (P.O. Box 318, Hana, HI 96713; tel. 248-7727), who offer a number of apartments, homes, and cabins in the Hana area, with prices beginning at around $50 per night.

Dining in Maui

RESTAURANTS IN THE KAHULUI-WAILUKU AREA: Excellent Chinese food can be found at **Ming Yuen,** 162 Alamaha St., in the Kahului Light Industrial Park, off Hwy. 380. The local people rave about both the Cantonese and Szechuan specialties here—the former light and delicate, the latter spicy hot at times—and we agree. Favorite dishes like almond duck, lemon chicken, mu shu pork, oysters with ginger scallions, and sweet-and-sour shrimp run from about $4.75 to $7.25. A whole fresh steamed fish is occasionally available, and a special treat. Dinner is from 5 to 9 p.m. daily; lunch, Monday through Saturday, from 11 a.m. to 2 p.m. (tel. 871-7787 for reservations).

Natural food fans will be happy to know about **McHealthy's,** right near the Kahului Airport, at 460 Dairy Rd., which serves up tasty entrees like char-broiled tempeh, chicken breasts, mahi-mahi with brown rice and garden salad ($2.95 to $4.75), plus stuffed potatoes, good salads, sandwiches, smoothies, and the like. Open daily until 6 p.m., only until 2 p.m. weekends (tel. 871-6618). And **Down to Earth Natural Foods** in Wailuku serves a hot vegetarian lunch special every day for under $4. They're at 1910 Vineyard St.

For a bit of local color along with a budget lunch, try **Naokee's Restaurant,** at 1792 Main St., in Wailuku (tel. 244-9444). At lunchtime, entrees like teriyaki steak, sirloin butt, mahimahi, etc., are just $3.95; an eight-ounce New York steak is $4.95; a one-pound New York steak is $6.95. And that includes rice, vegetables, potato or macaroni salad, and soup. Coffee is extra. At night, many varieties of steak, plus lobster, island prawns, etc., all served with soup, salad, coffee or tea, average $8.75 to $16.50 —still good value for the money. In Lahaina, look for Naokee's Too, a family-type restaurant, at 1307 Front St.

RESTAURANTS IN KIHEI: If your idea of a good meal is delicious Mexican food, frosty margaritas and daiquiris, a lively atmosphere, and a congenial crowd to enjoy it all with, you've come to the right place. Kihei has not one, but two, most agreeable Mexican restaurants, and the visitors are *loco* about both; take your choice, or better yet, sample them both. Across from Kamaole Beach Park at Kai Nani Village is **La Familia** (tel. 879-8824), a Maui institution for over a dozen years, in locations here and at Kaanapali Beach. The attractive dining room overlooks the ocean, the sunset, and all of that, but most of the action is right in the dining room, around the bar, and on the outdoor lanai; a lively crowd starts gathering as soon as the $1.25 frosty margaritas become available during the 2 to 6 p.m. Happy Hour. As for the food, served from 4 to 10 p.m., it's great and prices are reasonable: have some nachos or a Maui Wowie to begin, then plan on spending between $6.95 and $9.50 for specialties like macho burrito, tostada suprême, chili relleno. Combination plates run $8.50. Mini-desserts like Kahlúa pudding and such coffee-liqueur combinations as Peppermint Pattie (hot chocolate with peppermint schnapps and whipped cream) are great winders-up. Open daily, cocktails till midnight.

If we had a few years of our life just to laze away, we'd probably do it watching the water and the waves and the whales and the sunset on the huge, umbrellaed dining lanai of **Polli's on the Beach,** at Kealia Beach Center, 101 North Kihei Rd. (tel. 879-5275). Indoors, Polli's has an attractive Mexican environment (straw chairs, piñatas, tiles, etc.), and in both areas, good drinks (Happy Hour, 2:30 to 5:30 p.m.) and delicious and well-priced food: à la carte entrees like quesadillas, burritos, and chimichangas run from about $3 to $5; combination plates are $7.50 to $8.50; and appetizers go from $2.50 to $4. Fresh fish, lobster, and steaks are also featured. Dessert freaks should know about the buñelos—vanilla ice cream topped with cinnamon and pure maple syrup, atop a Mexican pastry base. Polli's is open daily from 11 a.m. to midnight, serving food from 11 a.m. to 3 p.m., and from 5 to 10 p.m. Sunday brunch begins at 9:30 a.m.

A great place to cool off on a hot Kihei night, the **Maui Outrigger,** 2980 South Kihei Rd., is housed in a low-slung wooden frame building directly on the waterfront. You could literally jump from your table onto the beach—but don't. Stay and eat. The food is good and the mood convivial. Fanned white napkins on red tablecloths, paintings on rock walls, flowers on every table, a lively atmosphere at the bar are background to a mostly seafood-and-steak menu that runs from $8.95 for the giant salad bar to about $14.95 for scampi. Catch of the day, surf and turf (filet and chicken or steak), and Makena teriyaki broiled chicken are all crowd pleasers; so are the pastas, priced from $10.95 to $12.95, including the salad bar. Early-bird dinner specials are often featured. Lunch—mostly burgers, omelets, and quiches—is served from 11:30 a.m. to 2:30 p.m., dinner from 5:30 to 9:30 p.m. The bar opens at 3 p.m. Reservations: 879-1581.

We've yet to find a Maui resident who doesn't sing the praises of the **Kihei Prime Rib House,** 2511 South Kihei Rd. (tel. 879-1954); once you've dined there, you'll know why. The rustic, South Seas–style building is decorated with handsome woodcarvings and original paintings; its dining room affords splendid views of the sunset over the ocean; and its kitchen is known for superb prime ribs, seafood, steaks, and a huge salad bar brimming with fresh, locally grown fruits and vegetables—one of the best in the islands. Prices begin at $8.95 for salad bar alone, and go up to $18.95; a special combination of prime ribs and scampi is very popular at $17.95. All entrees include either fettuccine or rice, and home-baked bread, plus your choice of salad bar, Caesar salad, or red snapper chowder. If you like to dine early, make reservations for the popular Early Bird Special, served every night between 5 and 6 p.m.: Polynesian chicken, prime rib dinner, or fresh island fish are $11.95. Dinner only, 5 to 10 p.m., with piano entertainment nightly.

A RESTAURANT UP-COUNTRY: Our favorite up-country Maui restau-

rant, right in the heart of Paia (which makes it an ideal stop to or
from Hana or Haleakala), is **Dillon's Hideaway,** 89 Hana Hwy.
(tel. 579-9113). Dillon's is very cozy, very relaxed, the kind of
place where you want to have a long, cool, tropical drink and rap
with the locals. But don't think that the relaxed attitude extends
to the kitchen: standards are strict; everything is fresh, cooked to
order, and delicious. The day starts early for travelers up and
about on the road to Hana: eggs Benedict (a special at $4.95 be-
tween 8 and 9 a.m.), french toast with Kahlúa, delicious frittatas
(open-faced vegetarian omelets), homemade quiches, and fresh
raspberry pancakes! Most of these goodies are available at lunch,
plus a mahimahi plate for $7.95, excellent hamburgers and sal-
ads, meatball heroes, and more. Dinner runs around $10 to $11
for a complete meal; your main course might be pepper steak, a
house pasta, or mahimahi. A vegetarian or meat lasagne with
soup or salad and French bread can do you nicely too, for $7.95
or $8.95. Burgers are on the dinner menu too. Have the home-
made cheesecake for dessert. The kitchen and bar are open con-
tinuously, with pupus available until closing. Dillon's is open
early to quite late.

RESTAURANTS FROM LAHAINA TO KAPALUA: The **Oceanhouse Restaurant,** on the waterfront at 831 Front St. (tel. 661-3359) has
been a local favorite for about 15 years now, known for consistently topnotch and super-fresh fish and seafood. The setting can
scarcely be improved upon, since the open dining lanai is right
out there over the water, just perfect for those magnificent Maui
sunsets. Come early, around 6, and you probably won't have to
wait for a table. The problem comes when deciding what to order
—if you dine with local Maui people, as we did, they'll all have a
favorite they claim is the best thing on the menu. The house specialty, scampi à la Oceanhouse—jumbo shrimp sautéed in garlic
butter with Maui onion, bell peppers, mushrooms, spices, and a
touch of bourbon and vermouth—*is* terrific, but then so is the
fresh fish, either baked in garlic butter and wine sauce, or sautéed
in champagne sauce. And then there's the blackened and fiery
red snapper, and the chicken with oyster dressing with ginger-
snap gravy, two selections with a Cajun-Créole accent. Entrees
run from $13.95 to market price (for the fresh fish), with almost
everything under $20, and include fresh vegetables, a choice of
potatoes or rice pilaf or fettuccine, plus bread. Desserts like
Black Forest cheesecake, chocolate torte soufflé, sweet potato/
pecan pie and bread pudding are just too good to pass up—so
don't. Lunch is fun too, featuring omelets, fish, and such intrigu-

ing sandwiches as marinated fresh ahi served open face on French bread for $7.25. Imaginative pizzas, pastas, salads, and quiches are also available.

The Oceanhouse is open every day, serving breakfast from 6 to 10:30 a.m., lunch from 11 a.m. to 3 p.m., dinner from 5 to 10 p.m. A seafood bar is open from 3 p.m. to midnight; there's bar service until 1 a.m. During the 3 to 5:30 p.m. Happy Hour, drinks are $1.25 and $1.50. There's also entertainment from 4 to 6 p.m., and jazz bands to midnight or later.

We—and scads of other visitors to Maui—have long had a special fondness for the **Lahaina Broiler,** on Front Street, corner of Papalua (tel. 661-3111). As you sit out on the big, open lanai with the sea smashing against the wall, viewing the South Seas nautical decor and enjoying the delicious food, you know that this is what Hawaii is supposed to be like. Steak and seafood are the big items here, and they are well priced. Dinners, served with soup or salad, french fries or rice, and hot rolls and butter, average $7.95 to $14.25 for entrees like shrimp curry, fresh island catch of the day, scampi, and top sirloin. For lunch, one of their sandwich plates—perhaps mahimahi almond sherry, or the Captain's Fish Platter for around $8.95, served with rice or french fries and a vegetable—makes a filling meal. The big nautical bar draws a lively crowd here until Lahaina quiets down, usually around midnight.

Another place that's immensely popular in Lahaina is **Kimo's,** at 845 Front St. (tel. 661-4811), overlooking the water, with glorious sunset views. It's exciting rather than peaceful, and packs in the crowds for good fresh fish of the day (the price varies seasonally), top sirloin or teriyaki sirloin, island specialties like huli-huli chicken (breast of chicken marinated in a ginger-shoyu sauce and broiled), or kushiyaki (brochettes of marinated chunks of sirloin and chicken breast), from $8.95 to $15.95. Along with your tasty entree comes a tossed green salad with a good house dressing, steamed herb rice, and a basket of freshly baked carrot muffins and French rolls. Special menus for kids, from $5.50 to $5.95. If you have room for dessert, try the Hula Pie—it's supposedly what the sailors swam to shore for—and Kimo's coffee, served up with a bit of macadamia-nut liqueur.

There are only a handful of fine French restaurants in Maui, so when a new one arrives on the scene, it's cause for celebration. And celebrate you will when you dine at **Gerard's,** a petite courtyard restaurant in the Lahaina Market Place, for chef Gerard Reversade is an unquestioned master and a visit here is a true experience in gourmet dining. The restaurant is tiny, with perhaps a dozen tables and booths, brick floors, plants, paintings by local artists adorning the walls. But don't let the casual atmosphere fool you: this food is elegant. Gerard creates a new menu every day (he doesn't like getting bored), depending on what's fresh in the market, combining the techniques of the classic French cooking he learned as a child in his native Gascony with island-inspired innovations. At a recent lunch, for example, we dined on salad niçoise with fresh ahi (local yellow fin tuna); one of his most popular appetizers is calamari with lime and ginger. Lunch is a modestly priced treat: for around $10 to $12, you could enjoy an appetizer like the exquisite cream of seafood soup, an omelet made with fresh black mushrooms or a New York steak and Maui onion sandwich for a main course, perhaps a dessert like fresh fruit with crème anglaise or chocolate Charlotte for dessert. Dinner is more elaborate, with most entrees between $20.95 and $24.95. These include a rack of lamb broiled with fresh mint sauce, fricassé of opakapaka with lime and ginger, confit of duck, rabbit with prunes, or whatever wonders Gerard dreams up for the day. Start your dinner with a salad dressed with raspberry vinaigrette, and be sure to have French champagne or wine with your meal (a glass is only $3.50), chosen from an excellent list. Gerard will probably stop by your table to make sure everything is perfect. And it will be.

Lunch is served every day but Sunday, from 11:30 a.m. to 2:30 p.m., and reservations are usually not necessary. They are, however, a must at dinner, served nightly from 6 to 9:30 p.m. Telephone 661-8939.

Chez Paul, at 830-B Olowalu Village (on the Wailuku side of Lahaina, about a ten-minute drive on Hwy. 30) is one of the first French restaurants in Maui, and it's still one of the very best. It's a small place, simply but tastefully decorated, and the kitchen is excellent: Cordon-Bleu trained chef and owner Lucien Charbonnier prepares different specialty entrees each day, depending, again, on what is in season, fresh, and available. Most are priced at $23.95 or $24.95 (only the vegetarian plat du jour is less, $18.95), and come served with soupe du jour or green salad plus vegetables. Scampi Olowalu (a house special of shrimp sautéed with white wine, garlic butter, and capers, also available as an appetizer), duck à l'orange, veal à la normande, and tournedos Madagascar are just a few of the enticing possibilities. Appetizers include pâté, escargots, fresh mushrooms and toast, to name a few. For dessert, treat yourself to the wonderful chocolate mousse or the superb fresh strawberries Grand Marnier. Dinner seatings are at 6:30 and 8:30, and reservations are a must: phone 661-3843.

Desserts are legendary at **Longhi's,** 888 Front St., where mango cheesecakes, chocolate-cake pies, strawberry shortcakes, and others have inspired poetry and rapture. Desserts run about $4 and are big enough and rich enough to share. Just about everything else at Longhi's (new menu daily, depending on what's fresh and in season) is special too, prepared with a gourmet flair. Dinner will cost about $10 to $20.

Dining at the big Kaanapali hotels is usually quite costly, but there is at least one very pleasant exception: **Apple Annie's Beach House,** just inside the Lahaina end of the Kaanapali Resort. The newest in the chain of Maui's popular Apple Annie restaurants, this one is a casual place, smartly styled in island decor. Omelets, salads, pizzas, and Mexican dishes, reasonably priced, are on the menu all day. Dinner specialties such as mahimahi in various styles and teriyaki or island-style chicken begin around $11. It's fun to sit out on the porch and have a few drinks while you wait for your meal. Apple Annie's is open from 11 a.m. to 11:30 p.m. every day.

The same people who run Kimo's in Lahaina recently opened **Leilani's on the Beach,** overlooking the ocean at Whaler's Village at Kaanapali, and it's been a winner from the very start. This is a picturesque, multilevel restaurant that makes artful use of wood, plants, tiles—the feeling is tropical all the way. And the food and service are tops all the way. At a recent meal, for example, our expert, witty waiter assured us that he had personally removed the calories from our Hula Pie and left them in the kitchen. Thus assured, we ate with relish. Everything here is delicious, from meats smoked in the koa-wood ovens or the lava-rock broilers to fresh fish of the day and specialties like scampi and Malaysian shrimp, $14.95 and $15.95 and excellent. Entrees run around $9.95 to $19.95 for the likes of baby back pork ribs, finger chicken, teriyaki sirloin, rack of lamb, and top sirloin. All dinners come with freshly baked bread, either steak fries or Oriental rice, plus chowder, bean soup, or green salad with a distinctive papaya seed vinaigrette. You won't go hungry here, but you'll probably want some wonderful desserts like the above-mentioned Hula Pie (we hope your waiter can remove the calories too), and the piña colada mousse. Have a drink to celebrate the sunset, or just the joy of being in Maui.

Good savings can be realized between 5 and 6 p.m. with the $8.95 early-bird meal, consisting of soup, salad, and entrees like teri brochette, mahimahi, half a chicken, sirloin, and New York steak. The Pupu Bar downstairs is the place for a lighter menu, including sushi, oysters, appetizers, and soups. Cocktails from 4 p.m., pupus and dinner from 5 p.m. nightly. Phone for reservations: 661-4495.

Where is Maui's best Chinese food served? We'd venture to say that it's at **Ming Court** at Whaler's Village, a sister restaurant to the popular Ming Yuen in Kahului (see above). Here, in a more elaborate setting (it's fun to dine out on the lanai overlooking the activity of Whaler's Village), the dishes are more elaborate too. Here's your chance to try some of the classics of Szechuan cuisine seldom seen around here, like the delicate minced squab with lettuce pockets, or the unusual smoked tea duck. For lovers of very spicy cuisine, chicken, shrimp, or scallops can all be ordered prepared in Kung Pao style: the "heat" comes from the dried chili pods they brown in the wok! Cantonese cooking is also expertly done here, and such classics as shrimp in lobster sauce, roast duck, and sweet-and-sour shrimp are all excellent. Most entrees cost from $8.50 to $12; a handful of vegetarian dishes go from $5.25 to $6.95; and there's an "all in one dinner platter" every night for around $10. On eight hours' notice, you can feast on that great delicacy, Peking duck, for $35, served in the Mandarin style. Desserts are quite unusual for a Chinese restaurant: we'd forgo fortune cookies any time for macadamia-nut pie or almond-amoretto mousse or buttercrunch cheesecake! Ming Court serves dinner only, nightly from 5:30 to 10 p.m. (tel. 667-7781).

Overlooking the ocean, and particularly lovely at sunset, **Erik's Seafood Grotto,** on the second floor of the Kahana Villa condominiums a few miles north of Kaanapali Beach, is a most attractive, moderately priced place in the Kahana area. Complete dinners here include seafood chowder or green salad, a basket of bread, and fresh boiled potatoes or rice pilaf. What to choose? Perhaps the house specialties of bouillabaisse or cioppino at $14.95 and $14.50; or curried seafood, crab imperial, lobster thermidor, coquilles St-Jacques, or a wide variety of other seafood specialties, priced from $11.95 to $17.95. Fresh-caught island fish—mahimahi, ono, ahi, ulua, snapper, or Hawaiian salmon—is priced as available. And as if that weren't enough, there's a large selection of mainland fish too. For dessert, we'd go with the fresh strawberries in Grand Marnier, topped by whipped cream, or the Kona coffee ice cream. A Sunset Dining Special is served from 5 to 6 p.m. at $10.95. Dinner is on from 5:30 to 10 p.m. daily. The lounge and bar are open from 11 a.m.

to 1 a.m., with Happy Hour and pupus from 12:30 to 3:30 p.m. (tel. 669-4806).

The same management also runs the excellent **Kahana Keyes Restaurant** in this area (tel. 669-8071), known for its terrific salad bar (one of the biggest and best on Maui), for $8.95 "Early Bird Special" dinners every night, and for other nightly specials. Entrees run about $10 to $20, and there's dancing and entertainment every night.

About one mile before you reach Kapalua, you'll find the Napili Shores Resort, and in its scenic restaurant, **Orient Express—** part Thai, part Chinese. The food is good and the setting is even better: the restaurant overlooks a Japanese carp pool and a fountain, set in a garden; sparkling beads of light in the ferns are reflected in the wide windows. There is Oriental statuary everywhere. In the midst of this loveliness, you can dine very modestly on Thai, Cantonese, and Szechuan entrees that run from about $6 for spring roll, up to about $11 for Mandarin fish clay pot. Fresh island fish, served in a yellow bean sauce or sweet and sour with fresh ginger, is market priced. You may want to try, as we did, the coconut chicken soup, made in a base of coconut milk and seasoned with lemon grass and other spices; and the house special, the chicken wings stuffed with ground pork and chicken, deep fried, and topped with sweet-and-sour sauce. Honey-lemon duck and garlic shrimp are also quite tasty. By all means, have the Thai coconut ice cream: it's made with fresh island coconut milk and topped with crushed peanuts—a winner at $2.50. The sweetness of Thai iced tea or coffee goes well with the spiciness of a meal like this (signify whether you want the Thai dishes mild or spicy when you order; they can be hotter than you expect). Ask about the Early Bird Special, served between 5 and 7 p.m. Open every day except Monday, from 5 to 10 p.m. Takeout is available. Phone: 669-8077.

Perhaps the most beautifully open-to-nature dining room in Maui is the one at the **Bay Club** at the Kapalua Bay Hotel. While the hotel is, indeed, expensive (see above), and dinner will probably run anywhere from $30 to $50 for food in the finest continental tradition, anyone with a few dollars in the pocket can have lunch here and enjoy the almost breathtaking views of sea and sky. The Bay Club is situated on a rise commanding a spectacular, multi-angled view of the ocean; the feeling is almost of being on board a ship. The atmosphere is serene, with deep, comfortable chairs, wood-and-wicker furnishings, artworks, and flowers everywhere. And lunch is not expensive. A variety of sandwiches, like smoked salmon with avocado and cream cheese, chicken salad on whole-wheat pita bread, croissant sandwich with prosciutto and Brie, are priced from $5 to $7. Daily specials will run about $8 to $9. Lunch is ready from noon to 2:30 p.m. daily. For reservations phone 669-5656, ext. 39; after 5 p.m., 669-8008.

Many local people claim that **The Grill & Bar** (tel. 669-5653) at Kapalua is consistently the best restaurant in Maui. Certainly it has a great deal going for it. Located between the Tennis Garden and the Golf Club, it offers fabulous views of the West Maui Mountains and Kapalua Bay in the distance. The wide glass windows look out over trees, plants—and tennis players. The Grill & Bar is run by the same people who do such a good job at Kimo's and Leilani on the Beach. Here, the specialties run to seafood dishes—fresh local fish, sherry-buttered scallops, shrimp and chicken, fettuccine pescatore, from $10.95 to $12.95—and poultry and meat dishes such as mixed grill, tournedos with béarnaise sauce, rack of lamb, and filet mignon and lobster, from $9.95 to $19.95. French bread plus baked potato or rice pilaf come with your meal. Dinner is served from 5 to 10:30 p.m., and lunch (burgers, sandwiches, salads, etc.) from 11:30 a.m. to 3 p.m. There's an excellent selection of house liquors and fine California wines.

In this same lovely Kapalua area, wend your way along a mile-long lane flanked by rows of Norfolk Island pine trees, and you will find yourself in the Hawaii of old. **Pineapple Hill,** one of Maui's finest restaurants, was the plantation home of David Thomas Fleming, a pioneer in establishing pineapples and mangoes on Maui. The old house has been lovingly cared for and is a gracious place for dining. Complete meals include salad, rolls and butter, and rice or vegetables along with your entree. One of the house specialties is chicken Pineapple Hill, oven-roasted and served in a pineapple boat. Our favorite is the shrimp Tahitian, jumbo prawns with a special seasoning, broiled in the shell and served with rice. Also good are the Alaskan king crab legs, rack of lamb, roast prime rib, and teriyaki steak. Dinners are priced from $8.95 to $18.95. Some of the vegetables are à la carte, prepared in a variety of interesting ways, and served in portions ample enough for two. For dessert, there's the champagne of ice creams—Häagen-Dazs. Cocktails are served from 4:30 p.m., dinner from 5:30 p.m. until closing seven days. For reservations, phone 669-6129.

The Sights and Sounds of Maui

Millions of years ago the sea bottom between the islands of

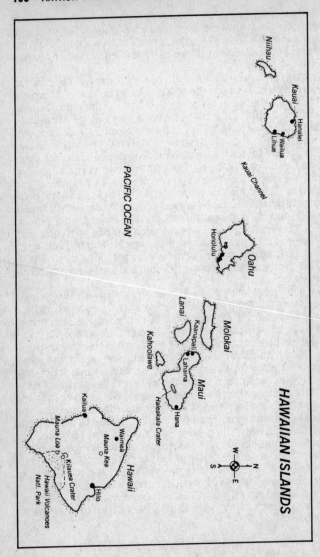

present-day Hawaii and Oahu erupted with surprising frequency. The results of Pele's work can be seen now as the islands of Molokai, Lanai, Kahoolawe, and Maui. The island of Maui, though, is by far the most glorious result of this constant volcanic action. The western end began as a separate island, with mountains that rise like leavened dough and fold upon each other as they run and spill at golden shores into the pounding surf. The eastern side of the island would have gained renown on its own by virtue of its awesome Haleakala Crater, where the sun rises as it must have on the first day of creation. But as time went on the two volcanic fountains feeding the growing islands caused the two land masses to meet and melt into one single island, creating the Maui that now exists. The ancient Hawaiians believed, though, that their own special god, Maui, pulled up both ends of the island from the sea bottom with his fish hooks. In any case, both versions of paradise are one for you to explore and enjoy, driving over modern roads with a minimum of effort. Plan on at

---

Buffet Bravos

Where do Maui families go when they want to celebrate something special? To Sunday brunch at the **Mayfair Buffet** of the Kapalua Bay Hotel, of course—and so should you. Actually, you can go any day between noon and 2:30 p.m. (avoiding the Sunday crowd) and feast on what is surely one of the most glorious spreads in the islands, for around $15 and not overpriced. The international chefs at Kapalua go all out for this one, proudly spreading their tables with gourmet treats, not the usual buffet table fillers. On a recent Sunday we counted seven hot entrees alone, including seafood Newburg, quiche Lorraine, sweet-and-sour pork, zucchini with mozzarella, and roast beef. The salad table numbers 25 entrees; the cold fish and meat spread includes sashimi and other island delicacies and crab legs every day. Tropical fruits, fresh fruit salads, and home-baked island breads (including Hawaiian sweet breads) grace the fruit table. And all this is prelude to the vast array of desserts—éclairs and lemon meringue pies and chocolate mousses and babas au rhum and such —all set out against a wall of flowing water. You eat as much as you want, and then come back for more—and more. The dining room, overlooking water and gardens, is a perfect setting for this fantasy meal. Don't miss. Reservations are required on Sunday: phone 669-5656, ext. 39.

least three days to see Maui: the first to explore Kahului, Wailuku, Lahaina and Kaanapali; the second to see the windswept wonder of Haleakala; the third either for the beach or for an excursion into the lush, tropical rain forest of Hana.

THE FIRST DAY—FROM KAHULUI AND WAILUKU TO LAHAINA: Let's suppose you begin your trip at the Kahului Airport. Head west on H-32, take a left and continue into Kahului proper. Kahului is important to Maui because it has the only deep-water harbor on the island (sugar is shipped from here), and there are several resort hotels on the waterfront. If you haven't gotten your muumuu yet, or if your child wants a swimming board, or you're just plain in the mood to shop, you've come to the right place. Both **Kaahumana Shopping Center** and **Maui Mall** are rewarding.

Kaahumanu is a giant complex, with **Liberty House, Sears, Shirokiya,** and other major establishments, plus one of our favorite island gift shops, **Nani Pacific, Center for Performing Plants,** which has everything from arts and crafts to Hawaiian bulbs and cuttings to miniatures for dollhouses and collectors . . . **Idini's Liquor and Deli** serves sophisticated fare—croissant sandwiches, salads, quiches —and is a good place for lunch when you get off the plane; so, too, is **Ma-Chan's Okazu-Ya,** a big favorite for local-style dishes. . . . Maui Mall houses huge branches of **Long's Drugs** and **Woolworth's,** good for reasonably priced souvenirs. . . . Don't miss **Island Muumuu Works** here, a wholesale outlet for a well-known manufacturer; beautiful muumuus and aloha shirts, too, are all about half the regular retail price. . . . **Sir Wilfred's Coffee, Tea and Tobacco Shop** also houses **Sir Wilfred's Caffee,** a great spot for espressos and cappucinos, as well as light meals; entertainment Wednesday and Thursday afternoon. . . . Bookish types should drive across Kaahumanu Avenue to the **Old Kahului Store** at No. 55; here they'll find **The Artful Dodger's Feed 'n' Read,** a bookstore cum coffeehouse with huge selections of used and new books and periodicals, art shows, classical music, free entertainment, light foods, and tables for lingering.

Back in the car, continue to drive to Wailuku along the valley floor on Kaahumanu Avenue; you'll pass both the Maui Pineapple Company (pineapple is important to the island's agriculture) and Maui Community College, a rapidly growing educational center on the island. **Wailuku,** the civic and business center of Maui, is Kahului's older sister. Market Street is the local business area, and Vineyard Street is where you'll find a health-food store, bookstore, and other establishments under the banner of the Hare Krishna people. Wailuku also has several beautiful new state and county office buildings, and it's past these that you take Iao Valley Road for a look at the **Maui Historical Society Museum** in the historic Bailey House built between 1833 and 1850. Historical displays date from prehistoric times to Hawaii's annexation in 1899. Hours are 10 a.m. to 4:30 p.m. daily; donation of $2 for adults, 50¢ for children.

If you have a few more hours for sightseeing, or if you want a pleasant buffet lunch, backtrack a little to Honoapiilani Hwy., make your right, and follow the signs to **Waikupu Village and Maui Plantation,** where you can learn all about Hawaiian agriculture on a 1½-hour Tropical Train tour ($5 for adults, $1 for kids), or visit pavilions and exhibits free. The Tropical Nursery provides good shopping, there's a buffet lunch for under $10, and delicious ice creams, fruit salads, and juices (tel. 244-7643).

Go back to Iao Valley Road now, for a drive through magnificent Iao Valley. Watch, on the right, for a mountain that looks uncannily like the profile of John F. Kennedy. Then proceed to **Iao Needle,** a 1,200-foot finger of lava scratching at the sky and draped in green cloaks of luxurious foliage that are common to this rainy valley. In fact, the clouds are likely to be heavy and brooding here, as if the local spirits were still mourning the slaughter that went on in this valley in 1790, when Kamehameha's men, armed with cannons, devastated the local forces of Kalanikupule. On the way to Iao Needle Lookout, do make a side trip to **Kepaniwai Park,** once the scene of a bloody battle in Hawaiian history, today a gardeny spot where local kids happily play in the swimming and wading pools.

On to Lahaina

Provided you haven't gotten lost in the shopping centers or stood gazing at Iao Needle for too long, this portion of your trip should not take much more than an hour. Now you can continue on to **Lahaina,** 22 miles from Kahului Airport on a road that curves along the western end of the island and allows you to survey some of its glorious beaches. Trace your way out of the valley, back to the outskirts of Wailuku, and take a right onto H-30 out of the city environs through the cane fields to where the road meets the ocean at Maalaea. (If you wanted to make a side trip to Kihei, you would have made a left a little while back, onto Rte. 31. There's not much in the way of sightseeing here, but you could have a swim at Kamaole Beach or Kalama Park and do some shopping at newly expanded Azeka Place.) Now every turn in the mountain road surprises you with oceanscapes that get more and more wild and spectacular. Continue on, passing a never-ending stretch of beach on your left; at some points the high-tide surf splashes right up onto the shoulder of the road. Soon you arrive at a busy intersection where Lahainaluna Road crosses the main highway. Turn toward the ocean and you're right in the heart of Lahaina, once the royal capital of Hawaii, the whaling center of the Pacific, and the scene of some of the most colorful—and violent—history of the islands.

Today the Lahaina Restoration Foundation is restoring many of the buildings and relics that remain from the old days when royalty walked the streets and whalers brawled in them. You can already explore **Baldwin House,** on Front Street, home of the devoted missionary Dwight Baldwin, who also doubled as a surgeon and doctor for Maui and its smaller islands. The Baldwin House has been lovingly restored, and a visit—personally guided —will give you a good insight into the incongruous blending of New England and the South Seas that marked the missionary lifestyle. Admission, which includes a free walking-tour map of Lahaina, is $2 for adults, free for children accompanied by parents.

Another of the foundation's restorations is **Hale Pa'i,** the House of Printing, on the campus of the Lahainaluna School, the oldest school west of the Rockies. It features a replica of the original Ramage Press and a large collection of early printing in the Hawaiian language. Closed Sunday; free. To reach it, just drive to the top of Lahainaluna Road.

The foundation also sponsors "The World of the Whale" exhibit aboard its floating museum **Carthaginian,** anchored just opposite the Pioneer Inn. The exhibit features a real 19th-century whaleboat discovered in the wilds of northern Alaska, and various multimedia displays on whaling, whales, and the reef life of Hawaii. Open daily; admission is $2 for adults, free for children with their parents.

Across the street from Baldwin House is the **Lahaina Library,** standing in the midst of what was once the taro patch of Kamehameha III. Behind this spot are excavations of the foundations of his royal palace; you can view them through glass panes on the ground level. Just behind that you can stand on the edge of the wharf at historic **Lahaina Roads** and maybe see a black stone in the ocean, the **Mauola Stone,** which was believed by the old Hawaiians to have sacred healing powers. Anyone who was ill could lie on top of the stone and be washed clean of his malady by the action of the waves. (Don't bother jumping in; it's only a legend.) It's interesting to gaze out across the water at the islands of Molokai, Lanai, and Kahoolawe, and to realize that you're on the precise spot where the whaling ships used to drop anchor over a hundred years ago. This spot is especially memorable at sunset, when half the island's population, it seems, turns out to watch the sun turn the sky to golden fire.

Turn left before you get to the town square and you'll end up at the **Pioneer Inn** (which you've seen in many movies), a hotel-hideaway with a long history of attracting beachcombers, movie stars in disguise, and other assorted notables for over half a century. It's a bit rundown now, but the old lazy, South Seas nautical flavor is still there, and it's fun to stop for a drink or a bite in its Harpooners' Lanai.

Across the street from the Pioneer Inn is a banyan tree that has been reaching out and monopolizing the town square for many years now. The locals will hotly defend its rank, size-wise, in comparison with other banyans in the world. It *is* big. The **Court House** faces the ocean behind the tree, and at the end of Wharf Street you'll find the reconstructed remains of an old fort that once stood someplace in the vicinity of the banyan tree. Rebuilding it at the original site would have meant that the tree had to go. Never! The tree remained, and the ruins of the fort were relocated.

Just off Front Street, on Prison Street, you'll get a taste of what awaited the whalers in town after the sunset drums were beaten each evening. You see, the whalers were not exactly popular among the kings and missionaries of Lahaina. For too long it was the habit of the native women to swim out to the ships with their own particular brand of aloha. When the missionaries decreed the end of such abominations, the sailors replied with riotings and burnings, even shellings of the mission house. So the custom developed that any sailor found ashore after the sunset curfew was immediately clapped into jail, where he might awaken the next morning to find his ship gone. **Hale Paahao,** the old stone jail, is still there.

You should also have a look at an important cultural contribution made to Lahaina by another group, the Japanese. Drive along Front Street and turn left on Ala Moana Street until you come to the Lahaina Jodo Mission. Here an enormous statue of Amida Buddha presides over the **Buddhist Cultural Park,** complete with a temple and a pagoda in the best tradition of Buddhist architecture. The statue was brought here from Kyoto to celebrate the centennial of Japanese immigration to Hawaii. There's an almost palpable serenity to this place, so drink it all in before you get back to the swinging world of present-day Lahaina.

Shopping Lahaina

Even more fun than seeing the historical sights is seeing the contemporary shops. New boutiques open almost weekly, it seems, and the place is a shoppers' mecca on the order of San Francisco's Sausalito. To get an idea, walk along Front Street for a few blocks and you'll find the likes of the **South Seas Trading Post**, with many rare and unusual items from the South Seas and the Orient, plus unusual low-priced gift items like hand-painted Kashmiri eggs at $6.50. . . . You can pick up whaling mementos of Lahaina at **The Whaler:** carvings and scrimshaw and ivory, boxes, prints, plus other nautical memorabilia. . . . **Far Out Fits, One World Family,** 726 Front St., has handcrafted clothing for kids and grownups, plus toys, books, and cards. . . . **Claire, the Ring Lady,** shows a smashing collection of loose stones, settings in gold, gold-filled, and silver, plus finished rings. We like the "Maui Diamond," a local quartz. . . . Art lovers should visit **The Art Affair,** in the **Whaler's Market Place,** for an excellent collection of arts and crafts, much of it by local artists.

The Wharf, across from the banyan tree in the center of town at 658 Front St., is a nifty little shopping world in itself, with scads of quality boutiques, fast-food and sit-down restaurants, a fountain and stage area for free entertainment, and a glass elevator that the kids will love riding. Some of our favorite shops here include **Artisans of Hawaii** for high-quality work by local artists and craftspeople, **Alberta's Gazebo** for exquisite gifts and ethnic clothing, **Ecology House** for products and educational materials dedicated to saving endangered species, and **Upstart Crow & Company** for a quality selection of books plus coffees and pastries in a European café setting. As you may have gathered by now, serious shoppers could spend eternity in Lahaina, but at this point we suggest that you take a short train ride (or drive) to Kaanapali and another exciting shopping complex, Whaler's Village.

The train ride is aboard the **Lahaina-Kaanapali & Pacific Railroad,** a replica of a railroad that carried cane between the villages of Lahaina and Kaanapali from 1890 to 1950. Now it carries visitors, especially those based at the Kaanapali hotels, who use it whenever they want to run into Lahaina. The train clickety-clacks through some perfectly beautiful scenery, the mountains on one side, the sea on the other. (Kids really dig it, especially the ferocious toot of the steam whistle.) Round trip is $7.50 for adults, $3.50 for children. Rates are subject to change.

Whaler's Village is a "shopping center" that's also a museum,

designed to recapture the late-19th-century years when both Lahaina and Kaanapali were major whaling ports. The decor is a
combination of New England and Polynesia, and outdoor displays and a small museum document the history and biology of
whales and whaling. If you're lucky, you may catch sight of some
humpback whales playing offshore; they are regular visitors December through May. The shops here are all attractive. **Ka Honu,**
for example, is unique in that it displays handmade Hawaiian
Christmas ornaments year round, perfect as gifts to yourself or
friends. Other handmade works are also special: bowls of koa
and milo wood, Hawaiian dolls of collector quality, needlepoint
kits and beautiful gemstone and jade jewelry. Prices range from
$2 to $2,000. . . . **Lahaina Scrimshaw Factory** has one of the
largest collections of quality scrimshaw anywhere, much of it
done by local artists who create everything from inexpensive gift
items and jewelry to collectors' pieces. In addition to whales'
teeth, they also work on ivories from nonendangered species,
that is, fossilized walrus and mastodon. (Other outlets are on
Front Street in Lahaina and at the Marriott Resort at Kaanapali.)
. . . **Super Whale Children's Boutique** has one of the best selections of kids' clothes we've seen anywhere in the islands, and the
sizes range from infants through 14 for girls, up to 18 for boys.
There are other Super Whales at the Pioneer Inn in Lahaina and
at Wailea Shopping Village in Kihei.

The **Tidepool Gallery** is outstanding, displaying unique shells,
jewelry, gift items. . . . So too, is **Whaler's Mercantile,** with intriguing personal accessories and giftware. . . . Check the fine
collection of books on Hawaii and many other subjects in the attractive **Book Cache.** . . . Buy an aloha shirt or a muumuu or
some island jewelry at the tasteful branch of **Liberty House.** . . .
And end with a banana daiquiri at the swinging **Rusty Harpoon,** a
meal or drink at lovely **Leilani on the Beach,** maybe a Mexican
meal at **Chico's Cantina,** or a swim at lovely Kaanapali Beach,
just beyond the shops.

On to Kaanapali and Napili

Back in your car, you can drive out of Lahaina in the Napili
direction, or you might want to take Lahainaluna Road to its beginning at the **Lahainaluna High School,** walk through the pleasant campus, and see the first printing press on the island. In any
case, your path will continue to lead you west as you follow either
Front Street or H-36 to the point where the two converge at the
site of the **Royal Coconut Grove,** an ancient spot favored by royal-

ty, whose restoration is another on a long list of projects of the Restoration Foundation.

Continue on H-36 and you'll pass the incredibly beautiful setting of the **Kaanapali Beach Resorts.** It's worth your time to take one of the daily guided tours of the glamorous Hyatt Regency Maui, or walk around on your own, admiring the gardens and plantings and the colorful birds that abound in the lobby and on the grounds. The shops here are noted for their architectural details (extraordinary ceilings, one in stained glass; railings of oak and teak, copper and brass), as well as their luxury offerings. Most impressive of all are the works of original art and sculpture in the passageways between the shops. Pay a visit to the spectacular new Westin Maui, another glorious conjunction of art and nature. You can swim anywhere along Kaanapali (beaches are public property), or drive on to **Honokawai Beach Park,** a mile or so ahead, where you could take out your picnic lunch. Several miles farther up the road, almost at the tip of the island, you'll come to the magnificent **Kapalua Bay Resort.** Here we suggest you get out, survey the grounds, maybe have a drink at the Bay Club, and admire the beauty, natural and man-made, all around you. Admire the beauty, too, of **The Shops at Kapalua,** a graceful setting for high-quality boutiques. A visit to **Distant Drum,** for example, brims with the excitement of crafts and artifacts from the cultures that surround the Pacific—perhaps Balinese temple ornaments, New Guinea wood carvings, rare masks from the South Pacific—collected by owner Candace Shaffer. Much of it is museum quality, but there are inexpensive treasures here too. **By the Bay** has extremely tasteful mountings of shells and coral for indoor decor; we like their branch-coral trees on koa-wood bases. **Ka Honu** is here with South Seas crafts, **Mandalay** with ancient Buddhas, and **Auntie Nani,** a branch of Super Whale, with a young teen department and lots of hand-made-on-Maui fashions. The **Market Café** has gourmet kitchen gadgets, cheese and deli sections, and, behind the swinging half-door, a real little café, where a well-deserved cup of cappuccino can bring your shopping labors to a close.

The good road continues just a few miles farther, to Honokohua; from there you'll have to double back the way you came, since the road continuing around the island is much too rugged for a small car.

THE SECOND DAY—HALEAKALA: Now you're set to visit Maui's Valhalla, **Haleakala,** the home of the great god Maui, and just as the proper home of a god should be, this is an awesome place. To reach it you'll have to drive 1½ hours from Kahului, part of it on a snaky highway high above the clouds. But it's worth whatever effort you have to make to see this sleeping giant, whose crater alone is 7½ miles long, 2½ miles wide. And it makes it even more exciting, as you scale its 10,000 feet, to know that the volcano is sleeping, dormant—not dead or extinct as is Diamond Head (or at least we hope it is). In other words, it *could* erupt in front of you. But don't panic; Pele has not visited here for some 200 years.

You'll want to make this trip on a clear day, so phone 572-7749 to check on weather conditions before you set out. Actually, the best time to see Haleakala is at sunrise; few things on earth can equal the sight, when it seems that the sun has risen only for you. Bring along a warm sweater or windbreaker, since it gets cool up here. And since there are no restaurants or gasoline stations once you pass the lower slopes, be sure to gas up, and you may want to bring a breakfast picnic.

Starting from Kahului, drive east of the city and follow the signs to the junction of H-36 with H-37. Continue on the Kula Road (H-37) and then to H-337, the Upper Kula Road. This is easy driving, but once you turn off to the left, on Rte. 378, you're on Haleakala Crater Road, and it's a winding two-way highway through the clouds. Check in at park headquarters to get maps and a general orientation. Camping, horseback riding, or hiking in the crater, over the same routes that once served as the main avenue of travel between the two ends of the island, is a magnificent experience. The rangers can give you all the details.

If, however, like us, you do most of your hiking in a car, there's still a great deal to see. You can get wonderful views of the crater at both **Leleiwi** and **Kahaluku** lookouts. If you're one of those lucky types who arrive when the sun is strong at your back, the clouds overhead misty, you might get to see your own shadow in the rainbow, a phenomenon known as the **Spectre of the Brocken.** And you may also experience the phenomenon of the double winds. The wind will be blowing right in your face as you view the crater, but then, if you just go back to the road and turn to face the other way, the wind will again be in your face. The effect is caused by the curling of the wind jets as they flow over the lip of the crater.

With or without spooky side effects, the view of Haleakala is awesome. You may also see some of the magnificent silversword plants that bloom in the lava between June and October. As tall as a man, they blossom once, producing purple-and-golden flowers, and die—leaving their seeds to grow again in the lava rock.

Now hop back into your car again and drive to the **Haleakala**

Observatory. Here your gaze encompasses some 30,000 square miles of the Pacific; and below you the crater, its kaleidoscope of colors changing with the sun and the clouds, creates an incredible light show that technology could never approach. Now take the Skyline Drive another half mile to **Red Hill,** the summit of Haleakala and the home of a satellite-tracking station. Stop a while to pay homage to the great god Maui, and down you go, to warmer climes and the golden valleys below. On the way down the slopes, you might stop in for lunch at scenic **Kula Lodge** in Kula. Not far from Kula, on Hwy. 37, you could make a side trip to Hawaii's first—and only—winery, **Tedeschi Vineyards,** which conducts free tours daily between 10 a.m. and 5 p.m. A shorter side trip, just a few miles off to the right, is a visit to the little cowboy town of **Makawao.**

THE THIRD DAY—HANA: Whether or not you decide to go to Hana depends on what kind of driver you are. Don't say we didn't warn you. It's rugged driving on a narrow, cliff-hanging road with many blind turns and potholes a plenty (especially on the last stretch, from Hana itself to the Seven Sacred Pools). There are no restaurants or gas stations. The views of dense tropical forests and cascading waterfalls are sensational though, and if you have the strength for it, well worth the effort. If it's all too much, relax and return to any of the dozen beaches we're sure you've already found.

If you do opt for Hana, head out of Kahului on the same road you took to Haleakala, but continue on Hwy. 36 and stay on it all the way. Coming up soon is **H.A. Baldwin Park,** a favorite picnic camping spot. Farther on you'll pass through **Paia,** a neat little natural life–style town where you might want to get some picnic fixings at **Pic-Nics** on Baldwin Avenue, or stop to see the imposing Japanese temple, complete with an immense gong. You can also make a little detour here to **Hookipa Beach,** scene of windsurfing championships. Back on the road, it's just you and nature —and a lot of other cars en route to Hana, which has lately been very much "discovered." Pineapple fields drop out of sight after a while as you swing and fly around the inside faces of many valleys, with waterfalls spilling over the mountaintops, rivers running under the roadway, and lush vegetation all around. The white-and-yellow ginger blossoms all along the way are so thick that the air is yellow and perfumed with their scent. (It's illegal to pick them though, so just admire them from afar.) One is constantly tempted to stop at a particular waterfall and admire its unique beauty, but we suggest that you keep right on until you get to **Keanae** and **Kaumahina State Park,** resplendent with flowers and shrubs. In the middle of Keanae town, you might want to stop off and stretch your legs at **Uncle Harry's Fruit Stand and Living Museum,** a charming family-owned operation where you can pick up handmade Hawaiian crafts, fruit, sandwiches, and souvenirs. About 800 feet past Uncle Harry's is **The Shell Stop,** the home of Anna Kapuna, who dives in local waters to gather her collection of Hawaiian shells. And across from The Shell Stop is **St. Gabriel's Mission** and the "Coral Miracle Church," named thus when an unusual storm in the 1860s tossed coral ashore and provided the villagers with the material to construct their church. Hana people still live in the same style their ancestors did many generations back. **Pua Kaa Park** is another place to stop for a look-see. One more possible side trip before you get into Hana proper is over a bumpy left-turn road that leads the way to the **Waianapanapa Cave** where poor Popoalea was slain by her jealous husband; the water is said to still run red with her blood every April. In Hana itself, you'll want to visit the charming little **Hana Cultural Center** right in the middle of town, to see old photographs, quilts, memorabilia from the near and far Hana past. You can swim at **Hamoa Beach,** at **Hana Bay,** or at the black-sand beach at **Waianapanapa State Park.** A must on your list of sights should be the **Hasegawa General Store** where, it is reported, you can get anything and everything your heart desires (just like at Alice's Restaurant) under one roof. A song was written about the store some years ago, and it has not changed in spite of all the hullaballoo.

Besides such novelties as this, you'll walk in the footsteps of illustrious ghosts in Hana. Captain Cook and his men dropped anchor here. The Hawaiian monarchs made this their vacation territory (they always picked the best places), and the missionaries were only too glad to follow them to enforce their teachings. If you're in a historical mood, you can even see the place where Kaahumanu, the favorite consort of Kamehameha, was born.

The main industry of Hana is the lovely and expensive Hotel Hana Maui, where you can treat yourself to dinner (see "Hideouts in Hana," above), or a superb buffet lunch. There's another good lunchtime buffet at the more casual **Hana Ranch Restaurant.** If you've still got the strength for more of this rugged driving, continue past Hana, about nine miles farther, to the site of the **Seven Sacred Pools.** Here one pool feeds into another and so on, creating an enchanting spot for a swim. And, of course, in true Hana fashion, there are waterfalls all along the way to the pools. Return home the way you came, since the road tapers out beyond this point and becomes just a rugged dirt path, suitable only for four-wheel-drive vehicles. Driving home is a bit easier, since you are on the other side of the road. The view is also extra-special from that vantage point. Return time should be about three hours, but do drive carefully. End your day, perhaps, with a super dinner at **Dillon's** in Paia, which we've told you about at the beginning of this chapter, or at **Mama's Fish House,** for super-fresh fish in an attractive, on-the-beach-setting. It's just outside of Paia on Hwy. 36, and open from 11:30 a.m. to 10 p.m. (tel. 579-9672).

Chapter XI

THE GARDEN ISLAND: KAUAI

WHERE DO HONOLULU RESIDENTS go when they want to get away from it all? To a magic island that any visitor can reach by spending less than 20 minutes on a jet. Only 95 miles northwest of the bustling freeways and crowds of Honolulu is a verdant little island that seems to have been sleeping in the tropical sun for centuries. It exudes a peace and tranquility that is decidedly not of the 1980s.

And yet, with its comfortable hotels and restaurants and golf courses and nightclubs and shopping centers, you couldn't exactly call Kauai behind the times. The only thing old-fashioned about it is the openheartedness of its people, the lack of pressure, the gentleness that is everywhere.

To our way of thinking, you should have at least four days to spend here, to discover the myriad beauties of this jewel-like island. For nature has been good to Kauai, creating craters and canyons (Waimea Canyon is even more spectacular, in some ways, than the Grand Canyon), mountains and rivers, glorious stretches of sparkling sand and graceful, palm-fringed beaches. The oldest of the islands in the Hawaiian chain, Kauai was born from the sea millions of years ago by violent volcanic eruptions occurring far below the ocean floor. Pele, the Hawaiian goddess of volcanoes (who, incidentally, is still revered by more than a few natives), made her first home here before moving on to the other islands; Kauai's volcanoes are now extinct. The centuries have turned the red volcanic earth green and glorious, and abundant rainfall has earned Kauai the title of "The Garden Island." But don't despair; rain falls where it's needed here, and only occasionally on tourists. Mount Waialeale, 5,240 feet high, receives something like 486 inches of rainfall a year, making it the second-

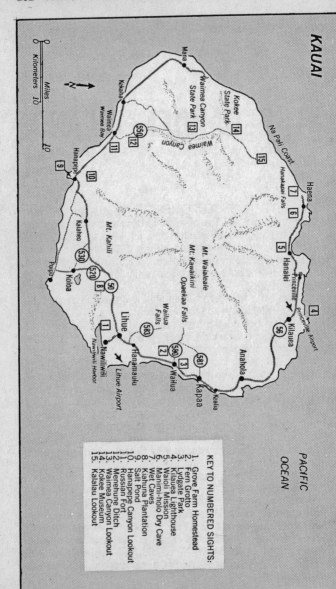

KAUAI

PACIFIC
OCEAN

KEY TO NUMBERED SIGHTS:
1. Grove Farm Homestead
2. Fern Grotto
3. Lydgate Park
4. Kilauea Lighthouse
5. Waioli Mission
6. Manini-holo Dry Cave
7. Wet Caves
8. Kiahuna Plantation
9. Salt Pond
10. Hanapepe Canyon Lookout
11. Russian Fort
12. Menehune Ditch
13. Waimea Canyon Lookout
14. Kokee Museum
15. Kalalau Lookout

wettest spot on earth. Other areas just a few miles away receive fewer than 20 inches. It rains in Kauai, but not enough to spoil your fun.

KAUAI—PAST AND PRESENT: Kauai has always been attractive to visitors. The very first were the Menehunes, who, according to legend, were here long before the Polynesians ever dreamed of leaving the South Seas. No one knows where these two-foot-tall gremlins came from (could they be the descendants of the lost colony of Lemuria? could a flying saucer have deposited them?), but whatever their origins, they accomplished remarkable engineering feats whose remains you can still examine. In about A.D. 750, the first Polynesians arrived, beaching their outrigger canoes on the banks of the Wailua River, on Kauai's north shore. It was along this side of the island that religious temples and villages sprang up. (Interestingly, an international yoga group has chosen this area as its headquarters; seems the vibrations are still special.) You can explore the remnants of these *heiaus* (temples) on the Wailua (sacred) River today. Capt. James Cook, the next notable visitor to the island, was heartily greeted on the southern shore, at Waimea. This deep-water harbor had become a favorite of the *alii* (royalty) who ruled here in pre-Cook days.

Kauai is proud of the fact that it is the only one of the Hawaiian Islands that was not conquered by Kamehameha the Great. The island was ceded to Kamehameha's federation in about 1790, and from then on its importance as a political power declined. The **Koloa** section of the island, though, is notably proud of its own contribution to Hawaiian politics, Prince Jonah Kuhio, Hawaii's first representative to Congress (1902-1922), and the much-beloved "People's Prince." (Kuhio Beach and Kuhio Avenue in Honolulu were, of course, named for him.) Each March 26 his birthday is celebrated with great pomp and pageantry, not only on Kauai but all over the islands.

The modern world is rushing in on Kauai, as it is all over Hawaii, but it is still a haven of peace and beauty. To see it properly, you will have to rent a car since there is a minimum of public transportation. There are sightseeing limousines and a limited bus service, but the best way to see the island is on your own. Seven or eight car-rental places are lined up in a stall across the road from the airport lobby at Lihue, and many rent inexpensive cars. Better still, make arrangements in advance with one of the major car-rental companies that rent on all the major islands: try **Holiday Hawaii Rent-A-Car** (800/367-2631), **Budget Rent-A-Car**

(800/527-0700), **Avis Rent-A-Car** (800/331-1212), all of which offer good flat rates for both stick-shifts and automatics.

Please note that the telephone area code for the state of Hawaii is 808.

Hotels in Kauai

HOTELS IN LIHUE: A convenient halfway point on the two major sightseeing excursions around the island, the minute town of Lihue makes a good tour base. And it's here that you'll find Kauai's newest and most spectacular resort—one of the most spectacular to be found anywhere, for that matter—the **Westin Kauai.** The $190-million seaside caravanserai that replaced the old Kauai Surf Hotel was in the construction stage as this book went to press, but it will very likely be ready by the time you read this. And advance plans indicate a world-class resort unmatched anywhere. Set in 200 acres of botanical gardens and lawns, fronting on a half-mile expanse of sandy beach that is bordered by a crushed-marble and mosaic-tile promenade, the hotel itself contains some 849 beautifully appointed guest rooms (including 29 suites), each with mountain or ocean view, mini-bar, and refrigerator. Horse-drawn carriages transport guests along a five-mile carriage road as they go from one part of the complex to another —perhaps to the 31,500 square-foot pool with its own island, fountains, waterfalls, rivers, and slides, which lights up at night to become one of the world's largest fountains; or to the Golf & Racquet Club, which boasts an 18-hole golf course, 12 tennis courts, and a stadium court with seats for 1,000 spectators; or to the sumptuous European health spa or the four-lane lap pool for serious swimmers. And, of course, the carriages will stop at the resort's bevy of restaurants and lounges, including Prince Bill's Restaurant and the Inn on the Cliff for gourmet dining with spectacular sunsets; Cook's on the Beach for indoor and outdoor informal fare; the Tempura House for Japanese delicacies in an authentic Japanese garden. Undoubtedly the resort will be a showplace of the islands, so whether or not you're planning to be a guest here (rates had not yet been set at the time of this writing, but they will assuredly be in the luxury category), you must stop by to have a meal or a drink, stroll along the grounds, and see the wonders that Christopher Hemmeter, the force behind this new tour de force (he is also responsible for the Hyatt Regencys in Waikiki and Maui and for the new Westin Maui) hath wrought.

For information and reservations, phone toll free 800/228-3000, or write the Westin Kauai, 1777 Ala Moana Blvd., Suite 221, Honolulu, HI 96815.

Located on 25 acres at Hanamaulu Beach, the new **Kauai Hilton,** 4331 Kauai Beach Dr., Lihue, HI 96766 (tel. 245-1955; reservations, toll free 800/445-8667), built adjacent to the Beach Villas, is a beautifully designed and appointed resort. The elegant, inviting lobby, with its sand-colored floors and columns and ocean-hued furniture overlooks the pool area and the beach beyond. Original paintings of Hawaiian subjects by such renowned island artists as Pegge Hopper and Kenneth Bushnell grace the walls. A few steps down from the formal lobby is a wonderful indoor lanai with white tables and chairs with cool green cushions. Guests gather here to play cards or board games—the concierge has a good supply—or just to visit and enjoy the very special ambience.

Outdoors, there are four tennis courts and not one, but three swimming pools, each connected to the others by small waterfalls and cascades; one of the pools is just three feet deep, lovely for little ones. The beach is great for sandcastles and walks, but swimming, alas, is not advised. Handsome suites are furnished in an oriental motif. Bedrooms have dressing tables, one or two double beds, original paintings, and upholstery and draperies in a variety of color combinations that are a feast for the eyes. Rooms are spacious and each has a lanai. Closets abound. The Beach Villas, too, are beautifully appointed; each Villa has a sitting room, one or two bedrooms, and full kitchen facilities. They face either the ocean or a lagoon on the hotel side. One-bedroom villas with lagoon view are $90 per day single or double; two-bedroom ones are $125. On the ocean side, one-bedroom villas are $115 per day; two bedrooms, $155. In the main hotel, standard rooms are $80; superior, $90; deluxe, $100, single or double; an extra person is $15. In keeping with Hilton's policy worldwide, there is no charge for children, regardless of age, when they stay in the same room with their parents. Room classifications are based on view. Suites start at $115. There are two restaurants here, Midori, the fine dining room, and the Jacaranda Terrace.

For reservations, you can call the toll-free number above. However, Hilton headquarters in Hawaii advises us that for answers to detailed questions, or to reserve suites, it is always best to contact the individual hotel.

Tucked away at 3115 Akahi St., near the Lihue Shopping Center, is the **Ahana Motel Apartments,** P.O. Box 892, Lihue, HI

96766 (tel. 245-2206), our favorite budget choice in the area. Mr.
and Mrs. Ah Sau Ahana have long provided simple but
sparkling-clean accommodations here, and their faithful following keeps returning year after year. Prices for these plainly furnished, homey units, all with television and many with kitchens,
are unbelievably good for this day and age. Single and double
rooms without kitchenettes are $16; kitchenette rooms are $22; a
one-bedroom apartment or studio for two is $22; and various
combinations of rooms with and without kitchenettes can be
worked out to accommodate large families with children. Newer
two-bedroom apartments, each with *two* bathrooms, rent for $38
for four. There is a charge of $4 for each additional person. Man-
ager Rosie Thigpen will make sure you're comfortable. Beautiful
Kalapaki Beach, a very short drive away, is yours to swim at.
Many of the regulars here are golfers, since the golf course at the
Westin Kauai is a few minutes' drive away, and the expensive
Wailua Golf Course is not far along Hwy. 56, nor is lovely Lydgate Beach. Write well in advance for accommodations.

HOTELS IN THE WAILUA-WAIPOULI AREA: It might be said that no
hotel in the islands is as Hawaiian as Kauai's **Coco Palms Resort,**
P.O. Box 631, Lihue, HI 96766 (tel. 822-4921; reservations, toll
free 800/542-2626 except California, 800/622-0838 in California),
close to the sea at Wailua Beach and a few miles north of Lihue.
Here you can live even more graciously than did the Hawaiian
royalty who once strolled along the banks of the palm-fringed lagoon around which the main hotel building and small cottages
are spread. The evening torchlighting ceremony is an authentic
moment relived—as the conch shell blows, the canoes arrive, and
one by one, scores of torches are ignited. And then, dining by
torchlight in the Lagoon Dining Room with its ancient fire pit,
you have the feeling that you are there by invitation of the old
Hawaiian *alii*.

The royal colors of red and gold are predominant from the
vaulted lobby to the extravagantly decorated rooms and cottages.
Standard, superior, and deluxe rates, for two, are $62, $75, and
$88. A variety of romantic luxury suites, popular with honey-
mooners, is also available, such as the Queen's Cottages at $115,
and the King's Cottages at $125, the Prince of Hawaii Cottage at
$155, and others, up to the Coconut Palace Suite at $300 for four
people. (Some of these are more lavish than a movie set. Would
you believe shell basins and lava-rock bathtubs, some outdoors in
secluded little nooks?) Each extra person is charged $10; Ameri-

can Plan is available at $53 per person, Modified American Plan at $41.

There's little chance of getting bored at Coco Palms, even if you scarcely leave the grounds. There are nine tennis courts and a tennis pro, the 18-hole Wailua Golf Course nearby, a shopping arcade, and three beautiful outdoor pools. Shows are presented every night in the Lagoon Dining Room. The only disadvantages that we can see are that you must cross the road to get to the beach, and the ocean can be a bit choppy at times. Otherwise, perfect.

About a mile past Coco Palms, on the ocean side of the road, is a more moderately priced hotel that is also very pleasant, the **Kauai BeachBoy** (tel. 822-3441). Rooms here are $60 standard, $68 superior, and $80 deluxe, single or double. And there's nothing skimpy about the rooms. Facing either the gardens or the sea, each of the 242 units has its own lanai, is air-conditioned, has two double or twin beds, a color TV, a small refrigerator, a lovely, large dressing room with a mirrored closet, tile bathroom with stall shower, and smart decor throughout, from the Polynesian-print spreads on the beds to lamps with coconut bases. There is a huge, almost Olympic-size swimming pool, the Pool Bar and Broiler Restaurant, and a nightclub close to the water. Of course there's the beach, and Kauai's purple mountains in the background (from your room you might catch a view of the island's legendary "Sleeping Giant" cliff formation). The Market Place, a Hawaiian-style shopping village, is just across the street. For reservations and information, write to AmFac Hotels, P.O. Box 8520, Honolulu, HI 96830; or phone toll free 800/227-4700.

Right next door to the BeachBoy is the also very attractive **Islander on the Beach**, 484 Kuhio Hwy., Kapaa, HI 96746 (tel. toll free 800/367-5124). The three-story buildings, grouped around a free-form pool, provide a plantation feeling, and ironwood trees form a protective windbreak against the sea. Entering the lobby, you could easily imagine yourself in a gracious southern manor house if it were not for the vivid, lighthearted colors and Polynesian art reflecting the spirit of the islands. The large air-conditioned rooms, all refurbished and redecorated, are attractive. Closets are roomy, and the bath is divided for dual use. Rates vary seasonally: from December 20 to March 31, oceanfront rooms are $96, single or double; ocean-view rooms are $85; garden-view rooms are $74. During the summer months, April 1 to December 19, the rates are $76 oceanfront, $65 ocean view, $54 garden view. A third person is charged $10.

The newest hotel in the Coconut Plantation area is a spacious, sprawling, island kind of place called **Sheraton Coconut Beach Hotel,** Coconut Plantation, Kapaa, HI 96746 (tel. 822-3455; reservations, toll free 800/325-3535). The decorative emphasis throughout is on the arts and artifacts of Polynesia, from the stained-glass Hokule'a (the hotel has chosen the legendary Polynesian canoe as its logo) and the mural *The Floating Island* by noted artist Herbert Kawainui Kane in the lobby, to such meticulous details as authentic tapa designs carved on the doorknobs of each individual room. The setting is a beautiful one, with groves of coconut palms, Norfolk pines, flowers, and tropical vegetation all about. The hotel is set on 10½ acres of Waipouli Beach, fine for snorkeling but a little rough for swimming; guests can use the large waterfront pool or try one of the good swimming beaches nearby. Tennis buffs have the use of three courts and have a tennis pro on hand; they can use the courts all day for $6, rent rackets, and have the use of a ball machine.

As is expected from a Sheraton, dining and entertainment facilities are top-notch, beginning with three-meal room service. The Voyage Room serves a splendid noontime buffet, plus breakfast and dinner; the poolside stand is popular for foot-long hot dogs with salad served from 11 a.m. to 4 p.m.; and the hotel's luau, held every night except Monday, is considered one of the best on Kauai. Within walking distance are all the restaurants and shops of the Coconut Plantation Market Place.

Rooms at the Sheraton Coconut Beach have all been tastefully decorated with authentic Polynesian touches, and over 70% of them have an ocean view. Rates for single or double rooms are $85 coconut grove view, $95 garden view, $110 partial ocean view, $120 ocean view, $135 oceanfront, $240 for suites. Portable refrigerators are available in the higher priced rooms. Third and fourth persons in the room are $15 each, and children under 17 stay free with their parents in existing bedding.

If you'd like to settle into this area and have a place with your own kitchen, you can't do better than at the **Plantation Hale Hotel,** Coconut Plantation, Waipouli, HI 96746 (tel. 822-4941), which has three swimming pools and some of the most eye-catching, luxurious rooms we've seen in the islands. The hotel is of the cluster type; there are several two-story buildings grouped around the three pools. Within are 160 air-conditioned units, all exactly the same. Each consists of a living room with sofa bed and a bedroom with two more double beds, all expensively decorated with beige carpeting and beautifully made cane furniture; a dressing room complete with built-ins; a large bathroom with tub and shower; a private lanai, and a full kitchen with a pass-through to a counter in the living room. The cost is $70 to $80, single or double. Although it has no restaurant, it is directly adjacent to Coconut Plantation Market Place with its several eating places, and there are other excellent restaurants less than a mile in either direction.

HOTELS IN THE POIPU-KUKUIULA AREA: On the dry and sunny leeward side of Kauai, about 14 miles south of Lihue, is a glorious area that comes as close to the real Hawaii as you can get. Around every bend another little garden curves down toward the sea, and the white, sandy beaches look out on a crashing, spectacular blue-green surf. Swimming is ideal here. If you want to settle down in Kauai, this, in our opinion, is the place to do it. But even if you have just a few days, it's a convenient base for island sightseeing.

Right on Poipu Beach, surely one of the loveliest in the islands, is the deservedly popular **Sheraton Kauai Hotel,** (reservations, toll free 800/325-3535 from mainland U.S., 800/268-9393 from eastern Canada, 800/268-9330 from western Canada), stretching across 20 acres of prime Poipu Beach property. The 340 guest rooms, split between a Garden Wing and Ocean Wing (the latter totally renovated and redecorated), are housed in low-rise, two-to four-story buildings set amid lush tropical gardens and meandering waterways. The Garden Wing, less than five years old, has spacious and modern rooms, all with air conditioning, television, radio, telephone, refrigerator, and private lanai. The Ocean Wing boasts 114 oceanfront guest rooms, plus suites. Entertainment and dining facilities are quite special. The Drum Lounge, perched alongside the ocean, features nightly entertainment. At the Pareo Pub, it's Menehune Magic Hour from 4:30 to 9:30 p.m. From noon to 4 p.m. light meals and snacks are as close as poolside at the Trellis Snackbar in the Garden Wing. And the Outrigger Restaurant serves all three meals with evening entertainment.

The Sheraton Kauai is just steps away from an excellent sandy beach, but the hotel also has two freshwater pools and a wading pool for the kids. For the tennis buff, a brand-new ten-court tennis complex is within walking distance of the hotel. Golfers have two championship 18-hole courses and a nine-hole public course within close proximity to the hotel.

Winter rates, single or double, begin at $90 for garden view, go up to $100 for pool view, $110 for partial ocean view, $140 for oceanfront, and to $195 for a one-bedroom suite with garden view. Summer rates are $85, $95, $105, and $135, respectively. Children under 17 stay free with their parents; an extra adult is $15.

For reservations, call the toll-free numbers above, or write to Sheraton Hotels in Hawaii, P.O. Box 8559, Honolulu, HI 96815.

Old Hawaii hands who remember the Waiohai Hotel at Poipu Beach should be advised that the new **Waiohai Hotel** (tel. 945-6121), risen from the rubble of the completely razed older hotel, bears no resemblance at all to its predecessor, which had the graceful charm of old Hawaii. But the new complex is modern and handsome in its own way, with lobby, corridors, and three restaurants open to the trade winds, the ocean, and the lush gardens. The elegant Polynesian motif is carried out in the guest rooms, furnished in rattan with Polynesian print bedspreads and big lanais. Some 460 units offer an incredibly wide range of accommodations, from the standard room with mountain view at $115 double, to the two-bedroom Waiohai Suite at $850 daily for up to six persons. The superior and deluxe one-room units are $150 and $180 daily, respectively. One-bedroom suites begin at $340 per day for two.

The Waiohai has everything one would require of a resort hotel: six tennis courts, an 18-hole golf course, a Clark Hatch Fitness Center, two swimming pools (three, if you count the children's pool), and most important of all, beautiful Poipu Beach.

For reservations, contact the central reservations office for AmFac Resorts Hawaii at P.O. Box 8520, Honolulu, HI 96830. You can call them toll free at 800/227-4700.

The older **Poipu Beach Hotel,** Waiohai's sister AmFac resort, has been newly renovated and absorbed into the grander Waiohai as its family wing. It's a low-key and pleasant spot. We've always liked the rooms here; they are large and nicely furnished, each with twin beds or a double bed and color TV. And every room has a compact little kitchenette as well as a dressing room—all of which make for very easy, very comfortable living. Every room is the same, but those that have a mountain view rent for $75 double, those with an ocean or pool view go for $85 and $98, single or double; suites from $190. There is a charge of $6 per extra person. There's a pool, of course, but you can practically fall out of your room onto the beach—it's that close. And it's a favorite snorkeling spot.

For reservations and information, contact, again, AmFac Resorts, P.O. Box 8520, Honolulu, HI 96830; or phone toll free 800/227-4700.

Kiahuna Plantation, R.R. 1, Box 73, Koloa, HI 96756 (reservations, call toll free 800/367-7052 from mainland U.S., or call collect 800/742-6411 from Canada and Hawaii), has gained a reputation for itself as one of the ultimate condominium resorts in the islands. Some 333 decorator-furnished one- and two-bedroom beach houses covering 200 acres ramble down to the water (only a few are at the water's edge), with more in the works. The luxurious, fully carpeted apartments have space to spare, beautiful appointments, either a queen-size bed or two twin beds in the bedrooms and queen-size hideabed sofas in the living room, and garden or ocean vistas. There's daily maid service, but no TV. Right at hand is the delightful Plantation Gardens Restaurant (see ahead) for continental dining.

Water sports are superb here, there are ten championship tennis courts, and an 18-hole championship golf course designed by Robert Trent Jones—all of which makes Kiahuna a mecca of sorts for the sporting set. One-bedroom apartments, which can sleep four, are $85, $95, $110, $150, and $215, double occupancy. Two-bedroom apartments, which can shelter six, are $155, $175, $190, and $280. Special vacation packages are available at attractive prices.

Now here's good news: lovely apartments at reasonable prices. **Sunset Kahili Apartments,** R.R. 1, Box 96, Koloa, HI 96756 (tel. 742-1691, or toll free 800/367-8047, ext. 212), are situated on a bluff, with a fine sandy beach just two blocks away. You have your choice of a one- or two-bedroom apartment. In either case, you'll have a fully equipped kitchen including a dishwasher and a laundry washer-dryer. Each apartment has beautiful, thick wall-to-wall carpeting, floor-to-ceiling draperies, and a private lanai overlooking the swimming pool and blue Pacific. Off-season rates, April 1 to December 14, are $51 for two people in a one-bedroom apartment with ocean and garden view, $56 with ocean and beach view; $71 for four people in a two-bedroom/two-bath apartment with ocean and garden view, $76 with ocean and beach view. During the high season, December 15 to March 31, rates for the one-bedrooms are $58 and $63; for the two-bedrooms, $79 and $85. Minimum stay is three days; rates get progressively lower the longer you stay.

Sharon and Robert Flynn, the hospitable owners/managers of **Garden Isle Cottages** in Poipu (R.R. 1, Box 355, Koloa, HI 96756; tel. 742-6717 from 9 a.m. to noon daily, Hawaiian time), have only a small number of cottages at their disposal; you'll be lucky and happy if you can get one. Their cottages are scattered along the Poipu shore, nestled in tropical gardens, and artistically decorated with batiks, tapas, and some of Bob's own sculpture and paintings. Sea Cliff Cottages are very large one-bedroom apartments overlooking a small ocean inlet, renting for $60 double. Hale Melia, across from the ocean, has a beautiful one-bedroom apartment at $60, and there are two studios, one at $36, another at $40. Hale Waipahu is a beautiful duplex with a 360° view from the highest point overlooking Poipu Beach; it rents for $95.

Attractive accommodations, budget prices, a warm and hospitable management, and an excellent location all combine to make **Prince Kuhio Condominiums** (Prince Kuhio Rentals, P.O. Box 1060, Koloa, HI 96756; tel. 742-1409) very, very popular in this area. Den and Dee Wilson, the charming owners/managers are on hand to make everyone feel right at home. Apartments are attractively furnished, fully equipped for housekeeping, and range from twin-bedded studios at $39 double daily ($234 weekly) and regular one-bedroom apartments for four at $46 daily ($276 weekly) to deluxe one-bedroom units for four at $55 daily ($330 weekly)—surely one of the best values in Kauai. Apartments overlook a garden and pool on one side, Prince Kuhio Park on the other. Good swimming beaches are a short drive away, and there's a good snorkeling beach right across the road. Also across the road is the terrific Beach House Restaurant.

THE GOOD LIFE AT PRINCEVILLE: Located on a lush green plateau that extends from the mountains through some 11,000 acres of rolling pastures, river valleys, and undeveloped forest lands down to spectacular white-sand beaches, Princeville at Hanalei is a multimillion-dollar planned resort where the living is easy and the outdoor recreational facilities superb: there's a spectacular Robert Trent Jones, Jr. 27-hole golf course considered one of the top 100 in the world, six outdoor tennis courts, facilities for swimming, sailing, snorkeling, trapshooting, horseback riding, and more. Accommodations in some 18 different condominiums and area resorts range from medium-priced to deluxe; there are about a dozen restaurants on the premises. And it's here that an enchanting new Sheraton hotel opened in 1986 to become an immediate hit.

Built in a series of three terraces on the face of Pu'upea Point, **the Sheraton Princeville Hotel**, P.O. Box 3069, Princeville, HI

96722 (tel. 826-9244; reservations, toll free 800/325-3535), over-looks Hanalei Valley, green mountains sparkling with waterfalls, across clear, blue Hanalei Bay to the ocean. The feeling here is that of a special retreat: the furnishings and appointments reflect the style of a gracious plantation of the Hawaiian Monarchy era. The central theme of the interior design is the Hawaiian quilt; a reproduction of an authentic Hawaiian quilt adorns each bed. Carpeting throughout the hotel reflects the green of the mountains and the burgundy of the Kauai sunset. The furniture that the missionaries brought from New England is faithfully reproduced in polished woods; for example, the color TV set in each room hides in a reproduction of a New England pie safe. The Lime Tree Lounge, the lobby bar, features handmade willow furniture in white with sea-foam green cushions; the Hale Kapa Restaurant shows a display of handmade quilts from Boston and Kauai; Ukiyo-E, the main cocktail lounge, is decorated in the style of Japan in the 1850s, with Ukiyo-E woodblock print designs lovingly etched on the mirrors. Café Hanalei serves breakfast, lunch and dinner in an open-air setting with a superb view of the bay. Nibbles, the hotel's signature restaurant, is decorated in the style of European royalty as it was copied by the Hawaiian monarchy. The 23-acre grounds feature a freshwater swimming pool and whirlpool spa, with an adjoining beach bar and grill. The calm waters of Hanalei Bay beckon to lovers of snorkeling and scuba-diving. The Princeville Golf Course and tennis courts are at hand.

Rates, single or double, are $120 daily for golf-course view rooms, $150 for bay views, $175 for ocean views. Suites begin at $350 per day. (Rates subject to change.)

Among the most popular condominium complexes here are the **Makai Club Cottages,** adjacent to the first fairway of Princeville's Woods golf course. They are completely equipped for easy living, and large enough—in the two-bedroom/two-bath units—to accommodate two couples with privacy. Rates for the one-bedroom units are $65 and $85; for the two-bedroom units, $105. For reservations contact Princeville Reservations Office, P.O. Box 3040, Princeville, HI 96722. Toll free from the mainland, phone 800/367-7090; in Honolulu, 524-5972.

Picture-perfect Hawaii is what we call **Hanalei Bay Resort,** P.O. Box 220, Hanalei, Kauai, HI 96714 (tel. 826-6522), a separately owned and managed luxury condominium hotel in the Princeville complex. The setting is a spectacular one, with the lobby and outstanding Bali H'ai Restaurant (more about which ahead) on the top level, and low-slung buildings winding down 20 acres to the white sands of Hanalei Beach below. Tennis players have 11 championship courts (three of them lighted), full pro shop and teaching program; golfers get a discount at the 27-hole Princeville "Makai" course surrounding the property. There are also two swimming pools and sauna, and good swimming in the ocean, which is, however, a long walk from many of the apartments (a roving jitney provides on-call service around the sometimes steeply sloped complex). Inside the buildings, which are named "Hibiscus," "Bouganvillaea," and the like, to correspond with the flowers growing outside their doors, are exquisitely furnished studio and one- and two-bedroom apartments, with plentiful space, rattan furniture, beautiful dressing rooms, large baths, complete electric kitchens, and coral fronds and other artful decorations on the walls. Prices for mountain-view apartments are $65 for a hotel room, $75 for a studio, $90 for a one-bedroom/one-bath suite, $105 for a one-bedroom/two-bath suite (up to four people), $125 for a two-bedroom/two-bath suite (up to four people). For ocean-view units, the rates are $75 for a hotel room, $85 for a studio, $105 for a one-bedroom/one-bath suite, $105 for a two-bedroom/two-bath suite (up to four people), $145 for a two-bedroom/two-bath suite, $210 and $350 (for up to six people) in the luxurious Bali H'ai and Alii suites. Add $10 more for a rollaway bed.

Dining in Kauai

RESTAURANTS IN LIHUE: Whether or not you're based in Lihue, you'll undoubtedly come into town and want to spend some time here, so it's fun to try some of the local restaurants that consistently serve up tasty food at very decent prices. Turn onto Kress Street in downtown Lihue and you can't miss the **Lihue Barbecue Inn,** 2982 Kress St. Owner Henry Sasaki has recently renovated this popular *kamaaina* place; now, with its new tropical decor, it's more cozy than ever. But the food is the thing here, with Japanese, Chinese, and American meals available. You could bite your nails at dinnertime (no nutritional value in that) choosing among dishes like fresh corned beef and cabbage, broiled teriyaki butterfish, teriyaki steak and shrimp tempura, seafood platter, and shrimp scampi, from about $5.95 to $8. There are also a few higher-priced specialties like island T-bone steak and lobster, up to about $14.95. Luncheon specials, ranging from $3.50 to $4.95 for a complete meal, include a variety of salads such as somen,

Chinese chicken, tofu, and taco. Try their exotic drinks; the "chichis" are excellent. And the mood is always friendly. Open every day but Sunday for breakfast, 8 to 10:30 a.m.; lunch, 10:30 a.m. to 1:30 p.m.; dinner, 4:30 to 8:45 p.m.

For the best steak in Lihue, we vote for **J. J.'s Broiler,** just down the main Hwy. 56 from the Lihue Shopping Center, on the road leading to the sugar mill. And from the number of local people who frequent J. J.'s, we're not alone in this opinion. Our favorite spot in this smartly styled restaurant is the courtyard with its statues. Specialty of the house is the Slavonic steak, at $10.95, with an exquisite flavor. (Gourmet food publications have been trying to wrest the recipe from owner Jim Jasper for years, but it remains a well-kept secret.) The price includes salad-bar helpings and freshly baked French bread. Or you might have the beef kebabs, mahimahi, teriyaki steak, tender smoked beef and pork ribs, scallops, or lobster, priced from $6.95 to $17.50. Salad bar and soup alone is $6.25. Dinner and cocktails from 5 to 10 p.m. Reservations recommended: tel. 245-3841.

The new Kauai Hilton offers two delightful dining possibilities: choose the exquisite Midori for a lovely splurge, or the attractive Jacaranda Terrace for a good meal at reasonable prices. **Midori** is exquisitely appointed. The eye is drawn to the very old, very precious and rare Japanese rice plates displayed in cases on the walls, as well as the jewel-like tones of the Oriental oil paintings and murals. The place settings are luxury plus: porcelain dinner plates are lavishly decorated with 24-carat gold, the wine and water glasses are crystal. Fresh flowers flank the beautifully carved, black marble column in the middle of the room. Cuisine at Midori is both Oriental and continental; among the appetizers, for example, you could have Molokai shrimp, veal carpaccio (marinated with herbs and avocado sauce), or beef samurai (stir-fried with spicy vegetables and cellophane noodles). Salads too are out of the ordinary; consider grilled duck breast on exotic greens, topped with a sesame-lime dressing; or the Midori salad of romaine, avocado, and watercress with goat cheese. There are less than 12 entrees on the menu; prices run from $17 to $23. Fresh fish of the day is a winner, whichever way you choose to have it—steamed with fresh herbs and threads of fresh vegetables, broiled and served with saké sauce and shiitake mushrooms, or sautéed and enhanced with papaya, ginger, and herb-lemon sauce. Other good choices include medallions of veal, beef tenderloin, New York steak, rack of lamb, breast of duckling, and baby onoma chicken. We like the baked Brie for dessert; cheesecake, fresh tropical fruit sorbet, and pastries are other tempting possibilities. Only dinner is served, nightly from 6 to 10 p.m. Reservations are an absolute must: tel. 245-1955.

Charming is the word to describe the **Jacaranda Terrace** at the Hilton, a real terrace overlooking pools and ocean, furnished in an off-white rattan; individual dining cubicles shelter lavender booths, each with an original painting on the wall. The menu might be termed "fancy coffeeshop"; both lunch and dinner offer green and pasta salads, sandwiches (fresh smoked tuna on grain bread, with cucumbers and sprouts, $5.75, is delicious), burgers, "Fitness First" specials (stuffed papaya, broiled chicken), fresh fruit and yogurt smoothies; and the dinner menu adds on some tasty and well-priced main-dish specialties. Plantation frittata, honey-dipped fried chicken, brochette of beef teriyaki, and linguine primavera go from $7.25 to $10.95; fresh island fish, fried coconut shrimp, chicken breast saltimbocca, and veal marsala run from $13.75 to $16.50. The roast prime ribs of beef, with fresh horseradish, served with baked potato and fresh vegetables, is very popular at $14.50. For desserts, go with the Hula Coupe at $3. Open every day.

Where do the local people take guests when they want to treat them to something special? To one of the nicest places around Lihue town, the **Hanamaulu Café,** two miles north of Lihue on Hwy. 56. While the indoor part of the café looks like just another pleasantly ordinary Oriental restaurant, the garden is something else again. Individual Japanese tea rooms look out on a beautiful garden with stone toros, bonsai, carp, all in a tranquil and moody setting. The nicest thing about all this is that you don't need a minimum group to get one of these *ozashiki* rooms (but it is a good idea to make reservations), in which you can order anything on the menu, even the $5.50 plate dinners. There's a variety of à la carte Oriental dishes at $4.50 to about $6. Or treat yourself to a multicourse Oriental banquet for about $10 per person. Cocktails are available. The sushi bar turns out delicate morsels of fish and vegetables, plus yakinukui dishes—meat, chicken, and assorted vegetables cooked on a special grill. The food is subtly seasoned—delicious! For reservations, phone 245-2511 or 245-3225.

If you're like us and the mere thought of Mexican food makes your mouth water, don't just sit there, hasten to **La Luna** at 4261 Rice St., a casual *fonda* with a spacious, covered outdoor dining area, a smartly decorated interior, a big bar, and lots of tasty dishes reasonably priced. You might as well start with a margarita magnifica or a tequila sunrise while they're fixing your appetizers; perhaps the super nachos or quesadillas at $4.50. Then on to combination plates and specialties like deep-fried burritos, chile relleno, and tostada suprema ($4.50 to $6.50). La Luna is open every day from 11 a.m. to 10 p.m., and there's live entertainment every night from 8:30. It could be Mexican music, it could also be country western—or whatever. Phone: 245-9173. *Simpatico*.

RESTAURANTS IN POIPU AND HANAPEPE: A spot as much favored by locals as tourists, **Plantation Gardens Restaurant** sits majestically in a seven-acre botanical paradise of cacti and rare plants. Part of Kiahuna Plantation (see above), the restaurant is a restored 19th-century plantation manager's home, an incomparable setting for dining on gourmet cuisine. You could begin, for example, by having a drink in the Poi Pounder Room (where Hawaiian calabashes and stone tikis are displayed in antique French armoires), or outside in the garden bar. Then on to dinner, perhaps in a Victorian drawing room, or in the main dining room, open on three sides to look out over lily ponds, cactus gardens, palm trees, and the blue Pacific beyond. The international menu features fresh local fish caught daily, imported seafoods, plus prime rib and steak. Most meat and seafood entrees run between $14.95 and $16.95, and along with your entree you get either a garden, Caesar, or hot spinach salad, or soup of the day, plus fresh vegetables and a basket of breads. Appetizers like crab-stuffed mushrooms with sautéed onion are delicious, and so are desserts like Naughty Hula Pie, a macadamia-nut ice-cream pie topped with chocolate sauce and whipped cream. Half a dozen light suppers—crab custard quiche, seafood crêpes, prime rib sandwich, and the like—are available from $9.95 to $10.95; three children's selections are $9.95. Plantation Gardens serves dinner only, nightly from 5:30 to 10 p.m.; the very popular bar is known for luscious tropical drinks and pupus in a relaxed setting. Reservations: 742-1695.

If you can manage to work out your itinerary to do so, you'll be well rewarded by being in Kauai on a Sunday morning. That's when you can join the island people in what is surely the most spectacular Sunday champagne brunch in the islands—at the **Waiohai Terrace** of the Waiohai Hotel. So famous is this brunch that people gladly wait in line for an hour or more to gain entrance (no reservations are taken); if you arrive by 9:15 a.m., we were told, you'll have your best chance of a short line. Once admitted, you'll be rewarded by a seat in a graciously decorated, open-to-the-sea room with the beautiful beach right in front of you. You'll also be rewarded with a view of half a dozen buffet tables laden with great delicacies—smoked fish and sashimi, many pastas, shrimp dishes, salads, prime ribs, flavorful pâtés, fresh fruits, hot breads, macadamia-nut pies, strawberry sherbets, special dishes that the chef has dreamed up that day. Omelets will be created at your command. New dishes are brought out frequently, and off you go to the table again—and again—and again. The servers estimate that most people spend about two hours eating here! The cost of this unforgettable repast, which includes champagne, is $19.50, and it's served between 10 a.m. and 2 p.m. A Hawaiian trio provides background music.

If you're not in Kauai on a Sunday, you can come to the Waiohai Terrace any night and dine on a delicious salad bar, also laden with many special dishes, plus grilled garlic bread, for $12.50. Regular meals start at about $13.75 for Kauai huli chicken, and go up to $17 (for prime ribs of beef), $19.50 (seafood platter), and higher. After your meal, take off your shoes, walk along the beach under the stars, and enjoy the special magic of the Kauai night.

A not-to-be-forgotten dining experience awaits you at **Tamarind,** Waiohai's incomparable continental restaurant, winner of the *Travel/Holiday* Award, and recently selected by a Honolulu critic as one of the top seven restaurants in the state. The setting is one of unsurpassed elegance, from the exquisite chandelier resembling two enormous seashells to the silken fabrics and brass decorations. Decor is in deep reds with rattan throne chairs; a candle and a bouquet of flowers adorn each table. Service is what you would expect in a fine European establishment, with a knowledgeable sommelier to help you choose the proper wines. And it's been a long time since we've seen a *porte-couteau,* the little crystal, dumbbell-shaped accoutrement on which a knife rests, but there was one on our table at Tamarind. Food is served on fine crystal and china, and it lives up to its elegant setting.

There's a mind-boggling assortment of chilled and hot appetizers from which to choose—such as lobster salad with papaya and fresh ginger, or escargot and shrimp on a bed of vegetable suprême with saffron sauce. And soups are unusual too; you might have chilled cream of chicken with almonds or even duck consommé with goose liver in a puff pastry. Although the crevettes et coquilles St-Jacques—shrimp and scallops sautéed with leeks and oranges—was intriguing, we opted for sautéed Hawaiian lobster, fresh scallops, and mushrooms in a basil-and-truffle lobster sauce on a pastry shell. Other selections from the fascinating menu include grenadine of veal, tournedos sautéed with truffles and wine, rack of lamb, and stir-fried lobster with Chinese black beans. Entrees are all à la carte and range from $18.50 to $24; appetizers and soups are about $4 to $8. The dessert cart offers extravagant cheesecakes, pies, fruit tortes, and our choice, a lovely flan accompanied by fresh strawberries and blackberries. The service and ambience are as outstanding as the cuisine and they all coalesce for a memorable evening. The Tamarind serves dinner nightly from 6 to 10:30 p.m. The lounge is open until midnight, with Kimo Garner's music from 7:30 to 11:30 p.m. Reservations are essential: tel. 742-9511.

For those nights when you don't feel like cooking in at the condo or going out to dine at someplace fancy, the **Koloa Broiler,** on Koloa Road, is a great compromise; cook your steak, mahimahi, barbecued chicken, marinated beef kebabs, or burgers right there, over the open grill. While everything's sizzling, you help yourself to salad bar and baked beans. And the price is right: $5.95 to $9.95 at dinner, the same at lunch plus a $3.50 hamburger. There's a lively bar, a pleasant lanai to sit on, and a good, casual time to be had by all. Open daily from 11 a.m. to 10 p.m. (tel. 742-9122).

Visiting Waimea Canyon is a Kauai must, and another Kauai must is stopping at the **Green Garden Restaurant** on Hwy. 50 in Hanapepe for a meal either before or after. Green Garden is a longtime *kamaaina* favorite (it has been run by several generations of the same family for almost 40 years), and it manages to serve delicious food at moderate prices in a spirit of real island aloha. The place does look like a garden, full of plants and flowers, done in a bamboo-and-white motif. The menu is a combination of Oriental and American dishes, with special kudos for the selections from the kiawe wood char-broiler, most from $6.50 to $14, a few going up to $23. These include pork chops brushed with butter or teriyaki sauce, "butterflied" rock lobster tail, sumiyaki (char-broiled beef kebab brushed with teriyaki), and steaks, from $6.50 up. They are served with fruit cup or homemade soup, tossed salad, and coffee or tea. Most complete dinners run $5.25 to $7.35, with such main-course choices as shrimp tempura, boneless teriyaki chicken, sweet-and-sour spare ribs, with all the extras. And you could also declare a special holiday and have a nine-course Oriental dinner on about a half-hour's notice! The Green Garden's homemade pies are a must: even the strongest will falter at the sight of their coconut cream or chocolate cream or their famous macadamia-nut and lilikoi pies.

The Green Garden is open from 6 a.m. to 2 p.m. and from 5 to 8:30 p.m., but closed Tuesday evenings (tel. 335-5422).

RESTAURANTS IN THE PRINCEVILLE-HANALEI AREA: Right in the little town of Hanalei itself, next to the Hanalei Trader shop, is a restaurant on the river called **Hanalei Dolphin.** Tiki poles mark the entrance, and inside, tapa-topped lacquered tables, glass-float lights, a redwood interior with a dramatic inlaid mural set the scene for relaxed dining. The food here has always been good, and a local friend swears that the Dolphin's teriyaki ahi (listed on the menu as fresh fish) is the finest to be found in Kauai (she also recommends fish over the steak here). Other favorites, from $9.50 to market price include Alaskan king crab, haole chicken (boneless breaded breast with parmesan cheese, with a side of sweet-and-sour sauce), two kinds of shrimp (char-broiled or baked in a butter sauce and topped with sour cream), and an excellent New York cut of teriyaki steak. Light dinners, with choices of broccoli casserole, clam chowder, or salad, are $8. All entrees are served with family-style salad, steak fries or rice, and hot homemade bread. Home-baked desserts are another plus for the Dolphin (they've got a whopping-good Mud Pie), as well as solid appetizers like ceviche and New England clam chowder. Dinner only, 6 to 10 p.m. (tel. 826-6113).

All steak lovers in these parts are unanimous in singing the praises of the steaks at the **Beamreach Restaurant,** in the Pali Ke Kua complex at Princeville. Well, of course you could have some very good fish and seafood dishes here, but why bother, when you can savor the likes of an exceptional steak teriyaki (featured in *Bon Appétit* magazine), an equally tasty chicken teriyaki, a terrific ground sirloin, filet mignon, and more. Prices start at $7.95 for the ground sirloin and go up to about $19.95 for the steak-and-lobster combo. You'll have more than enough to eat, since your entree comes with a good salad bowl and a choice of baked potato or rice, but you may want to start with the cheese board or chile among the appetizers to go along with your strawberry daiquiri, the house specialty. Beamreach has an open feeling with its beamed ceilings, attractive nautical decor, and view of the golf course. Reservations: 826-9131.

RESTAURANTS IN THE WAILUA-WAIPOULI-COCONUT PLANTATION AREA: For an elegant evening in Kauai, head for the luxurious **Coco Palms Hotel.** Make your reservations before 7:30 in the **La-**

goon **Dining Room** so you'll be seated for the impressive torch-lighting ceremony, done with great authenticity and a true feeling of the olden days. Dinner features good continental dishes. The menu changes every night, but typical appetizers include lomi-lomi salmon, tropical fruit, and potage St-Germain. Your main course could be roast capon or teriyaki steak, Polynesian shrimp tempura or Wailua beef brochette. You'll also get salad, vegetables, and potatoes with your main dish, and a choice of dessert—perhaps orange chiffon pie or the famed Coco Palms sundae (vanilla ice cream with coconut syrup and coconut topping)—for an all-inclusive price, from $14.50 to about $23. Around 9 p.m., when you're sipping your coffee, the evening show gets under way; it's always pleasant, featuring traditional island entertainers. There is no cover charge. Reservations: 822-4921.

Another good Coco Palms possibility: the buffet brunch every day from 10 a.m. to 2 p.m., at around $9.50, filling and delicious.

Just north of Coconut Plantation Market Place and its attractive fast-food stands are many restaurants in the little town of **Kapaa**, all catering to the large crowd of visitors and condo dwellers in this part of the island. Two tried-and-true favorites on Kuhio Hwy. here are **Kountry Kitchen** (tel. 822-3511), which offers wonderful omelets for breakfast; burgers, sandwiches, reasonably priced entrees for lunch; and excellent dinners, which feature barbecued spare ribs, sesame shrimp, fresh local fish, quiche, etc., at prices of about $6.15 to $8.25; and **Ono-Family Restaurant** (tel. 822-1710), also known for terrific breakfast omelets, very good fish sandwiches and burgers plus plate lunches at noontime, and such dinner specialties as pork chops, ribs, or teriyaki chicken, between $7.75 and $10.95.

After Dark in Kauai

Nightlife in Kauai is where you find it. There's nothing spectacular enough to warrant a 40-mile drive, but wherever you are, something will be going on—perhaps Hawaiian entertainment, rock music, or just soft sounds to sip your cocktails by. Most of the big hotels provide Hawaiian shows for their dinner guests. And we should tell you that here in the neighbor islands Hawaiian shows are usually relaxed, informal affairs, much less pretentious than those in Waikiki. Besides, you'll probably recognize the faces of the entertainers: they may be the hotel clerks or bus-boys or cab drivers you met during the day! In the islands, everybody dances, everybody sings, and surprisingly well. Unless it's a dinner show, a drink or two gets you a ringside seat for the action;

unless there is name entertainment, there's usually no cover or minimum charge.

LIHUE: A walk around the glamorous new **Westin Kauai Resort** will be entertainment in itself, and the new hotel (still a-building at this writing) will doubtless have a bevy of nightspots, including a disco . . . **Gilligan's** is a popular disco venue at the also lovely new Kauai Hilton at Hanamaulu . . . And down by the wharf at Nawiliwili Harbor **Club Jetty** continues to be the local hangout, as it has been for years, alternating between live band and disco until the wee hours.

COCONUT PLANTATION-WAILUA-WAIPOULI: There's a lot of action at the hotels out here. At the **Sheraton Coconut Beach Hotel** there's entertainment from 7 every night at **Cook's Landing,** plus terrific luaus nightly except Monday. Admission of about $33 for adults, $20 for children, includes one-hour bar, buffet dinner, and show. . . . Another top luau is held on the same nights at the **Kauai Resort Hotel** for $32. . . . **The Lagoon Dining Room** is the place for the Coco Palms dinner show, every night at 9: it's either Larry Rivera or varied singing and dancing groups . . . A swinging disco called the **Boogie Palace** packs in the crowds at the **Kauai BeachBoy Hotel,** every night from 9 on. There's a $1 cover. . . . A far-out disco is the **The Vanishing Point** at Waipouli Plaza, a mile past Coconut Plantation, with live music and disco from 10 p.m. to 4 a.m. every night. Cover charge is $1 weekdays, $2 weekends.

POIPU BEACH: The best entertainment in the area takes place on Sunday and Wednesday nights with the weekly Polynesian Revue and dinner at the **Sheraton-Kauai Hotel;** Chief Henry Taeza and his troupe of dancers and musicians provide the entertainment, and the Sheraton chefs whip up an international buffet table with over 50 dishes. The cost is $31 for adults, $21 for children . . . There's also nightly entertainment at the **Drum Lounge** of the same hotel . . . Over at the **Poipu Beach Hotel's Mahina Lounge,** it's live disco and rock music from 9 p.m. to closing.

HANALEI: The luaus at **Tahiti Nui** (tel. 826-6277) are so much fun that people call from the mainland to make reservations! They're held Monday, Wednesday, and Friday nights, and cost only $20. Tahiti Nui's Louise and her friendly crew have been at this funky tropical café for over 20 years and know how to make sure everybody has a good time. Dinner—fresh South Pacific catch, stuffed calamari, chicken curry, smoked ribs and steak, from $8.95 to $13.95—is on every night.

The Sights and Sounds of Kauai

Since you cannot circle entirely around the island of **Kauai** and see it all in one day, you must plan on at least two full-day sightseeing excursions. The trip to **Waimea Canyon** (the southern and western route) is best made on a clear day; call the weather bureau before you go. If it's foggy, take the eastern and northern trip first. Both trips are about 40 miles from Lihue each way, and since each offers a full share of gorgeous little beaches as well as awesome natural wonders, you should plan to leave early in the morning, pick up a box lunch in town for a picnic (or check the restaurant selections above), throw your bathing suits and suntan lotions into the backseat, and head off for an adventure.

WESTWARD TO THE CANYON: Get thee to **Lihue,** the center (for all practical purposes) of the island and the site of a delightful shopping complex in the center of town. Nearby, at 3016 Umi St., Suite 207, you will find the offices of the **Hawaii Visitors Bureau,** where you can pick up a variety of information.

Your next stop in Lihue should definitely be the **Kauai Museum,** a two-building complex at 4428 Rice St., housing a splendid collection of Hawaiiana (quilts, calabashes, furniture, artifacts, etc.) as well as the permanent exhibit, "The Story of Kauai," which includes a video showing the highlights of Kauai's scenery. Note the Museum Shop, with many fine Hawaiian and South Pacific items. Open Monday to Friday from 9:30 a.m. to 4:30 p.m. Admission is $3 for adults; children under 17 get in free with an adult.

Now cross Eiwa Street and walk to the site of the new **Civic Center,** whose daring architecture is strikingly modern in this setting. Back in your car now, follow Rice Street until you almost reach its junction with Hwy. 50. To your left is the quaint little **Haleko Drive** and four restored homes once belonging to sugar plantation workers, which now house several restaurants, including **J. J.'s Broiler** and the cozy little **The Eggbert's.**

Now follow Hwy. 51 to **Nawiliwili** (the place where the willow trees grow). Once one of the most bustling harbors in the island, it is just a shadow of its former self. The biggest attraction here is lovely **Kalapaki Beach,** one of the best in Kauai, the town beach that residents share with guests of **The Westin Kauai.**

After a swim here (highly recommended), you might head for some most entertaining shopping at the huge **Kukui Grove Center,** about a mile from the airport on Rte. 50. We could get lost for days here at **Rainbow Books,** browsing through a quality selection, checking out the wonderful art collection at **Stone's Gallery** in the rear, or dining on heavenly pastries and coffees at **Rainbow Coffees,** which sits right in the middle of the store. Other personal favorites here are **See You in China** for crafts and clothing by local artists, and **Butterflies Too?** for imaginative gifts —jewelry, belts, baby clothing, quilts, etc.—all in the shape of, or decorated with, butterflies. Popular restaurants include **Rosita's Mexican Restaurant** for good food and drinks, and the **Kukui Nut Tree Inn** for pleasant and inexpensive family-type meals.

Poipu

About 14 miles out of Lihue you head into the tranquil **Koloa** region of Kauai, where a recent restoration has created **Old Koloa Town,** with some enjoyable restaurants (see the preceding chapter) and shops, and a historic site here and there like the old Koloa Hotel built in 1898 for traveling salesmen from Honolulu. After you've browsed a bit and maybe had some ice cream at Lappert's, get back into the car, swing off the main drag onto Hwy. 52 and follow the markers to Poipu Beach. On Kiahuna Plantation is a remarkable botanical garden whose Hawaiian name is **Pa'u A Laka,** the Skirt of Laka, goddess of the hula and sister of the volcano goddess, Pele. It is believed that this site was once the training grounds for her disciples. The place abounds in history as well as horticultural beauty (a cactus garden, an orchid garden, a plumeria plantation), and you are invited to walk through the gardens free; markers identify plants. The gardens are, alas, smaller than they once were, but still beautiful.

Now you continue on to the glorious **Poipu Beach** region. Although luxury hotels abound along this stretch of crystal and golden sand, the very best beach, the one to which even the hotels send their guests, is the Poipu public pavilion. It's the perfect place for a picnic and a swim.

Continue along the Poipu shore highway and you will come upon the monument, on the right side of the road, commemorating the birthplace of Prince Jonah Kuhio Kalanianaole, who represented Hawaii in the U.S. Congress from 1902 to 1922. Up the road, the **Kukuiulua Small Boat Harbor** is the best place to take in, in one swoop, the grandeur of the south shore of Kauai. Set your sights now for the **Spouting Horn** blowhole on your right, and then drive on down the highway to see it close up. A lava tube under the black rock funnels the force of the waves into a veritable geyser; the effect is spectacular.

Back on Hwy. 50 now, watch for the HVB marker and the sign indicating **Olu Pua Gardens,** just past the junction of 50 with 54. Here you'll find another horticultural fairyland (they really mean it when they call Kauai the "Garden Island"). On 12½ acres of land that was once a plantation manager's estate is an island-within-an-island of floral beauty. Open for guided tours only, on Monday, Wednesday, and Friday at 9:30 a.m., 11:30 a.m., and 1:30 p.m. Admission is $6 for adults, $4 for senior citizens. For reservations and information, tel. 332-8182.

Back on Hwy. 50, you'll come to the HVB warrior pointing directly to the lush and lovely valley of **Hanapepe.** It's a fine miniature of some of the grander valleys you'll see on Kauai. If you're hungry, stop for lunch at the **Green Garden.** The **Salt Pond Pavilion** is a good spot for a picnic lunch and a swim; turn toward the ocean on Hwy. 543 outside Hanapepe. Down the other fork of the highway are located the ancient salt ponds where the *Hui Hana Paakai O Hanapepe* still practice the ancient art of salt-making. These drying beds are almost 200 years old.

On you go now, hurtling into the historic town of **Waimea** where Captain Cook first landed in 1778, looked around him, and claimed the Sandwich Islands for England. You'll first pass a state marker indicating the site of a Russian fort where a member of the Alaska Fur Trading Company, hoping to capture the island for his czar, built—and watched crumble—the walls of his six-pointed fort. Parking facilities have already been built, but until the complete fort is restored there's not much to detain you here.

Now watch for the sign leading through a quiet valley up to the site of the **Menehune Ditch.** Those busy little gremlins were at it again. Here they built an aqueduct to feed mountain water to the highlands of the valley. All that remains is an expanse of cut-stone bricks, two feet higher than the road and 200 feet long, inscribed with markings whose significance the archeologists can only guess at.

To the Canyon

Just outside Waimea, take the Waimea Canyon Road on your right. Don't continue to Kekaha, since most of the beautiful beach here, the area's major charm, has been closed off by the army. Winding and doubling back in the most vicious of manners, the Waimea Canyon Road carries you higher and higher into the cool, crisp **Kokee** region, 3,600 feet above the green seas of Kauai. The scenery is spectacular: on one side stretch sloping mountainsides emptying into the ocean, and on the other drops the magnificent Waimea Valley. You can get different perspectives on the valley from numerous roadside clearings, but we suggest you wait until you reach the **Puu Ka Pele Lookout.** There, below you, is the Grand Canyon of the Pacific, a ten-mile-long, mile-wide gorge, the result of an ancient crust fault that split miles of solid stone into a maze of jagged ridges. A rainbow of colors dances along the peaks, spiraling and cascading down the mountain slopes.

Before you reap the full gift of the canyon at **Kalalau Lookout** farther up, relax for a few minutes at the **Kokee Museum,** right next to the **Kokee Lodge Restaurant.** Just after you pass this point, follow the signs to Kalalau Lookout. Driving the winding road for these last few miles, you will pass the Kokee tracking station, now world-famous for its part in the success of the Apollo 11 mission to the moon. It was from this site that a laser beam was flashed to reflectors that Neil Armstrong had set up on the lunar surface.

At the end of the road is a sight that may make you forget the moon and stars and your own petty concerns as you stand at the edge of the world: suddenly, 4,000 feet below you, past long-abandoned cliffs that once supported ancient villages, the turquoise ocean crashes noiselessly on far-away beaches. White birds glide to and fro on gentle breezes. It is rumored that a wise man once lived here in a cave by the sea; he never came back to civilization again. You may not want to, either; if you must, your drive from Kalalau Lookout to the highway will be about an hour's worth of concentrated driving.

THE NORTHERN AND EASTERN ROUTE: As you start out on your second exploratory tour of Kauai—this time along its eastern and northern shores—you might keep one thing in mind: if there is something spectacular to see, the Menehunes made it. And if they didn't, the gods did. In any case, you will find this end of the island steeped in a mythology that lends an aura of mystery to the breathtaking sights.

Again, plan on a full-day trip, and be sure to take along your bathing suits and perhaps a picnic lunch. Head out of Lihue and past the airport on H-56 until you go through the little village of **Kapaia** just a mile away. If you go too fast you might miss the sign for **Wailua Falls,** four miles mauka of the main highway. Don't attempt to drive up the road past the falls; just enjoy the peacefulness of the area.

Heading down the road, you'll pass the Wailua Golf Course on your right, just before the entrance to **Lydgate Park,** a beautiful beach area that is open to the public and snuggles right up to the grounds of the Kauai Resort Hotel. The beach is safe and great fun for children; rest rooms and showers are provided. Just up the road from this spot you approach the Wailua River. Turn left before you reach the bridge over the river and drive to the **Wailua Marina,** where you can hop a boat to the magnificent **Fern Grotto,** where ferns form a frame for a cave under a waterfall. A 1½-hour cruise is $7.

Just behind the marina (take the access road on the Lihue side of the bridge, you'll find **Smith's Tropical Paradise,** where you might stop to visit a 220-acre botanical garden (admission $3 for adults, $1.50 for children). You can also see the gardens here if you come back for their luau and Polynesian show (tel. 822-4111 for information), so for now, make your way back to H-56 and turn left just before the sign for the Coco Palms Hotel. Now you're on **Kuamoo Road,** formerly known as the King's Highway, upon which the corpulent *alii* of old Hawaii were borne by their servants (their feet were too holy to tread common ground). Just up the road is the **Holo-Holo-Ku Heiau,** where human sacrifices were offered up to the gods, and not too long ago. Up a skinny stairway on the right side of the *heiau,* you'll discover an old Japanese graveyard, bespeaking the settlement of Orientals that grew up in this area many years back. Continue on the road to its conclusion at the head of **Opaekaa Falls,** where white birds soar in silence above the steaming, rainbowed waterfalls. Shrimp used to gather at the foot of the falls to spawn, and the tumbling motion that the churning waves put them through suggested the name—Opaekaa, rolling shrimp. Newly opened here is the **Kamokila Hawaiian Village,** where you can take an informative and entertaining guided tour ($5 adults, $1.50 children) through a tasteful restoration of an ancient settlement. Open Monday through Saturday, 9 a.m. to 4 p.m.; tel. 822-1192.

Once you turn around and head back to H-56, you can take the one-way fork off Kuamoo Road that leads, as the signs indicate, to the **Bellstone,** just beyond the place where the king's home and temple were once located. One of the rocks here is supposed to respond with a clear, bell-like tone when you hit it with another rock. We've never figured out which one, but you're welcome to try your luck. The rock was once used to signal news of danger from the sea—possibly in the form of enemy canoes—or to ring out the news of a royal birth.

At the base of Kuamoo Road now, you'll be passing the beautiful grounds of the **Coco Palms Hotel.** If it's lunchtime, stop in for the lovely buffet. This has always been a very special area. Long before the days of tourists, Hawaiian royalty lived here, and the lagoon was a series of fishponds. The old days are recalled each night in torchlight ceremonies at 7:30 p.m.

You'll certainly want to make a stop at the **Market Place** at Coconut Plantation, coming up now on the ocean side of the road, and the temptation will be to stay *too* long here; what with something like 70 shops, about a dozen restaurants or tempting ethnic snackbars, a twin-movie theater, and even colored fountains and an irrigation system that the kids can have fun playing with, it may be hard to tear yourself away. You'll recognize a number of places from Honolulu, like **Liberty House, Andrade,** and **Crazy Shirts.** But don't miss some local favorites like the **Pottery Tree,** whose wares, all created by Kauai craftspeople, include beautiful batik wall hangings, batik clothing, pottery, planters, and the like. **Waves of One Sea** is the place for international gift items, many from Indonesia, Bali, and the Orient; and **Kahn Gallery** shows outstanding arts and crafts by island artists. If you can, come back to the Market Place on a Thursday, Friday, or Saturday around 4 p.m., when they present free Polynesian shows. Bring the cameras.

Back on the highway, you'll soon notice an HVB marker indicating the **Sleeping Giant** rock formation, and you can pull off the side of the road to figure this one out. It's our favorite rock formation in the state, since, unlike the others, very little imagination is needed to see that it does indeed resemble a reclining Goliath. He was, in fact, the giant Puni, who befriended the Menehunes. Once, while he slept, enemy canoes threatened the shoreline, and the little men threw boulders onto his stomach to wake him up. He swallowed a few and died in his sleep, but a few stones ricocheted off his belly and destroyed the invaders' canoes.

Past the little town of **Kealia** (where once the Waipahoe Slide beckoned visitors but is now closed) you go, and perhaps stop at **Anahola Beach Park** for a picnic. Beyond the beach turn-off point you can get a good view of lovely **Anahola Valley.**

A possible side trip is in Kilauea, to the **Kilauea Point National Wildlife Refuge.** The old Kilauea Lighthouse here is no longer operative, but the view from a high bluff overlooking the sea is spectacular, and it's a great spot for watching unique Pacific sea birds. The U.S. Fish and Wildlife Service is in charge and can provide helpful information at the Visitor Center and bookstore. Open daily except Saturday, from noon to 4 p.m.

It seems hard to believe that **Kalihiwai Bay,** which you come upon next, was once the scene of savage tidal waves that twice, in 1946 and 1957, destroyed its little village. All is peaceful here now, and the road continues along, winding upward until it affords one of the most splendid views in the island of **Hanalei Valley.** Neatly terraced and squared off for irrigation purposes, with its rice paddies, taro patches, and the Hanalei River far below, it looks remarkably like a bit of the Orient.

Now you might want to take a few minutes out to visit **Princeville at Hanalei,** a luxurious resort complex described in the hotel section (above). Take a drive through the complex, stop in to see the stunning new Princeville Sheraton Hotel, and soak up the views. **Chuck's Steak House** here is an old island favorite.

Now proceed to quaint Hanalei Valley itself, where the surfers hang out. You might want to have a look at the 1837 **Waioli Mission House,** a small historical house-museum (open Tuesday through Saturday, 9 a.m. to 3 p.m.), perhaps check out the new **Chin Young Village Shopping Center,** a rather sterile, if serviceable, replacement for the funky old general store that was here for eons. Next door to the Dolphin Restaurant is **Ola's,** where you can find lovely handcrafted items, plus tasteful toys, books, and clothing for children.

Continuing on, you'll skirt a cliffside road that looks out over the much-photographed **Lumahai Beach.** It's one of the most beautiful in the islands, but just to look at. Rocks and currents make it unsafe for swimming, which may be the reason for its untouched appearance. Don't attempt to thread the path down the mountainside to the beach. There's great swimming coming up ahead.

Now your drive takes you through the enchantingly beautiful Haena region, over narrow one-lane bridges, into country that is truly unlike anything else in the islands. Soon, on the left side of the road, you'll see the **Manini-holo Dry Cave** and, a little bit past that, two wet caves, **Waikapale** and **Waikanaloa.** Both figure in the mythology of Kauai, and sometimes the islanders swim in them. But that's a bit dangerous and besides, you're practically at **Ke'e,** one of the most serene of island beaches. Park where the Na Pali trail begins (devoted hikers claim it is unforgettable). Here, under the towering Na Pali cliffs, once the scene of Hawaiian religious rituals, you can bask in the sun, swim in safe waters, let the rest of the world go by and not miss it a bit.

Kauai has spectacular regions not accessible by car: you may want to consider hiking the Na Pali Coast, taking a boat expedition (**Na Pali Zodiac** runs some terrific ones; tel. 826-9371), or, best of all, a helicopter flight. For many, swooping down the walls of Waimea Canyon, flying into the mists of Mt. Waialeale, experiencing the wilderness areas and remote beaches of Kauai constitute an extraordinary, almost mystical experience. All of the helicopter companies are good: some well-recommended ones are **Menehune Helicopter** (tel. 245-7705), **Papillon Helicopters** (tel. 826-5691), and **Will Squyres Helicopters** (tel. 245-7541).

NOW, SAVE MONEY ON ALL YOUR TRAVELS!
Join Arthur Frommer's $25-A-Day Travel Club™

Saving money while traveling is never a simple matter, which is why, over 24 years ago, the **$25-A-Day Travel Club** was formed. Actually, the idea came from readers of the Arthur Frommer Publications who felt that such an organization could bring financial benefits, continuing travel information, and a sense of community to economy-minded travelers all over the world.

In keeping with the money-saving concept, the annual membership fee is low—$18 (U.S. residents) or $20 (Canadian, Mexican, and foreign residents)—and is immediately exceeded by the value of your benefits which include:

(1) The latest edition of any TWO of the books listed on the following page.

(2) An annual subscription to an 8-page quarterly newspaper *The Wonderful World of Budget Travel* which keeps you up-to-date on fastbreaking developments in low-cost travel in all parts of the world—bringing you the kind of information you'd have to pay over $25 a year to obtain elsewhere. This consumer-conscious publication also includes the following columns:

Hospitality Exchange—members all over the world who are willing to provide hospitality to other members as they pass through their home cities.

Share-a-Trip—requests from members for travel companions who can share costs and help avoid the burdensome single supplement.

Readers Ask . . . Readers Reply—travel questions from members to which other members reply with authentic firsthand information.

(3) A copy of *Arthur Frommer's Guide to New York*.

(4) Your personal membership card which entitles you to purchase through the Club all Arthur Frommer Publications for a third to a half off their regular retail prices during the term of your membership.

So why not join this hardy band of international budgeteers NOW and participate in its exchange of information and hospitality? Simply send $18 (U.S. residents) or $20 U.S. (Canadian, Mexican, and other foreign residents) along with your name and address to: $25-A-Day Travel Club, Inc., Gulf + Western Building, One Gulf + Western Plaza, New York, NY 10023. Remember to specify which *two* of the books in section (1) above you wish to receive in your initial package of members' benefits. Or tear out this page, check off any two books on the opposite side and send it to us with your membership fee.

It's 2 am.
It's far from home.
It's more than
a tummyache.

American Express Cardmembers can get emergency medical and legal referrals, worldwide. Simply by calling Global Assist.℠

What if it really is more than a tummyache? What if your back goes out? What if you get into a legal fix?

Call Global Assist – a new emergency referral service for the exclusive use of American Express Cardmembers. Just call. Toll-free. 24 hours a day. Every day. Virtually anywhere in the world.

Your call helps find a doctor, lawyer, dentist, optician, chiropractor, nurse, pharmacist, or an interpreter.

All this costs nothing, except for the medical and legal bills you would normally expect to pay.

Global Assist. One more reason to have the American Express® Card. Or, to get one.

For an application, call 1-800-THE-CARD.

Don't leave home without it.®

If you lose cash on vacation, don't count on a Boy Scout finding it.

Honestly. How many people can you trust to give back hundreds of dollars in cash? Not too many.

That's why it's so important to help protect your vacation with American Express® Travelers Cheques.

If they're lost, you can get them back from over 100,000 refund loca tions throughout the world. Or you can hope a Boy Scout finds it.

Protect your vacation.

 Travelers Cheques